Qualitative Research in Sport and Physical Activity

Qualitative Research in Sport and Physical Activity

Ian Jones, Lorraine Brown and Immy Holloway

Los Angeles | London | New Delhi
Singapore | Washington DC

Los Angeles | London | New Delhi
Singapore | Washington DC

SAGE Publications Ltd
1 Oliver's Yard
55 City Road
London EC1Y 1SP

SAGE Publications Inc.
2455 Teller Road
Thousand Oaks, California 91320

SAGE Publications India Pvt Ltd
B 1/I 1 Mohan Cooperative Industrial Area
Mathura Road
New Delhi 110 044

SAGE Publications Asia-Pacific Pte Ltd
3 Church Street
#10-04 Samsung Hub
Singapore 049483

Editor: Katie Metzler
Assistant editor: Anna Horvai
Production editor: Ian Antcliff
Copyeditor: Kate Harrison
Proofreader: Neil Dowden
Indexer: Martin Hargreaves
Marketing manager: Ben Griffin-Sherwood
Cover design: Jennifer Crisp
Typeset by: C&M Digitals (P) Ltd, Chennai, India
Printed by: MPG Books Group, Bodmin, Cornwall

Library of Congress Control Number: 2012937454

British Library Cataloguing in Publication data

A catalogue record for this book is available from
the British Library

ISBN 978-1-4462-0744-4
ISBN 978-1-4462-0745-1 (pbk)

Contents

About the authors

Ian Jones is Associate Dean for Sport at Bournemouth University. His main research interests lie in the field of sport and leisure behaviour, specifically sport fans and spectators, and the concept of 'serious leisure'. He is co-author of *Research Methods for Sport Studies*, and co-editor of several other books, including *Serious Leisure: Extensions and Applications*, *Sport Tourism and Sustainability*, and *Leisure Cultures: Investigations in Sport, Media and Technology*.

Lorraine Brown is Senior Lecturer in Tourism Education at Bournemouth University. Her research interests include cross-cultural interaction, the impact of prejudice on the sojourn experience and the outcome of culture contact. She is interested in qualitative methods generally.

Immy Holloway is Professor Emeritus at the Centre for Qualitative Research, Bournemouth University. She was the founder member and one of the co-directors of the Centre for Qualitative Research at Bournemouth University before retirement and still works there part-time. Having taught and supervised qualitative research for several decades, she is still actively pursuing her interests by supervising PhD students as well as writing articles and books. Some of the latter have been translated into several languages.

Preface

Sport and physical activity is an area of study that is, as Brustad (2009) notes, particularly suited to qualitative research. There has, undoubtedly, been a significant growth in interest in such approaches within the subject, and it is within this context that this book has been written for those students of sport and physical activity undertaking, or considering undertaking, qualitative research, particularly those at undergraduate and Masters level. We hope that doctoral students will also find the text useful as an introduction to some of the key issues related to qualitative research, as well as those students who may not be considering such approaches, but would wish to gain an understanding of some of the key concepts in qualitative research as part of, for example, a broader research methods programme. The text will be of interest not only to sport sociologists, but also to those from all disciplinary approaches, such as sport psychology, sport management and the broad range of sport sciences.

The text is designed to provide readers with a detailed outline of the processes involved in planning, undertaking, analysing and writing up qualitative research in the sport and physical activity arena. The aim of this book is to provide students with a theoretical understanding and a practical knowledge of the qualitative research process as it applies to sport and physical activity. There are four main parts to the text, these being:

Part I: Introducing qualitative research in sport

This part (Chapters 1 to 5) will introduce the nature of qualitative research, and its place within the study of sport and physical activity. It will outline some of the key ethical issues, before describing the qualitative research process. The role of the literature in qualitative research will be described, as will the nature of sampling for qualitative research.

Part II: Collecting qualitative data

The second part (Chapters 6 to 8) of the book outlines the various methods of data collection, detailing the use of one-to-one and focus group interviews, as well as observation and participant observation.

Part III: Choosing the research approach

Part three (Chapters 9 to 13) explores the different approaches available to the qualitative researcher. As such, it will outline grounded theory, ethnography, phenomenology, narrative research and mixed methods research.

Part IV: Analysing and reporting qualitative data

The final part of the book (Chapters 14 to 16) outlines the key issues in analysing data, focusing on thematic analysis. Issues related to the quality of the data obtained are discussed, followed by the concluding chapter on writing up and disseminating the research.

Our goal was to write an accessible text that would be both useful and informative to the reader. We are aware that some of the qualitative research literature in sport and physical activity can be viewed by the novice researcher as difficult, or even impenetrable at times, using a language unknown to students beginning their research journey. Hopefully, the key ideas have been presented here in such a way as to encourage rather than deter students but without, we hope, being over-simplified.

Ian Jones
Lorraine Brown
Immy Holloway

PART I

INTRODUCING QUALITATIVE RESEARCH IN SPORT

1

Qualitative Research and Its Use in Sport and Physical Activity

All research is concerned with seeking the answers to specific questions, and qualitative inquiry is no exception to other social science approaches. Qualitative social research – an umbrella term for a group of approaches which take a similar worldview – focuses specifically on the under-standing of social phenomena and the ways in which people make sense and extract meaning from their experiences, while quantitative research refers to a systematic examination of phenomena through testing a hypothesis – a statement of a relationship between variables – and focuses on measurement; however they are not incompatible, and nei-ther is one form superior to the other. Qualitative and quantitative researchers answer different questions, use different procedures and need different skills.

The main characteristics of qualitative research

The essential traits of qualitative research explain its character. They are:

- Flexibility, coherence and consistency
- Priority of data
- Context sensitivity
- Thick description
- Immersion in the setting (natural setting)
- Insider/outsider perspectives
- Reflexivity and 'critical subjectivity'

Flexibility, coherence and consistency

Qualitative researchers need flexibility – the design of the study to be carried out is emerging and evolving rather than wholly predetermined. The research can change in the early stages and be adapted according to developing ideas. As Patton (2002) notes, qualitative research is neither unilinear nor straight-forward, but is iterative. It uses the skill of 'tacking', going back and forth between the data collection, analysis and findings. This means that qualitative researchers make sure that their work is always 'grounded in the data'. The strategies used are more open-ended and flexible, and give the participants the freedom to respond in their own way, enabling researchers to follow up on anticipated and unanticipated areas in both interviews and observations. The research relationship too has inherent flexibility and might change over time. More so than in other types of inquiry, researchers can evaluate ideas, take them back to the data, and explore them and modify or reject them. Nevertheless, qualitative research should still stay true to the principles and procedures of each specific approach, which should be followed so that inner consistency and coherence can be established (Holloway and Todres, 2003).

Priority of data

Qualitative research is initially inductive, which means that the researcher moves from specific instances to discover patterns or regularities or even tentative hypotheses (or working propositions). Thus the data in qualitative research have primacy, and inductive reasoning does *not* start with a hypothesis (or theory). The patterns in the data allow theories to develop. Inductive reasoning allows more flexibility and exploration, especially in its early stages. However, there can also be a deductive element in that the working propositions are followed up and explored (and in some forms of grounded theory even tested) until researchers come to a broader conclusion or theory, for example the study by Roberts et al. (2001) on athlete perceptions of sports equipment under playing conditions, where the initial inductive analysis generated a number of themes that were subsequently tested deductively.

Context sensitivity

Qualitative research is context-bound; it is not located in a vacuum but always tied to its context, which refers to the locality, time and culture in which it takes place, and the values and beliefs the participants – and researchers – hold. As Patton (2002) observes, qualitative research takes a holistic perspective – it portrays the whole of the phenomenon under study. To be aware of the context, researchers need context sensitivity or context intelligence. They can only make sense and grasp meaning through contextualisation. Context is important throughout the process of the research; it influences the way in which participants and researchers think and behave. Of course, the unique context of the research makes generalisations difficult though not impossible (this will be discussed in Chapter 15). Sport and physical activity take place in particular contexts or settings which will impact on both the nature of the activity and the experiences of the participants. Thus context sensitivity is crucial for a full understanding of the data generated.

Thick description

Closely linked to context and contextualisation is 'thick description', a concept developed by the anthropologist Geertz and discussed by Denzin (2001). Thick description refers to detailed, contextual description that includes feelings, meanings and intentions of people. The use of quotes from participants enhances the description and makes it more vivid. Thick description portrays the context of the participants' lives, their culture and the meaning they attach to their actions and words, showing both general traits and specific patterns in the group under study. It is not merely factual description but needs to be grounded in a theoretical base.

Immersion in the setting

For thick description to be possible, researchers immerse themselves in the setting and situation which they study and engage fully with the participants, specifically in participant observation and interviews. This means spending time in the setting with participants to learn about their thoughts, feelings and actions. Researchers build a relationship of trust with the people whose world they study. Through this, critical events are observed, feelings uncovered and routine behaviours understood. It would be difficult to analyse and interpret data from sport fans, for example, without ever having been to a game. Similarly gaining an understanding of the experiences of elite athletes may prove to be difficult if the researchers have had no exposure to sport at a high level themselves.

Insider/outsider perspectives

In qualitative research, writers differentiate between insider and outsider perspectives, the 'emic' and the 'etic' view (terms developed by Harris in 1979, though not first used by him). The emic perspective refers to the participants' understanding and voice, from those who are insiders in the group and setting that researchers study. Patton insists that it is important to be empathetic and non-judgemental, however. The outsider, 'etic' view – that of the social scientist, the researcher, who takes the research to a different level – is less empirical or concrete than that of the participants. This level is more abstract and theory-based as well as having more general applications (see Chapter 15 on transferability). The theoretical framework will not be predetermined but links directly to the data analysis and findings. A qualitative account which lacks proper analysis, interpretation and theory does not suffice.

Reflexivity and 'critical subjectivity'

Reflexivity refers to the location of the researchers in the study, 'the situated self'. Their values and beliefs – as well as their status and place in a hierarchy – affect the research they carry out. They need to reflect on their position in the study and how their own assumptions influence it. In qualitative research this is called 'reflexivity'. Researchers are participants in the research and cannot distance themselves from it; indeed they acknowledge their assumptions and their involvement in the research. Self-referencing is not easy; qualitative researchers are often criticised for self-indulgence. They need to be part of the study without smothering the ideas and voice of the participants. Reflexivity goes on throughout the research; the research diary will chart the process of reflexivity. Throughout the inquiry researchers reflect on their own assumptions (or bias, a term from quantitative research and rarely used in qualitative inquiry). Reflexivity also takes into account the philosophy, ideology and worldview in which the research is based.

Research can never be neutral and wholly objective. Qualitative researchers take their own subjectivity as a resource, drawing on their own experience to assist in understanding participants: 'researcher subjectivity impacts upon how the research unfolds and is interpreted' (Bott, 2010: 161). Prior knowledge becomes part of the research though it cannot direct it. Researchers need a critical stance to their own assumptions and predispositions while focusing on their participants' ideas.

Qualitative research in sport and physical activity

The very nature of sport and physical activity makes it a rich area of investigation for the qualitative researcher. Its social, cultural, political and economic importance, its pervasiveness at all levels of society, the key issues raised by participation (and non-participation), the embodied nature of the phenomenon, the uncertainty of outcome, and the varied experiences of both fan and player are just some of the characteristics that make it interesting in qualitative research terms. Brustad (2009) summarises the role of qualitative research in sport and physical activity succinctly, suggesting that:

> Sport is an entirely human endeavour. Our involvement in sport and physical activity is full of personally and socially generated meanings as our participation occurs in interaction with other individuals in various social and cultural contexts. Qualitative researchers in sport and physical activity have an essential role in uncovering the meaningful nature of this involvement. Without this contribution, we will never have a good understanding for why completing a marathon could transform a person's life, or how burnout is experienced by adolescent or elite athletes … we need to better understand the lived meaning of the experience and qualitative/interpretive forms of research provide us with important tools for achieving this goal. (p. 112)

Despite this, as Hunger et al. (2003) note, early approaches to sport science research were dominated by quantitative research, adopting methodologies largely inspired by the natural sciences. Despite Whitson arguing in 1976 for the use of phenomenological methods within sport, it was only in the late 1980s, as the field of sport science matured, that the use of qualitative methods began to be debated, let alone implemented to any significant extent among scholars in the field, for example through the call of Martens (1987) for greater consideration of the use of qualitative research in sport psychology. Since then, as Kerry and Armour (2000) suggest, qualitative research methods have become increasingly popular, particularly in the fields of sport pedagogy, sociology, philosophy and psychology. However, it must be noted that in some domains, such as sport management and sport science, quantitative approaches are still dominant.

Arguments about the relative merits of qualitative and quantitative research in sport and physical activity have existed for many years. However, Li et al. (2008) suggest: 'these two research approaches answer different types of questions and both can facilitate an understanding of the field' (p. 41). Thus, as Smith and Gilbourne (2009: 1) observe, 'for some time qualitative inquiry has been recognised as a legitimate area of scholarship within the sport and exercise sciences', and even in disciplines where quantitative research prevails, there is still a clear increase in the use and perceived legitimacy of qualitative studies. Li et al. (2008), for example, demonstrate a significant growth in the number of academic articles published in key sport management journals since 2001.

Despite the growing acceptance of qualitative research in sport and physical activity, its use is, on the whole, relatively restricted methodologically. As Krane and Baird (2005) point out, although the acceptance of qualitative research in sport psychology has grown steadily, 'more attention to methodological diversity is needed' (p. 87). The authors suggest an over-reliance on 'one-shot interviews that are often highly structured' (ibid), a point reinforced by Brustad (2008) who argues that reliance on such approaches will limit the potential knowledge generation that is a key strength of qualitative research. Indeed, a survey of the literature suggests that the most commonly adopted qualitative method is the semi-structured interview. It is gratifying, however, to record a gradually increasing diversity in both methods and approaches adopted by qualitative researchers in sport and physical activity, as a number of the case studies presented in subsequent chapters demonstrate.

2

Ethical Considerations in Research

The need and moral duty of researchers to protect participants in the research process is well documented. According to Mason (2002), qualitative research raises a number of ethical issues which should be anticipated in advance, so that researchers can take into account how their actions may affect participants. It is paramount that ethical issues are considered before, during and after the research process. This is particularly true of qualitative research because of its processual and flexible nature. Ethical considerations need to be made in the following situations:

- When choosing the topic and aim
- When gaining access to participants
- When conducting the research
- When writing the report and disseminating the data.

When writing a research proposal, a key issue to be addressed is the extent to which ethical issues have been covered. Research proposals will be considered by an ethics committee; in some cases, students will be advised to reconsider certain issues, and to resubmit their proposal, and it has often happened that proposals have been rejected on the grounds that the research might harm either participants or the researcher, not only in terms of physical harm, but also social and psychological harm.

It is important that the researcher continues to consider ethical issues throughout the research process; that they are not forgotten once approval to conduct the research has been given. Simply gaining ethical approval at the start of any study is not enough. Guillemin and Gillam (2004) distinguish between procedural ethics, denoting the steps that need to be followed to gain approval from ethics committees and gatekeepers, and ethics in practice, relating to the issues that arise on a daily basis during research. Ethics in practice should be continually addressed throughout the research process. All ethical issues that have been considered should be discussed by the researcher in a distinct section of the methodology.

Recruiting participants

Gaining access to participants is one of the first steps in research, and it can be ethically difficult (Daymon and Holloway, 2011). Formal permission is required first of all from the gatekeeper to the research setting. The study of Groves et al. (2003) for example – exploring children's experiences of physical activity through the use of 'PE diaries' and subsequent interviews based on the contents of the diaries – required permission from the gatekeepers, in this case the teachers from the school, before they were able to approach parents for consent. As well as simply providing access to a pool of individuals, gatekeepers may also have a role in selecting appropriate participants in sensitive topics, for example the investigation by Partington et al. (2009) into dependence in surfing used initial discussions with a gatekeeper to select appropriate individuals based upon participation in what were defined as 'big wave' events. The gatekeeper subsequently contacted those deemed to fit the criteria, and consent was gained to participate in the study, leading to the recruitment of 15 interviewees. Alternatively, researchers might put notices in public places, such as through social media, on notice boards, on online fora and in newspapers. This can be ethically problematic, as the researcher has no control over the volunteers who come forward; they might be vulnerable and in need of sensitive handling. If participants are accessed through a gatekeeper, the latter needs to be assured that the researcher will behave with integrity and honesty and that there will be some benefit to the community in participating in the research. Much thought and preparation need to go into approaching gatekeepers, as access can be denied if it is felt that the research findings might damage any stakeholders, especially if the research topic is a sensitive one.

Using a gatekeeper when researching sensitive subjects: attitudes towards doping and anti-doping in sport

A gatekeeper can have a valuable role in creating trust among participants, especially when researching sensitive subjects. This was the case with the study by Bloodworth and MacNamee (2010) of attitudes towards doping and anti-doping in sport. Initial contact made directly from the research team to athletes resulted in a very low response, which was perhaps unsurprising given the nature of the study. Thus, there was the need to consider an alternative strategy. In this instance the strategy was to recruit a number of gatekeepers, such as coaches and performance directors, who, having a much stronger position in terms of access and trust with potential participants, were able to recruit a final total of 40 athletes to participate in subsequent focus groups.

Research may also be seen as an intrusion, a disruption to everyday operations. Daymon and Holloway (2011: 63) advise that, in order to be successful, 'access should be negotiated with a great deal of diplomacy, honesty and tact'. In online investigations, thought needs to be given to whether or not permission will be sought from gatekeepers to conduct, for example, an observational study. In a public forum, it might be argued that the researcher does not need to obtain consent from either gatekeepers or participants. However, in a closed forum which requires membership, the researcher's identity and role should be declared, especially if their role goes beyond passive observation.

Informed consent

Voluntary informed consent shows 'respect for autonomy', which is a key ethical principle (Gillon, 2003). Ethical approval to undertake the study should be sought from the departmental or University Research Ethics Committee, and thereafter from the main gatekeeper to participants, if appropriate. When access is gained via a gatekeeper, the principle of obtaining informed consent from the participants to whom access is required should also be adhered to (Brewer, 2000). Participants should be informed of the aim of the study and the use to which data will be put before data are collected. Informed consent is central to research ethics; if due process is followed, participants should be able to think carefully about and decide on their involvement in the research. Gratton and Jones (2010) emphasise that informed consent should involve giving partici-pants all the necessary information for them to make a fully informed decision as to whether to participate in the research or not, and ensuring that participants understand the explanation, and do not consent to something that they do not fully understand. In qualitative research this information should not, however, be too detailed at the start of an interview, as the ideas should emerge rather than be directed; nevertheless the communication of the overall aim and full discussion at the end of an interview will ensure informed consent.

Participants should also be assured of their right to withdraw from the project at any time, even halfway through an interview, for example. It is also important that pressure is not placed on participants to be involved in the research, whether tacitly or forcibly. The researcher should offer special con-sideration to participants who cannot take complete responsibility for their own decisions, such as children, older or ill people and people with learning difficulties (Daymon and Holloway, 2011). Research should be conducted with these groups only after careful reflection, and for students, only after discus-sion with their supervisors. It is advisable that a blank copy of the informed consent form provided to participants is placed in the appendices of the research report. All signed copies should be kept in a safe place by the researcher in case of complaints upon release of the report.

In observational studies, it might be tricky to obtain informed consent from all the actors in the setting, though consent should be obtained from *key informants.* It is important in a longitudinal study, where participants come and go, to obtain consent on a regular basis. Observations of anonymous groups or crowds in public settings need no consent, for example a large group of spectators watching a sporting event.

Gaining valid informed consent when researching lifestyle physical activity among individuals with severe mental health problems

The study of certain vulnerable groups raises a number of ethical issues, which are acknowledged by Soundy et al. (2007) in their paper on lifestyle physical activity among individuals with severe mental health problems. To ensure valid informed consent, as advocated by Gratton and Jones (2010), a number of exclusion criteria were identified:

1 Individuals with coexisting alcohol or drug abuse disorder.
2 Those who could not give informed consent.
3 Individuals identified by gatekeepers as not suitable or for whom the task would provide an unacceptable burden.

Any individuals demonstrating these criteria were not invited to participate. Of those that were subsequently eligible, participants were not interviewed unless they clearly demonstrated that they understood both the nature and duration of the interviews, and had provided written consent.

Deception in research

It is widely agreed that deception in research violates important ethical principles; it specifically contravenes the principle of informed consent. Thus it will be frowned upon if the researcher deceives participants as to the nature of the research or if they hide their identity or lie about the use to which data will be put. It can be argued that if participants are made aware of the research aim, then the data will be skewed. However, it can be further argued then that it is in the interests of the research to withhold key information. This relates to the 'observer effect', the influence of the researcher's presence on the setting. Thus in participant observation, a covert stance may be adopted, either to protect the researcher from harm if the research setting is unpredictable, or to collect more naturalistic data that are untainted by the presence of the researcher. As Lugosi (2006) argues, concealment is sometimes necessary, it is often unavoidable, and critics of covert methods should not stop the researcher from adopting a covert stance. Nevertheless, Brewer (2000) maintains that covert methods are defensible only when access is likely to be closed. If researchers are convinced that some measure of deception is necessary, they must be prepared to justify their position during both the proposal and writing-up stage.

Confidentiality and anonymity

At the start of the project, the researcher should assure participants that their identity will be protected and that confidential data will not be revealed (unless the participant makes a clear wish for their identity to be revealed, and this does not allow any third parties to be subsequently identified). This is a challenge in qualitative research, which generates rich data that are revealed in the final written account. Researchers must ensure that they alone have access to raw data, which must be stored in a secure location. Identifying information must be kept separate from the data so that participant identity cannot be discovered. Patton (2002) recommends that recordings should be erased shortly after data collection, but many universities or funding agencies wish them to be kept for a number of years. Furthermore, if interviews are not transcribed by the researcher, careful thought needs to be put into the decision as to who will do the transcriptions; commitments to confidentiality will have to be made (written and signed), but the individual must be judged to be trustworthy in the first place.

Rejecting anonymity: the role of sport in rehabilitation following spinal cord injury

Kavanagh (2012) undertook a narrative study of the role of sport in rehabilitation following spinal cord injury. As far as confidentiality and anonymity are concerned, Lucy Shuker, the participant in the research, insisted on being identified in the research report in order that she, and her story of rehabilitation, may act as inspiration to others. Thus, both her name, and a number of clearly identifiable characteristics and elements of her background were presented.

In the final report, pseudonyms (rather than numbers) should be used to protect identity, and demographic details should be scrutinised so that participants cannot be tracked by, for example, nationality, age or gender. Researchers must consider whether participants' identity might be exposed in the research report, thus key biographical data such as age and profession might be changed or not mentioned. In some cases, the name and location of the institution participants work in might be changed to a pseudonym too. It is imperative that participants and institutions are not exposed to risk through the dissemination process. In some cases, participants may insist that the research report is not made available for public consumption until a certain period of time has elapsed. This relates to the principle of confidentiality, which requires the researcher to withhold information that the participants have asked them to keep private. Revelation of sensitive information could put an individual or an organisation at risk. This is particularly relevant to organisations whose profitability may suffer if key information is released to their competitors.

On the other hand, Guillemin and Gillam (2004) raise two contentious issues. If wrongdoing is reported during the interview process, should the researcher contact the relevant authorities, or do they observe the commitment they have made to observing confidentiality? Second, what if a participant reveals information that they insist is incorporated into the final report but that may place them in danger if disseminated by the researcher? These are defined by Guillemin and Gillam as ethically important moments, requiring careful thought on the part of the researcher, who may need to seek advice before they take action.

Hadjistavropoulos and Smythe point out that the identities of third parties mentioned by participants also require protection. In a survey of qualitative theses over a six-year period, they found that all contained reference to third parties who might be identified by others or by the parties themselves: 'the narrative information is so detailed that the third parties involved would easily recognise themselves. The main ethical problem stems from the fact that these people did not give consent for stories to be circulated about them in this way' (Hadjistavropoulos and Smythe, 2001: 170).

Safeguarding third parties when researching referee communication in rugby

Mellick and Fleming (2010: 301) discuss issues of disclosure, defined as 'the unwitting revelations about an identifiable individual or group of individuals who have not been consulted about and consented to the revelations', with reference to the doctoral study of the first author on referee communication in rugby. Four connected themes regarding disclosure were identified:

1 The impossibility of gaining prior voluntary informed consent given the emergent nature of the study.
2 The anonymity of those involved and the need to present the narrative in such a way as to conceal identities. Two possible 'errors' are identified. First, being able to identify actors based on information presented throughout the narrative particularly if that information is central to the analysis; and second, mistaken identity whereby it may be possible to implicate another person entirely.
3 The risk of harm – for example, Mellick and Fleming's study identifies the potential impacts upon the future careers of third parties such as coaches and mentors.
4 Violating privacy – for example, a dialogue with a mentor who didn't envisage their words being made public through the research account.

Avoiding harm

The researcher must adhere to the principle of non-maleficence. The research should not do harm to participants or institutions through identity exposure or through the revelation of information that can cause damage to individuals or organisations. According to Williams (2003), being ethical is about achieving a balance between being an objective researcher and being a morally bound citizen: social research should not create harm or distress even if the outcome may be beneficial to society. Neither should it cause harm during the data collection stage. For example, during an interview on a sensitive topic, the researcher must be careful not to cause undue distress to participants.

Collecting data on sensitive topics: exploring body image

The exploratory study of Grogan and Richards (2002) of body-shape ideals, body esteem, exercise and diet among boys and young adults demonstrated a clear understanding of the need to ensure participants were as comfortable as possible with the data-collection process. To achieve this, first they chose focus groups, whereby participants would interact with, and be supported by their peers, a strategy which would also 'shift the balance of power away from the researcher and towards the research participants' (p. 222). Second, pilot work suggested that participants would be more comfortable discussing the issues with a female facilitator. Finally, again as a result of pilot work, it was determined that participants felt more comfortable with smaller groups, thus leading to the decision to restrict the focus groups to four participants.

Mason (2002) states that the in-depth interview can feel to participants like a therapeutic encounter (though this is, of course, not its aim) with the following consequences: the participant may suffer distress during the interview and the researcher must be prepared to offer comfort; the interview may raise uncalled-for self-knowledge that carries repercussions beyond the research encounter; and the researcher may need to provide follow-up care and possibly recommend further support. The research experience may be a disturbing one, as participants may experience unnecessary anxiety: attempts must be made to minimise disturbance, and special care should be taken where participants are vulnerable (Brewer, 2000). As Hadjistavropoulos and Smythe (2001) note, an already depressed participant could suffer a worsened negative mood state through the elicitation of sensitive information. They also state that extensive questioning could undermine the defensive strategies that participants have created to protect themselves from harm. Furthermore, Guillemin and Gillam (2004) state that the intimate atmosphere associated with the in-depth qualitative interview can lead to the disclosure of information not directly related to the research topic, but to which the interviewer has to respond. It may be worth considering counselling training for researchers into sensitive research topics, so that participants can be treated with care.

Avoiding harm to the researcher

It must not be forgotten that the research might do harm to the researcher, and that possible risks need to be identified at the proposal stage. For example, the research topic may be a sensitive one that is close to the researcher's heart, and for that reason, it may have a negative emotional impact. Furthermore, it may be difficult to achieve a distance on a familiar topic; data collection and interpretation may suffer. Another issue to consider is the research setting – at no point must the researchers be placed in danger, for example if the data are to be collected at night or in an isolated location or in a neighbourhood known to be dangerous. It is therefore always important to tell a friend or colleague of the place and time of the research as well as to take a mobile phone. Universities will generally insist upon the researcher completing a risk assessment before such research is carried out, and will refuse permission if the dangers are felt to be too significant.

Breaking the law as a researcher: participant observation into football hooliganism

Whilst we would suggest that student research should never involve partaking in criminal activities, the issues associated with such research do provide an interesting ethical dilemma to the researcher. Pearson (2009) outlines a number of problems that he encountered through his covert participant observation in the field of football hooliganism. Whilst acknowledging the desirable ethical standards associated with observational research, he also discusses the tensions between ensuring those standards are adhered to, and the need to create an accurate picture of the phenomenon, especially when the activity involves breaking the law. If researchers refuse to break the law, then their position may become threatened, not only through loss of their 'research position', but also through potential physical harm. If researchers fully immerse themselves with the activities of the group, then richer and more accurate data may be forthcoming, yet this may well involve participation in criminal activity. As Pearson notes, there is no 'right answer' to this issue. He discusses his own compromises, such as committing 'lower level' offences, those being defined as activities that would not cause physical harm to another person, such as running on to the pitch, or smuggling alcohol onto trains where it had been banned. Some activities, however, such as racist chanting were not undertaken as a result of the researcher's own moral and ethical position. Given the lack of formal guidance, the need for researchers to justify their own approach becomes extremely important. As Pearson suggests 'covert methods should be justifiable if they achieve the aim of enhancing understanding of otherwise "hidden" areas' (p. 252).

The principle of beneficence

The researcher must bear in mind the principle of beneficence in research. Not only must the research process not incur damage, but it must also, if possible, do good. This might mean that participants reap benefits from participation; for example, Corbin and Morse (2003) state that there is a quid pro quo in interview research in that the participant enjoys being listened to, and the interviewer gains access to valuable data. Furthermore, the outcome of research might be positive in that the research findings, if carefully disseminated through a range of media, can lead to changes in practice for the better. Thus the research is beneficial to society. Action research in particular has the potential to lead to positive outcomes for communities, given its grounding in a commitment to culminate in the empowerment of those involved in the research. As Halai (2006) notes, a key element of action research is the sense of ownership of the research problem and the process being used to address it. Finding a solution to a problem is on the agenda from the outset.

Exit strategy

Rapport between researcher and participant is crucial to the success of qualitative research, and it is something that the researcher has to work hard to achieve and sustain. Particularly important is the creation of an atmosphere of trust, intimacy and confidentiality (Mason, 2002). Indeed, according to Warren and Hackney (2000), a hallmark of post-modern, qualitative research is that the interviewer can come to be seen as a confidant(e) or best friend. As Hammersley and Atkinson (2007) point out, it is important that the researcher realises that the interview may be an important part of the participant's social life. This has ethical implications in terms of consideration of participants' feelings and expectations, and is all the more pertinent to research with potentially vulnerable interviewees. Brewer (2000) states that the possibility of the burden of long-term commitment should be anticipated at the planning stage; researchers may need to be sensitive to the fact that participants may desire more contact after the research has finished than the researcher is prepared to offer, and this needs to be prepared for. Indeed, researchers may have to carefully negotiate their exit strategy, which may demand sensitivity to participant needs. This is all the more pertinent to research conducted in a setting in which the researcher is involved professionally or socially. It is also important for researchers to consider the impact of exit upon themselves, especially given the strong connections that may develop over an extended period of fieldwork.

Reflections upon leaving the world of the wives of professional athletes

Ortiz (2004) reflects upon some of the issues he encountered when leaving the social world of the wives of professional athletes, both in terms of the impact upon participants within the study and the impact upon himself as

(Continued)

(Continued)

researcher. As a male researcher, entering that particular social world posed a number of challenges. However, Ortiz was able to gain acceptance, trust and rapport, and immerse himself for a period of three years, to the extent that he was involved in activities such as babysitting and house-hunting with participants. The difficulties in exiting were closely related to the aspects that allowed him to collect rich data, for example the social isolation experienced by wives and the lack of social support from others. This strengthened the bond between researcher and participants; however, as Ortiz notes, 'as I left their world of isolation and perhaps neglect, I felt guilty as if I were betraying them' (p. 473). He concludes by noting the importance of the qualitative researcher identifying appropriate exit strategies that minimise the 'disruptive, emotional and problematic nature of leaving the field' (p. 483).

Authentic representation of the data

The researcher has an ethical duty to represent the data they have collected as faithfully as possible; this relates to the principle of veracity, or truth-telling. This links with to one of the criteria for ensuring validity, that of credibility (see Chapter 15). When writing up the research report, the researcher must strive to create an accurate portrayal of the research setting and participants, to tell their story in a way that would ring true for them and which carries resonance. Though problematic, it is often recommended that a member-check be conducted, so that the researcher's account can be verified and commented on by participants. As Hadjistavropoulos and Smythe (2001) point out, however, reading the researcher's interpretations of their own narrative can undermine participants; it can carry a psychological risk. Thus care should be taken over the parts of the report shared with participants.

Summary

Ongoing debates over ethics have led to researchers being more informed, reflexive and critical (O'Reilly, 2005). Guillemin and Gillam (2004) argue that researchers should hold themselves up to critical scrutiny throughout the research process. A reflexive stance should be adopted, serving as a check on the researcher, making the researcher alert to ethical tensions and to their responses to them. The key principles are as follows:

- The researcher must obtain informed consent
- Principles of anonymity and confidentiality must be adhered to
- Care must be taken not to cause harm to participants
- An accurate representation of the data must be created
- Researchers must try to do good with their research

3

Developing the Research Question and Writing the Proposal

The first step in the research process is to discover a suitable topic and research question. Qualitative inquiry needs no hypothesis as its data have primacy and it does not start with a fully developed theoretical framework. Researchers, of course, do not start with 'a blank sheet', as they already have some ideas about the topic and area of study – though they should set aside assumptions and preconceptions. After deciding on the topic and research question, researchers need to develop a plan of action and write a proposal (always following the guidelines of the institution where they wish to enrol and register, or the funding agency from which they want to obtain funds). Students should not forget that they must be interested in the topic, otherwise they will never write a good piece of research; enthusiasm and interest are particularly important in qualitative inquiry because data collection and analysis take place over a long time period. The plan and design of the research should reflect the research question or problem and show how it might be answered or resolved.

The topic and research question

The research topic of sport students or other researchers involved in sport and physical activity will obviously have a basis in this particular area; for instance, it might be sport participation, sport fandom, or sport and social exclusion among the many varied research topics that exist within such a diverse field. Punch (2006) suggests that researchers ask themselves what they are trying to find out about a specific topic, and how the emerging questions can best be answered. This might lead to a straightforward question such as: 'What are the experiences of career termination among professional athletes?' It could also be an evaluation of a programme, such as the impact of a healthy walking pro-gramme upon older people. The research question is crucial not only for the proposal but also for the whole process of doing qualitative research. Luckily, qualitative researchers are allowed to be flexible – indeed flexibility is an impor-tant element of qualitative inquiry – and the initial question can change during the course of the proposal (and occasionally even afterwards, although in an undergraduate project or a Masters dissertation, change is not usually advisable, otherwise the study might never get off the ground). An example of this was the lead author's own PhD thesis which initially focused upon fan satisfaction in English football, but gradually evolved into a study exploring the concept of fandom as social identity (Jones, 1998). In the evolution of the research focus, the disciplinary boundaries of the study shifted from management to sociology. This type of change is a fundamental characteristic of qualitative research, and one that should be anticipated by the researcher (and the research supervisor). If students already know much about the topic and area they research, the question is probably not suitable for qualitative research, which often takes place in 'uncharted waters'; that is, in areas where not much research has been carried out before.

The topic of the research leads directly to the research question or research problem. For instance, the topic of research might be 'injury in competitive sports', while the research question could be: 'How do competitive female athletes cope with career-threatening injury?'

The research question or problem is often based on the following:

- The researcher's own personal experience as player, fan, coach or other role within sport and physical activity
- Academic reading as part of a sport or physical activity-related programme of study
- A topic that has been covered in the media

The topic should be researchable, doable in the time available, as well as relevant and interesting. One occasional misconception among students is that research into the higher levels of sport is somehow 'better' than, for example, research into lower-level amateur sport. In reality, some of the most interesting questions are to be found at the lower levels of the participation pyramid, or even in informal, non-competitive activities.

Research-ability

The topic and research problem must be researchable in the first instance. Only too often students wish to explore a philosophical question that requires an essay rather than a piece of empirical research. One of the characteristics of research is that it adds to, rather than simply evaluates, existing knowledge. If a topic does not require data, it is not researchable. The research question should direct the researcher to collect data that will help answer the question posed. Thus the following questions are not researchable: 'Should parents force their children to exercise?' or 'Is bullying by sport coaches wrong?' Moral or philosophical questions are not researchable.

Do-ability

The researchers should be able to conduct their study in the time-frame available. It is not appropriate to choose a problem that needs many years of immersion in the setting for a Masters dissertation. If not enough participants are available or willing to take part, some qualitative approaches are not doable – though of course others, such as phenomenology, do not need many participants. If the gatekeepers, those who allow access to participants, are unwilling to grant this entrée, the study is not feasible. The researcher should also be capable and knowledgeable enough to undertake the study. Students will need to convince their supervisors that they have the time and skills to carry out the research. Thus, time-frame, availability of participants, and researcher capability are important elements of do-ability or feasibility.

Relevance and interest

The topic should be relevant, that is, it should directly concern issues of sport and physical activity and it should be important and interesting for the readers of the final study. Advancing knowledge in the field is always a wish of researchers, and even an undergraduate project is an exercise in doing research which extends knowledge. Indeed, some undergraduate dissertations have been published, in collaboration with the supervisor, as journal articles. This is also a common phenomenon at postgraduate level, if the study has been well executed. Finally, as we said before, researchers themselves need be interested to be able to sustain their enthusiasm through much of the research process.

The selection of a topic and its conversion into a research question takes time and thought. It should be discussed with potential supervisors, other experts and peers. The research question for qualitative work must fit a qualitative approach; research questions with factual content are not suitable. Sometimes authors write about 'the research problem' rather than the research question: researchers might find something puzzling in a situation or setting that they want to explore, such as athletes' experiences of using sport psychologists, to cite just one example. If the topic or problem is not relevant or important, readers will find it boring to read.

Qualitative researchers formulate their question in a broad rather than a detailed way,. As the study proceeds, researchers become progressively more focused on specific issues that emerge in the early stages of their research from their observations and interviews. For example, a study that started by looking at the experiences of overseas football players finished by becoming an examination of host–visitor relations within a specific community.

Potential researchers also need a research design that best fits the research question or problem. For instance, if a theory is needed, researchers might develop a grounded theory study; if they are investigating a culture or subculture, they can take an ethnographic approach; whereas an exploration of the life world requires a phenomenological approach. In the early stages of the study, researchers can be flexible about the research question, but eventually they will need to be more specific so they do not get confused. The contribution to knowledge in the area of study must be stated, though this need not be dramatic and world-changing, as the potential work is only the first step in becoming a researcher. Distinctiveness from other studies in the field, especially for undergraduate and Masters research, is generally a much better aim than high (and often unachievable) levels of originality, and will demonstrate whether the dissertation is worth being carried out.

Writing the proposal

After making decisions about the topic, the approach and methods to be adopted, researchers are generally required to submit a proposal. A proposal is a plan of the potential research although it is not rigid and absolute as qualitative research is flexible and evolving. The proposal will describe clearly the research design: *what* will be done, *how* it will be done and *who* will be involved (Kilbourn, 2006). The most important issue is to produce a convincing argument for the intended research.

The purpose of the proposal

The proposal should show that the student or researcher is able to carry out the research and has the skills and knowledge to do so. It also allows the relevant department to assess whether the expertise and supervisory capacity are in place to supervise the proposed study; for instance, a student might wish to explore the role of exercise in the lives of people with mental health problems. This would require expertise in both the relevant fields of exercise and psychology. Finally, it may also outline the importance of the research. This may be either in terms of adding to academic knowledge or the potential practical implications of the study when it is complete.

The qualitative proposal is just an outline plan; the study might change and evolve over time. Usually research committees will be aware of the differences between qualitative and quantitative research, but it might be useful to explain why the proposal differs from proposals based on the quantitative approach. Morse (2003a) suggests that research committees judge the proposal on the quality of the idea in the proposal and the perceived competence of the researcher; hence the presentation of the proposal must demonstrate these. It is understood that the first proposal of a new researcher will not be evaluated as harshly as that of an expert in the field. It is important to add that a different type of proposal will be required from a funding agency, a doctoral research degree committee, and a dissertation coordinator for undergraduate and Masters programmes.

Length of the proposal

The length of the proposal varies across institutions and funding agencies; thus guidelines should be checked. As an example, a Masters student at Bournemouth University is required to write a 1200-word proposal, whereas for a potential doctoral student, the length is 1500 words.

Proposal contents

The proposal will generally include:

1   An initial working title (which can be changed before submission of the work)
2   An abstract
3   The introduction (which contains the background, rationale, initial literature review and aim)
4   A potential methodology (including approach, methods, sample, analysis and ethical considerations)
5   A short overview of expected implications for practice
6   A timeline or timetable for the study

These elements are mirrored in the final report which will be more extensive of course, to include findings, conclusions and implications for practice.

1. The working title

The title should reflect the aim of the research and must be clear and concise. If a title and abstract are interesting, they spur on the reader to read the rest of the work. Words such as *an investigation*, *a study*, etc. are unnecessary and can be avoided. The working title should neither be too long nor should it be formulated as a question, but it can have a subtitle. A department sometimes allows the title to be changed (in the doctorate by the time of the intention to submit, and in a Masters dissertation, changes are usually only allowed at an early stage).

Examples of potential titles

- 'Leisure, stress, and coping: the sport participation of collegiate student athletes' (Kimball and Freysinger, 2003).
- 'Black football players on a predominantly white college campus: psycho-social and emotional realities of the black college athlete experience' (Melendez, 2008).
- 'A grounded theory of young tennis players' use of music to manipulate emotional state' (Bishop et al., 2007).
- '"Shaking it off" and "toughing it out": socialisation to pain and injury in girls' softball' (Malcom, 2006).

---

2. The abstract

Sometimes an institution requires an abstract even for a proposal. This is a short outline or summary of the proposed research. It includes the topic and research question, the rationale, the proposed methodology and methods. Hence the main points are: *what* will be done, *how* it will be carried out and *with whom* (the participants). The abstract is the part of the proposal that the research committee sees first, thus it is important to present it with clarity and without mistakes. It should have enough information so that readers can overview and appraise the study quickly; indeed sometimes it guides the evaluators to read on rather than having doubts about the project at the very beginning.

3. The introduction and literature overview

This is sometimes called the introduction only (the institution often has a pro forma for a proposal). Here the researcher acquaints readers with the topic and area of study; it indicates the research question, and where the boundaries of the study will lie, i.e. what it will include and exclude. It is important to highlight the relevance of the research. If it is uninteresting or trivial, readers won't be drawn to the study. Thus the significance of the research must be identified. Researchers must also explain how the findings might extend knowledge in the field and they must point out implications for practice. The proposal puts the research question in context. Here researchers give the background to the study and explain why they wish to undertake it. At this stage, they also might explain their own background and its influence on the study, and how they arrived at the research question.

The initial literature review, which includes a critical discussion of some important foundational and key up-to-date studies in the field, will identify the gap in knowledge for the area of study and how and why the student intends to fill it (often jokingly called by supervisors 'not re-inventing the wheel'). All researchers need to demonstrate some familiarity with the field (hence the advice to get acquainted with the most important studies at the very beginning). From this background and initial literature review emerges the aim of the research. Some universities require objectives, the steps needed to achieve the aim, but in qualitative research they are not necessary as they arise in the course of the work. For the qualitative research aim, verbs such as *explore, examine, understand* are usual at this stage.

Examples of aims

- 'This study aims to provide a rich description of participants' experiences of watching their chosen team abroad.'
- 'This research aims to examine the perceived social impacts of a mega sporting event by members of the host community.'
- 'This dissertation aims to offer a detailed account of the surfing subculture within a tourist destination.'

In the final write-up, the introduction and literature review are often separate chapters, but there might not be space for extensive discussion in a proposal. Our own university has specific headings for the research proposal, so the researcher needs to check the guidelines of their own department or programme.

4. The methodology

The methodology needs to be justified to the research committee and potential supervisors. Why qualitative research? The researchers should show that they understand qualitative research and its basis, its aims and its distinctiveness from quantitative research (although they do not need to dwell on the latter). Included in the discussion is also the 'why not'. It is important to remember that the student need not go through all research approaches in detail to confirm their own selection (although we have heard some supervisors suggesting this), but that they justify their own approach in particular and in some detail. The question *why* is thus more important than the question *why not*, so it's best to start with the former. The researcher should also suggest the potential sources of data (for instance, interviewing, participant observation, documents or other visual data, etc.). If interviews are used, which

type – in-depth and unstructured or semi-structured? Fully structured interviews are, of course, not used in qualitative research (see Chapter 6).

a. The sample

The purposive and judgemental sample is chosen carefully from the appropriate group (see Chapter 5). Students need to state the sample size; how many
people will be included in their initial sample. There is always a possibility to
add to the sample, as the sampling frame is not rigidly fixed at the beginning
of the study. Exclusion and inclusion criteria need to be given. Who is not part
of this study and why not? Who will be included and why? The way the
researcher gains access to the sample also needs to be outlined.

b. Ethical considerations

Ethical issues need a short paragraph at this stage to show the research committee that they have been considered and that the student has gained (or will
gain) permission from the university ethics committee.

c. Data analysis

There should be an outline of the envisaged analysis, although at this stage it need
not be too detailed. The analysis must fit with the approach that will be used.

d. Validity (trustworthiness)

New researchers might not know much about validity, but they should consider, even at this early stage, how they will ensure that their study has validity
(see Chapter 15).

5. Potential outcomes

It is obvious that researchers cannot make a firm statement about the outcomes of the research, and it is hazardous to make a firm and absolute statement about this, especially as qualitative research is flexible and changes
during its process. Students could however suggest what impact or use the
research might have for their field.

6. The timeline

Universities are concerned about student completion and researchers should
stay within the guidelines for this. It is desirable and sometimes required to
have an exact timeline for the research. It should be noted that the literature
search and review are ongoing throughout the study (see Chapter 4).

Sometimes researchers fall at the first hurdle. In our experience, proposals are usually returned to students by dissertation coordinators or rejected by research committees for the following reasons:

- The proposal is poorly structured and worded, portraying a lack of commitment.
- Care should be taken over presentation, which can influence the reviewer's judgement of the proposal.
- The title is unclear.
- The research aim is unclear.
- There is no rationale for the topic chosen.
- Insufficient detail is offered on methodology.
- Reference to the literature is lacking or inadequate, on both topic and methodology.
- There is a clear misunderstanding of the methods to be used.

The importance of the proposal

What is the significance of the proposal? First, it opens the door to life as a researcher (this is especially significant to PhD students who cannot start their research journey if their proposal is unsuccessful); second, it shows a clear plan of action, instilling confidence in potential supervisors in the do-ability of the study; third, it highlights the relevance and timeliness of the research; fourth, it indicates the researcher's grasp of the subject and the methodology to be used; and finally, the gap in existing knowledge is established. Research can be a long, time-consuming process, and the proposal is an important first step in ensuring that the final outcome will be successful.

Summary

- The research question is more focused than the broader research topic
- The research should be doable, relevant and interesting
- The study will change during the research because qualitative inquiry is flexible and depends on what is found in its process
- The proposal is an action plan of the research – it needs to give a clear idea of what is going to be done and how

4

The Role of the Literature in Qualitative Research

The role and location of the literature represent key distinguishing features of qualitative research. Qualitative and quantitative literature reviews differ both in their nature and scope. Whilst quantitative researchers generally carry out an extensive literature review related to their topic, a different type of review is required in qualitative research. This chapter will point out the differing uses of the literature in a piece of qualitative research. It must, however, be emphasised that there is not a 'one size fits all' approach to the use of the literature, and there is variation among institutions, and guidance should be taken from supervisors prior to undertaking a review of the literature. Similarly, the attitude of journal editors and reviewers towards the place and function of the literature in qualitative research varies considerably, thus research students need to make themselves explicit to the reader so that examiners or journal editors understand the role of the literature, especially for journals that publish little qualitative research. Occasionally, papers might need to be amended depending upon the nature of the journal; again, this is something for which students need to seek guidance.

The literature and the proposal

The research proposal, whether for an undergraduate or a postgraduate dissertation or a PhD, will include a section on the existing literature related to the research topic. As well as an awareness of the state of knowledge and understanding of an area of research, the researcher should also show some knowledge of the methods used in previous studies. Furthermore, researchers will specify the contribution to knowledge that the proposed research will make, to demonstrate that it is needed to fill the gap in knowledge about the field of study. It is important to be able to show how the research is related to existing work. The rationale for, and the position of, the proposed study in the larger literature must be clear. Indeed, Creswell (1994) advocates drawing a figure or map of the existing literature, which indicates how the proposed study fills a gap. Therefore, some familiarity with the literature is required even at this early stage. The role of the initial literature review at the proposal stage is thus threefold:

- To establish the state of knowledge in the field
- To identify gaps and to show how the proposed research will contribute to existing knowledge
- To support the choice of approach taken

It is important to show that a search of the literature has been made, but it is equally imperative that the researcher does not force the research into a particular direction. Thus researchers may scan the relevant literature and can store useful sources for a later stage in the research process, but they will try not to let their reading influence the primary research that they conduct, by, for example, making presuppositions about what they may find or by asking leading questions in interviews. Creswell (2007) states that the emergent design of qualitative research must be reflected in the proposal which should not be prescriptive because the research process may evolve as data are collected; the sample and setting may be revised, and new avenues of exploration may be pursued.

The literature overview

At the start of the research, once the proposal and topic are accepted, it is common for qualitative researchers to undertake an overview of the literature. This is not an exhaustive review as undertaken by quantitative researchers, as the bulk of the literature in qualitative studies is tied to the themes that emerge from analysis. It is an initial rather than a comprehensive review. In a doctoral thesis, for example, it is not uncommon to find a literature section of just 25 pages at the start of the thesis. (The findings or the discussion chapter engages the researcher in a subsequent dialogue with the literature that is directly related to the findings, and which might not have been covered in the initial review.) It must be noted, however, that some qualitative researchers advise that little or no literature should be explored before primary data are collected, so that assumptions cannot colour the findings collected. This is, as Chenail et al. (2010) state, a find-ings-driven strategy whereby emerging findings dictate the literature accessed. However, researchers take different approaches to the use and role of the literature, and the novice researcher needs to be aware that examiners and reviewers may not share the same views as the supervisory team (and student of course). For this reason, Wolcott (2009) advises stu-dents and researchers to seek guidance and to make their choice of how to use the literature explicit. Some familiarity with the literature is desirable however, particularly about the theoretical concepts that might be involved in the research. In the literature section or chapter, the researcher should reference key studies of previous research on the topic, including findings and method of these research articles. This shows that duplication hasn't taken place and identifies a gap in knowledge and in methodology, and lends credence to the rationale for research. Researchers use the review to point to gaps in the literature that their study will address. For example, existing research may take place in a different context from theirs, it may be dated, it may have a different aim, it may adopt a different approach – or indeed, it may be full of flaws that must be pointed out and examined. As Creswell (2007: 40) notes, new research may need to be conducted 'when partial or inadequate theories exist'. It is of importance that the new research should illuminate the topic from a different perspective; it may be that the approach or the setting or the participants or the aim will be different from those covered in existing research.

It is very rare that no, or very little, previous research has been done on a topic. Often, when inexperienced researchers cite a total lack of literature, it is as a consequence of their search strategy, especially in terms of the actual focus of the study. Thus, a student exploring the adoption of sport psychology by coaches, for example, may suggest a lack of literature after undertaking a specific search focusing on all these terms together. By recognising that in this case, however, the study is not about sport coaches, but rather about the adop-tion of ideas that simply explore this notion within a sport-coaching context, suddenly a wide range of relevant (albeit non-sport-related) literature becomes available. It is here that looking to the parent discipline, such as psychology or sociology, rather than focusing purely on sport-related sources, can be use-ful. If, however, there is a genuine lack of any relevant literature, then this makes the overview difficult. Conversely it does demonstrate the need for the researcher's contribution to an important topic. If too much material exists in the field, there is no point in doing the research – adding to an already exhausted field of research – unless it can be shown that a radically new per-spective is needed.

Critical treatment of the literature is paramount. Researchers should critically evaluate, rather than simply describe what has already been done in the field. As Gratton and Jones (2010) point out, a critical stance is needed towards both content and method; it is not sufficient to present a list of what research has been done before. Critical analysis should not, however, just focus upon the negative aspects of existing research, but should also acknowledge the particular strengths of any studies. Adopting such a critical stance further supports the rationale for the research both in terms of addressing the weaknesses of past studies, but also potentially exploiting the strengths of other studies. The literature should not just be a summary or description of what the articles or books contain. Being critical and analytic in this context, the researcher asks the following questions:

- Did the research fulfil its stated aim?
- Are there shortcomings such as inconsistencies or contradictions?
- Are the arguments persuasive and convincing?
- Are they supported by findings?
- Does the research lack evidence?
- Have the authors neglected contrary occurrences?
- Do they show bias for or against certain types of information?
- Do the authors have credibility?

In the initial review, the methodological approach adopted by the authors cited also needs to be described and critically discussed. It is important to have a grasp of the research methods used by researchers in the field, and to identify the weaknesses of the methods they have used. This might involve reference to the research approach adopted, to the sampling techniques used and to methods of analysis. In the methodology chapter, of course, it will be important to cover the literature on the chosen methodological approach, covering the evolution of its use, both generally and in the chosen field.

The inductive approach

Qualitative researchers adopt an inductive approach to inquiry – in other words, they let the data lead them; they (and the literature) do not lead the data. Inductive reasoning proceeds from specific cases or observations to general principles. Meanwhile, Spradley (1979) advises that researchers start their research with 'an attitude of almost complete ignorance' (p. 4), while Fetterman (2010: 1) states that researchers begin 'with an open mind, not an empty head'. Related to this, phenomenologists refer to the process of bracketing (see Chapter 11), which entails the suspension or putting aside of prior knowledge – including that of the literature – so that it doesn't colour or influence data collection.

> ### Assessing prior knowledge and attitudes through bracketing
>
> Cope et al. (2010) explored the role of the 'cancer' within sport groups (i.e. an athlete who expresses negative emotions that spread destructively throughout a team). A strategy of 'reflexive bracketing' was used to identify the primary researcher's existing ideas and values regarding the idea of the 'cancer' and its subsequent effects upon the team. To do this, a member of the research team led her through the initial interview guide and asked her to provide responses to each question. The intention of the strategy was not to 'remove' pre-existing ideas, but rather to assess them in order to allow them to be accounted for in the subsequent analysis. The bracketing process identified a number of assumptions held by the lead author, for example that there were individuals who likely fulfil the negative role of 'cancer' within most teams or, at the very least, that most coaches had come in contact with a 'cancer' at some point in their coaching career. It also allowed the primary researcher to identify that she had previous experience as a coach interacting with an individual occupying the role of a cancer, and felt that it was important to control and manage such individuals.

Thus, it is important to set aside the preconceptions and assumptions that are born from both experience and familiarity with the literature, but one cannot pretend that one knows nothing. It must also be pointed out that in the case of semi-structured interviews, questions may often derive from previous experience and from the literature consulted.

The influence of the inductive approach comes to the fore in both the approach to data collection and in the presentation and discussion of findings. As stated above, the literature review is processual – it is directed by the findings collected by the researcher. Qualitative research is, nevertheless, not always purely inductive. Some approaches such as grounded theory suggest that researchers sometimes move between induction and deduction as they follow up findings and search for the concepts that emerged in further interviews or observations (though many qualitative researchers disagree). Indeed, Strauss and Corbin (1998) advise that researchers examine provisional hypotheses or working propositions; this seems to be a form of deduction.

The ongoing dialogue with the literature

The bulk of the literature in qualitative research is tied to the themes that are generated by analysis. Literature directly related to the findings is critically reviewed as the research proceeds. The researcher provides an audit trail of what has been done, including the literature reviewed, to enhance clarity and credibility. A dialogue between the relevant literature and the primary data takes place throughout the findings and/or discussion chapters. The literature helps to illuminate and interpret the data (Wolcott, 2009), and it can be used to answer questions posed by the data. The function of the literature at this stage is threefold:

- To compare findings with those of others
- To examine whether the research literature confirms or challenges findings
- To identify an original contribution.

As soon as researchers start analysing the data, they look at the directly relevant literature related to their findings – some of which they might have already collected but not read in detail at the beginning. Wolcott (2009) argues that the researcher must become a master of the literature related to the themes. Some students make the mistake of only perusing the research in their own specific field; as we noted earlier, there is often a wealth of literature in the broader disciplines – for instance a concept like 'thrown in at the deep end' or 'working in the dark', previously examined concepts in teaching or nursing might have relevance when discussing how people take up a new sport or when novice coaches deliver a session without having any idea about what they are supposed to do. Researchers can thus broaden their search and examine studies that are directly relevant to the themes or categories which they discover, and this may take them outside their area of comfort. The inductive nature of qualitative research means that an interdisciplinary focus to the analysis is often needed, so it is important not to be restricted to the researcher's 'home' discipline.

The next step is to compare the findings of the literature with one's own. Sometimes it confirms one's own findings, occasionally it contradicts (disconfirms) or challenges them. It is the researcher's job to interpret similarities and differences, and to highlight plausible reasons for any differences that may exist. Where one's own original contribution is established, this should be highlighted, and should be clear, rather than hidden away.

In the final chapter or section of the research report, conclusions are drawn from the researchers' own data, which are related back to the aim of the research. However, findings should be contextualised, and it is appropriate to show where their own work is located within existing research. Before submission, it is advisable to scan the literature again to add relevant up-to-date material which might interact with the findings. Time may well have elapsed between data collection, analysis and interpretation, and the final write-up.

We would like to emphasise that qualitative researchers are flexible in their approach to the literature. While we would advocate integrating the literature in the findings or discussion chapter (or the chapter that collates the findings and discussion), writers employ a variety of ways to weave the literature into the study, as shown in the following examples:

Examples of different types of literature review

- The report of a study in a journal article on how football goalkeepers cope with negative media content (Kristiansen et al., 2012) seems to have a relatively short initial literature review with discussions of coping among athletes and the stressors they experience. The researchers justify this by explaining that there is relatively little research on this aspect of media pressure on football goalkeepers. These and other aspects became a matter for dialogue and integration with the findings of the researchers. This is a relevant example of qualitative research where not much research has been carried out on the specific topic.
- A phenomenological study of young adult women exercisers' body self-compassion by Berry et al. (2010) locates the research within the literature of self-compassion, self-esteem and exercise behaviour. This is a fairly lengthy review of linked concepts. The rest of the 'body-related' literature is woven into the discussion.
- On the other hand, Darko (2011) has a lengthy review of the literature in the introduction to her study on rugby players' body anxieties as well as a large section in her research about visual methods. There is not much literature in her findings or in her discussion of the research.

Keeping track of references

It is vital from the start of the research process to maintain and regularly update the list of references, including all the necessary bibliographic detail to suit the referencing style used by the researcher's institution. We know from bitter experience that one sometimes forgets details, and if the article or book cannot be found again and the deadline is imminent, an important reference may have to be deleted. If research findings are to be published in a book or journal, it is important to check on the referencing style used: reformatting a reference list can be onerous, and time should be allowed for this stage of the write-up. It is advisable to note down the full names of authors as some journals require the use of first names, not just initials; it also establishes the gender of the writer. Poor referencing can negatively impact on both reviewers' and markers' judgement of a piece of research, or even result in a submission being returned for correction.

Summary

- Quantitative and qualitative research differ in their treatment of the literature
- The literature review in the early stages of research helps to establish the gap in knowledge and the rationale for the research
- Analysis of primary data leads the researcher to the rest of the relevant literature
- The literature helps to illuminate and interpret the data collected

5

Sampling

Sampling can be described as the purposeful selection of an element of a whole population to obtain data relevant to your study. In qualitative research, sampling strategies are different from those used by quantitative researchers; probability sampling, for instance, is inappropriate in qualitative research. There are various sampling methods to be used, the choice of which is dictated by the research topic. At the start of the research, researchers must ask two questions: *what* to sample and *how* to sample. It is important in the methodology section of the research account to describe and justify the sampling strategies used and to explain how access was gained to the participants.

Purposive sampling

According to Creswell (2007), purposive sampling means that the researcher chooses participants and settings that will inform an understanding of the research question. The selection of participants is criterion-based, that is, certain criteria are formulated, and the sample is chosen accordingly. Sampling units are selected in line with the purpose of the research, therefore the term 'purposive' or 'purposeful' sampling is used. Sandelowski (2000) points out that the goal of purposive sampling is to gain rich information according to the purpose of the study. Individuals are sampled for the information they can provide about a specific phenomenon. As Mason (2002: 121) states, 'essentially the work you are asking of your sample is to help provide you with the data which you will need to address your research questions'. For instance, the study by Thomas et al. (2011) into the characteristics of robust sport confidence used focus group interviews. Given the suggestion that elite performers have a greater awareness of robust self-confidence, a purposive sample was adopted based upon defining elite performers as those who had received international honours or those who had represented their country at a major event such as the Olympic Games. The sample is thus specified in advance, once the aim and research focus have been chosen. Purposeful sampling may also refer to the research setting or to decisions on *when* to sample.

Participants may be chosen by the researcher, or they may be self-selected. Sometimes researchers can easily identify individuals or groups with special knowledge of a topic; occasionally they advertise for participants who have insight or knowledge of the research topic. Identification of a particular population provides boundaries between those who are included in and those who are excluded from the study: inclusion and exclusion criteria must be specified to the reader.

Sampling types

There are various types of sampling, which may be combined in a single study (Creswell, 2007). The most commonly used are as follows:

- Homogeneous sampling
- Heterogeneous sampling
- Total population sampling
- Chain referral sampling (snowball sampling)
- Convenience or opportunistic sampling
- Maximum variation sampling
- Theoretical sampling

Homogeneous sampling

This involves individuals who belong to the same subculture or have similar characteristics. The sample can be homogeneous with respect to one variable only – for instance, occupation, marital status, age or gender. The important variable should be established before the sampling starts.

Homogeneous sampling: identity formation and adaptation to retirement from competitive sport

The study by Lavallee and Robinson (2007) examines the factors influencing identity formation and adaptation to retirement from competitive sport through the use of semi-structured interviews. The authors chose homogeneous sampling, identifying criteria for the recruitment of the sample. All participants were former female gymnasts aged between 22 and 25 years old, each having competed at least at regional level. Given the suggestion of a link between ethnicity and athletic identity, it was also decided that all participants would be British. They noted that in terms of capturing the experience of a specific group, 'the use of a small homogeneous sample was particularly beneficial' (p. 139). They suggested, however, that the study was also limited by its sport- and gender-specific focus.

Heterogeneous sampling

A heterogeneous sample, also known as 'maximum variation sampling', contains individuals with differing experiences. It may include, for example, participants of varying age, of different nationality and economic status. It can also include variations in settings. Given that the researcher will access a wide range of perspectives, the sample will be relatively large. Mason (2002) similarly refers to representational sampling whereby the researcher aims to achieve a representative microcosm of the population by collecting data from participants who vary in terms of key variables.

Heterogeneous sampling: perceptions of sport and business leaders

Weinberg and McDermott (2002) compared and contrasted the perceptions of sport and business leaders through 20 semi-structured interviews with what they termed 'leaders'. A heterogeneous sample was chosen in terms of ethnicity, gender, employment and experiences of both success and failure. The authors selected their approach in order to achieve a representation from a wide cross-section of organisations and positions within those organisations.

An extension of heterogeneous sampling is a type of 'maximum variation sampling' which aims to recruit participants whose characteristics vary as much as possible. For example, Soundy et al. (2007), in their study of lifestyle physical activity among individuals with severe mental health problems, selected a maximum variation sample based on weight, gender, perceived physical activity and mental health.

Maximum variation sampling: athletes' experiences of rehabilitation and recovery from anterior cruciate ligament injury

The study by Olofsson et al. (2010) investigated athletes' experiences of rehabilitation and recovery from anterior cruciate ligament injury using semi-structured interviews with seven participants. These were 'selected to reach a maximum variation sample according to gender, age, activity level, time between injury and ACL reconstruction and time between surgery and the interview' (p. 50). It was felt that participants 'in this study corresponded well to the mixed group of patients who have undergone ACL surgery' (pp. 55–6).

Total population sampling

A sample is called a total population sample when all participants from a particular setting are selected, as is often the case in ethnography.

Snowball sampling

Using this sampling method means that participants nominate others with knowledge of the research topic. Researchers use snowball sampling (also known as 'chain referral sampling') in studies where they cannot easily identify participants; where participants are not easily accessible; or where anonymity is needed, for instance in studies of the maltreatment of athletes.

Snowball sampling: volunteering in sport among older adults

Hamm-Kerwin et al. (2009) explored the factors associated with volunteering in sport among older adults through 20 semi-structured interviews. They initially generated their sample through contacting the presidents of a number of community sport organisations who were asked to identify any volunteers who would be eligible based on the researchers' criteria, and likely to be willing to participate. This allowed seven participants to be identified for initial interviews. These participants were asked to identify any volunteers who met the criteria of the study, allowing an additional 13 participants to be recruited.

Convenience or opportunistic sampling

With this type of sampling, the researcher exploits any opportunity they can, however unexpected, to collect data. This method may be adopted when the researcher finds it difficult to recruit participants, thus any chance to collect data must be seized. Convenience sampling was adopted in Gearity's (2011) study of athletes' experiences of poor coaching using a sample of 16 current or former athletes drawn from the author's own university. Sampling also refers to the choice of setting, as reflected in the study by Warner and Griffiths (2006) of exercise addiction, which focused on three gyms in the West Midlands region of England. These gyms were chosen simply, as the authors point out, because they were the three main gyms in the home town of the first author.

Theoretical sampling

Theoretical sampling, which is most associated with grounded theory (see Chapter 9), develops as the study proceeds; it cannot be planned in advance. After data have been collected from the initial purposively chosen sample, researchers select their ongoing sample on the basis of the concepts that emerge during analysis. Sampling can stop when data saturation has been reached, that is when no new ideas arise that are of value to the developing theory.

Sampling decisions

Researchers make their sampling decisions early on in the research project, often at the proposal-writing stage. It is important that qualitative researchers offer a clear account of, and rationale for, their sampling decisions in the methodology section of their research account. In a doctoral exam, questions about the sample are likely to be posed, and the researcher must be prepared to give a fluent account and justification of their decisions. Sampling strategies can make a difference to the whole study; clearly, the data collected will vary among participants (Mason, 2002). A sample can be described in terms of people, time or setting. Researchers have to decide who to sample, when to sample and where to sample: they cannot investigate everything, but it is important to justify what was investigated.

Qualitative research is characterised by flexibility, thus sampling decisions often continue to be made after the initial data have been collected. This is because the research focus may change or expand as the research progresses, depending on their initial findings. This is especially the case in grounded theory and ethnography. Thus, the sampling strategy differs from quantitative research where respondents are chosen before the project begins.

Inclusion and exclusion criteria

When accounting for their sampling strategies, researchers need to state what their inclusion and exclusion criteria are. For instance, for ethical reasons, vulnerable adults may be excluded from a study, as may children. A study of football fandom may exclude those with only a casual interest in the sport, or a particular team, unless the aim is to investigate external perceptions of fandom. The exclusion and inclusion criteria depend on the aim of the particular study.

Defining criteria: the roles of significant others in adolescent swimming patterns

Fraser-Thomas et al. (2008) explored the roles of significant others in adolescent swimming patterns. Criteria for participation in the study were as follows:

a. Swimmers were to be aged between 13 and 18
b. A minimum of four years' competitive swimming experience was stipulated

(Continued)

(Continued)

c. Involvement in a minimum of ten hours training per week was required. These criteria were produced to eliminate younger sport 'samplers' and older swimmers whose withdrawal from participation may have been a natural transition at the end of their education. This allowed a clear link between the overall aim of the study and the choice of participants to be demonstrated.

Sampling parameters

Decisions on time and location of sampling must be made explicit by the researcher. The criteria for selection must be clearly identified. Research may be conducted in a variety of contexts or in one single setting, such as a school, a competition or a training ground; and data could be collected at different times of the day, week, month or year. These are significant factors in the type and quality of data collected.

Choosing the setting: the influence of physical education on self-image

The study by Perrin-Wallqvist and Carlsson (2011) investigated the influence of physical education on self-image from a phenomenological perspective. The importance of participants being willing to share their experiences with a stranger was acknowledged by the researchers; thus they determined that an important criterion regarding the setting was that the study be conducted at a school 'where there was a good environment for implementing interviews' (p. 937). The setting was chosen due to good contact between the researchers and the physical education teachers where there had been previous collaboration and where the PE teachers had good personal knowledge of the pupils and thus guided the selection of the interviewees.

Sample size

Sample size varies among qualitative studies, and is dependent on a number of factors, including the research aim and the time available. In qualitative research, the sample is usually small as the focus is on depth; generalisation is not the aim. A note of caution is sounded here: some funding agencies, journal editors and even external examiners may question a small sample size through a lack of understanding of the aim of qualitative research. This often leads to the choice of a large sample, in an effort to placate external bodies, but this is not advised, as a very large sample might result in a loss of depth and richness, and thus may actually be counter-productive.

Students often ask how big a sample should be, and although there are no fixed rules, a guideline offered by Holloway and Wheeler (2010) is as follows: a homogeneous group might contain six to eight participants, while a heterogeneous sample might contain between 14 and 20 participants. A quick review of studies using qualitative methods will show, however, a wide variation in sample size. Each research approach will also carry differing implications for sample size. Whereas narrative and phenomenological researchers may interview as few as one to three people, grounded theorists will usually seek an interview sample of around 20, and ethnographers will seek data from as many people in the research setting as possible, though they will also interview key informants. The most important factor to consider is how many participants will offer the data needed to answer the question in mind.

Examples of sample size

There is a diverse range of sample sizes within the sport and physical activity literature. To demonstrate this diversity, three studies can be highlighted:

- Kavanagh (2012) used a sample size of one in her narrative study of recovery and rehabilitation from spinal cord injury.
- Fletcher and Arnold (2011) conducted a study of performance leadership in elite sport, which involved interviews with 13 national performance directors.
- McDonald's (2007) study of Kalarippayattu (a Keralese martial art) involved a total of 41 interviews. Heterogeneous sampling was used.

Mason (2002) states that sample size does not preoccupy many qualitative researchers who seek through their sample not representativeness but to provide 'a flavour – sometimes a very vivid or illuminating one' (p. 126) of life for the target population.

Reaching saturation point

Data saturation means that all data of significance to the research aim have been collected. *Theoretical saturation* indicates that no new concepts that are important for the study have emerged. Saturation does not mean that nothing new can be found; it is rather tied to the research aim. According to Bowen (2008), it is challenging for researchers to recognise saturation point, and for this reason, he advocates that claims that saturation point has been reached should be supported with evidence.

Accessing the sample

Practical and ethical questions of access must be considered when choosing the sample. It may prove difficult to obtain access from gatekeepers to the desired research setting; much – sometimes wasted – time can be spent on negotiating access. If positive relationships can be made with gatekeepers, however, then access becomes easier; for example, Thomsen et al. (2004) used in-depth interviews with 41 athletes to examine how adolescent female volley ball players constructed meanings from photographs of athletes in sport magazines. Given the age of the participants, permission was required from the coaches to allow participation in the study. Support from the gatekeepers allowed the researchers to access a very large sample, in qualitative terms. Had such co-operation not been forthcoming, then access would have been impossible. Furthermore, the researcher may have a clear sample in mind, but may be concerned that it may be disturbing to approach potential participants if the topic is a sensitive one. Thomas et al. (2007) argue that too little attention is paid to the emotional labour put into the process of recruiting participants, which is a time-consuming stage in research.

It is also possible that targeted individuals may not want to participate in the research project or they may offer less time than is needed for an in-depth interview, for example. Clark (2010) cites several factors that motivate people to participate in research, including personal interest, enjoyment and curiosity; these may not always be present in potential recruits. This may be the case even in a situation where gatekeeper access to an organisation has been granted. We have experienced ourselves a number of situations where the identified sample has been unwilling to give up their time, leading to the abandonment of the research project. In such a scenario, the researcher must have a 'plan B' with alternative sampling strategies. Time may also pose a problem: the researcher may plan to conduct 20 interviews, for example, but may run out of time, under-estimating the time and personal resources needed to conduct qualitative research, such as the time required to transcribe interviews. This may have consequences for the quality of data collected.

Referring to the sample

The way researchers refer to their participants varies, as the literature shows, from subject to respondent to participant to informant to co-researcher. Though 'respondent' is commonly used by quantitative and occasionally by qualitative researchers, we would not recommend its use because the term implies a passivity that runs counter to the freedom offered to the participants to express themselves. The same can be said for the term 'subject', which suggests a lack of power and a subjugation to the researcher. Meanwhile, whilst anthropologists and ethnographers commonly refer to 'informants' – those members of a culture who 'inform' the researcher about their world – it has been suggested that it carries negative connotations, being linked to the word 'informant' as used by the police, with a suggestion of providing privileged information about a group without the knowledge of others, often for personal gain. The term increasingly used by qualitative researchers is 'participant', which implies collaboration between the researcher and the researched, and is one that we would suggest is preferable.

Summary

- Sampling is usually purposeful and criterion-based, chosen in accordance with the research aim
- The sample in qualitative research is generally small
- Sampling refers to participants, time and setting
- Sampling is not always fixed before the study starts
- Sampling decisions must be made explicit
- Ethical issues in accessing participants must be carefully considered, and should be discussed in the methodology

PART II

COLLECTING QUALITATIVE DATA

6

Interviews

Interviewing has become a valuable source of data for students and professional researchers alike as they feel able to gain an insider view on the experiences of participants and the meaning they give to these experiences. These first-person accounts are strategies for exploring in depth the thoughts and feelings of participants as well as offering an insight into phenomena of interest to researchers in the sports and physical activity arena. As we have noted in Chapter 1, interviews are, by some considerable way, the most common qualitative data collection method in sport and physical activity.

Many research texts now use the term 'conversation with a purpose' to define the in-depth interview (quoting the expression used by Beatrice and Sidney Webb who carried out social research around the turn of the last century). As with participant observation, the researcher is the main research tool in interviews; interviewer and interviewee become 'conservational partners' (a term used by Rubin and Rubin, 2005: 14). However, interviewers go beyond conversation, as they have an agenda and a research focus in mind; this is the case in both formal and informal interviews. Interviews need to be prepared, or at least reflected on – even when unstructured – so that the most can be made of the research encounter.

Students sometimes feel that carrying out interviews is an easy and quick way of doing research, but the process of doing and analysing interviews demands complex skills in both areas. In terms of undertaking interviews, students commonly experience difficulties in their first effort, often developing their interviewing skills only after several attempts. This can obviously be an important issue to consider if a small sample size is anticipated.

The purpose of the interview – the 'why' of interviewing – is to uncover the world of the participants, their thoughts and feelings on a phenomenon, and an account of their experiences. For instance, the research question might be to examine motivation among elite female triathletes as Waddel-Smith (2010) did, or the thoughts and conflicts of mothers who surf (Spowart et al., 2010) or indeed to explore the life-course perspective of young athletes (Phoenix et al., 2007). Researchers also attempt to find the meaning which people give to these experiences. This way, they extend their knowledge of a phenomenon and the understanding that participants attach to it. Priority in qualitative interviewing is given to the ideas of the participants rather than the researcher's agenda which, however, still has to be taken into account for the fulfilment of the aim of the study. Interviews are especially useful when they explore areas and phenomena about which little is known. Findings can lead to the generation of new concepts and theories, and potentially help in the formulation of a new research agenda.

Types of interview

The qualitative interview has different forms depending on the agenda of the researcher. The two main types are the unstructured and the semi-structured interview. Both are in-depth interviews and elicit rich data. Most qualitative interviews, whether unstructured or semi-structured, become progressively more focused as the interview unfolds, determined by the issues raised by participants. New lines of inquiry may emerge for which the researcher had not prepared, and if relevant and of interest, they can be pursued.

The unstructured interview

The researcher who uses unstructured interviews allows the participant to take some control of the interview. It starts with a broad question and an *aide mémoire* which is a list of topics that might be covered depending on the direction of the interview. None of the questions, apart from the first, are predetermined but develop in the process of interviewing when they might become more focused. The researcher and the participants are free to take up important issues which arise in the course of their interaction and in particular can follow up unanticipated ideas which previously had not occurred to them.

Example of an unstructured interview

'Tell me about your experience of running in the marathon.'
Aide mémoire:

- Feelings while running
- Interaction with other runners
- Coping with pain
- Emotions after the run

Unstructured interviews are flexible and allow participants and researchers to pursue their interests. In particular, the control and the direction of the interview lie with the participants who divulge the thoughts and feelings they want to disclose. Unstructured interviews allow participants a greater voice – they can express themselves in their own words and at their own pace – and they thereby minimise the influence of the interviewer (Denzin and Lincoln, 1998). Researchers have minimal control over the process and the interview can take a long time. They may occasionally find that the participant talks about issues unrelated to the research; indeed, the unstructured, in-depth interview might have a high 'dross rate' (material of little use for the agenda of the researcher) because of the control enjoyed by participants. Seidman (2006) recommends that the researcher might try to 're-direct' the participants to fulfil their agenda; however, this term is problematic in qualitative research which should be focused on guidance not direction.

Unstructured interviews: exploring the experiences of long-distance walking

Crust et al. (2011) explored the experiences of long-distance walking through the use of unstructured interviews in their phenomenological study. This was seen as an appropriate approach given the lack of understanding of the activity in the literature. The authors stressed the need for the participant rather than the interviewer to be regarded as the expert. Six interviews, each lasting between 30 and 60 minutes, were undertaken. All used an opening question of: 'What was it like to walk a long-distance footpath?' (p. 246). Follow-up questions formed part of 'the natural flow of conversation' (p. 246). Prompts were used to elaborate on experiences such as: 'Can you tell me a little more about that?' and 'Can you tell me how you felt?'

The semi-structured interview

As we noted earlier, interviews are the most common method to be found within qualitative studies into sport and physical activity. Of the different types of interview, the semi-structured approach is by far the most common type to be found in the literature. Semi-structured or focused interviews consist of more specific questions, found in an interview guide. The latter term is preferable to 'the interview schedule', used by quantitative researchers, because the guide is less rigid and fixed. Although the main focus is on the topic area of interest to the researcher, the participant nevertheless has some control over direction and focus; the agenda is still flexible and depends on individual responses. Although some questions might be pre-planned, the response often dictates further questions and generates more ideas and a different formulation of the questions in the process of the interview, hence no one qualitative interview is exactly like another. Indeed, the interviewer can jettison planned questions if the participant raises new and interesting topics or if a few questions are covered in depth. Furthermore, the interview guide may evolve as interviews are conducted. However, as the name implies, the semi-structured interview has some structure and researchers tend to follow their agenda to a greater extent in order to achieve a specific aim of exploring a phenomenon or eliciting participants' thoughts and feelings. Though the sequencing and exact wording of questions will not be the same through all interviews, the researcher will ask most of the questions in the interview guide. The semi-structured interview can save time and effort because it has a clearer focus from the very beginning; the dross rate is rather lower than in an unstructured interview. In their paper, Jowett and Timson-Katchis (2005) include an interview guide consisting of 15 questions that were asked to parents during semi-structured interviews. Here are some of the questions they asked:

1   Why did you wish your young child to start swimming?
2   What sort of opportunities have you provided to your child in starting and continuing their sport participation?
3   In what ways has the organisation of the sport enabled or hampered the opportunities you could possibly have taken?
4   What were the main reasons that determined your decision to select that coach over another for your young child?
5   What do you think is the impact of the opportunities you have provided in determining the developing partnership between your child and their coach?

Even with such a guide, however, it is important for the researcher to be able to adapt, modify, add and omit questions depending upon the responses from the participant. This can be a difficult skill to learn, and will often develop as the researcher becomes more experienced.

Using-semi structured interviews to explore the role of public sector tourism planners capitalising on sport event tourism

In a study of the role of public sector tourism planners capitalising on sport event tourism, Wright (2007) justified his choice of a semi-structured interview with 11 representatives of New Zealand-based tourism organisations. He suggested that because 'a certain degree of basic structure was deemed necessary to avoid the respondent drifting too far from the topic', the semi-structured format was preferred, allowing both the researcher and the respondent some flexibility and freedom to develop their own narratives during each interview (p. 349).

The structured or standardised interview

Though many research methods texts refer to three types of interview, qualitative researchers tend not to use standardised interviews because they are pre-planned and rigidly applied. They do not offer the advantages of flexibility and spontaneity that are typical traits of qualitative research (on the other hand, consistency can be more easily established). This type of interview is more suited to a quantitative survey in which the interview *schedule* contains strictly structured, pre-planned questions, all asked in the same order. Structured interviews may contain open questions, but even then they cannot be called qualitative because the structure imposes some rigidity. In qualitative research, structured questions can be used to find facts on a face sheet, such as socio-demographic data (e.g. age, occupation, qualifications, or gender).

Variety of interviews

Interviews can take various forms. They might be formal or informal, indeed they can be just chats with participants who will be more relaxed in social situations than in formal interviews. These are referred to by Mason (2002) as opportunistic conversations.

Subtle differences exist in the variety of research approaches although they share commonalities. Phenomenological interviews are unstructured, and focus on a specific phenomenon such as the pain of a long-distance runner. The aim of the phenomenological interview is to go beyond specific cases and to find insights that are shared among human beings – the 'essences' or 'essential structure' of the phenomenon. Meanwhile, grounded theory interviews proceed in a different way, as the researcher follows up concepts which emerge in successive interviews (theoretical sampling). Ethnographic interviews are more discursive and explore the culture of key informants; both formal and informal interviews are used in an ethnographic study.

Less traditional than face-to-face interviews, the use of online and computer-mediated research tends to be popular with students, and its popularity is only likely to grow. In 2001, Seymour argued for the use of new technologies in data collection, valuing the freedom IT gave to interviewers and participants alike to choose their own time to go online. Indeed, the growth among researchers of IT use in data collection has been fast. Interviews can be conducted by email, through an online chat room or special interest forum, and by Skype. Researchers can also use online fora where messages and replies stay in place for a while, easing data collection. A disadvantage of conducting an interview by Skype (or by phone) is that the conversation cannot be recorded easily, putting pressure on the researcher to take notes or to recall what was said.

The individual one-to-one interview on email can be described as either synchronous or asynchronous (Mann and Stewart, 2000). The former takes place in real time and is immediate, the latter in non-real time where participants can hold an email conversation with the researcher (and others if emails are shared among a group of people). Internet researchers maintain that these conversations are difficult, especially if they involve cross-cultural or cross-national research because of different time zones. The advantages are the spontaneity and immediacy of responses between participant and interviewer, and the lack of reliance on 'time and space' as Seymour argues.

An easier and possibly more productive way of doing internet research is through asynchronous email, which records a conversation between interviewer and participant(s). Participants cannot be labelled or stereotyped because visual cues about appearance and tone of voice are absent. Hence electronic research provides a more egalitarian forum and is less intrusive; the interviewer effect does not work as strongly as it might in face-to-face interviews; furthermore, participants can choose their own time to respond. They are able to reflect on their words and those of the interviewer or other participants. The procedure works best when the research dialogue is an ongoing process over time.

Using asynchronous and synchronous email interviews: constraints to participation in Parkour, and brand communities in English professional football

An example of an asynchronous email interview can be found in Bavinton's (2007) examination of the constraints to participation in Parkour. As part of a mixed-methods study, interviews were carried out with 14 participants. Given the geographical spread of the sample (eight from Australia, three from the US and three from the UK), asynchronous email interviews were deemed to be the most appropriate means by which to have a conversation with the participants who could respond to contact at their leisure.

Kerr and Emery (2011) examined the brand community of Liverpool FC overseas to explore first how fans may benefit from being members of such a community as well as identifying opportunities for sport marketers to capitalise on 'brand admirers' (p. 202). Given the geographically dispersed nature of these communities (for example, Canada, Indonesia, Norway and Australia), synchronous online interviews were identified as an appropriate method. Thirty interviews were conducted using instant messaging technology in an interactive forum, each lasting approximately one hour. Interviews were instantaneously transcribed through messaging software. The authors identify the key strength of the online synchronous approach to be that it kept the conversation spontaneous.

Telephone interviews, though rare in sports and physical activity studies, can provide additional information if observation and/or face-to-face interviews have been previously carried out. Alternatively, they allow researchers to communicate with participants to whom they have limited access, for instance, immediately after an event such as a marathon when the participants don't wish to talk, or when the setting is closed to others – such as a private gym. They can also be used where students lack access to participants who live at a distance, and they add to other methods of data collection (Mann and Stewart, 2000).

A disadvantage of telephone interviewing, similar to that of the e-interview, is the lack of social context if the interviewer has not met the informant before. Telephone interviews are generally much shorter than face-to-face interviews; often they tend to be more focused and semi-structured, and the interviewer collects fewer, and more superficial data. The interaction between interviewer and interviewee is less intimate or intense, and Opdenakker (2006) argues that the lack of 'social cues', such as facial expressions and body language, are a hindrance to the interaction between interviewer and informant. This observation can be applied to the e-interview too (but also note the advantages).

Using telephone interviews: parental influences on coach/athlete relationships

Jowett and Timson-Katchis (2005) explored the influences that parents exert on coach/athlete relationships. Fifteen participants (five coach–athlete–parent triads) were interviewed by a researcher trained in telephone-interview techniques. As the authors note, there are both strengths and weaknesses to this approach. Strengths included the elimination of travel time and costs; access to populations that would otherwise be impossible; and the notion that telephone-collected data is not distinctly different in quality than that collected face-to-face. For this particular study, the authors suggest that, for the athletes in particular, telephones were a habitual communication method. They do, however, acknowledge that such interviews lack non-verbal communication and visual cues.

Asking questions

Interview questions differ from research questions. Research questions in qualitative research, as said before, are broader questions which the researcher attempts to answer in the study or problems which need to be solved, while interview questions are more specific and can be seen as steps on the way to achieving the broader aim of the research. Kvale and Brinkman (2009: 135–6) list question types, some of which are illustrated below:

1   Introductory questions – these are usually broad and serve to get participants talking, in a bid to relax them.
2   Follow-up questions – these 'hook into' the ideas of the interviewees and follow up on what they say. Researchers deeply explore concepts that emerge from the interview. For this part of the interview, the use of prompts is important.

3   Detailed questions – these are more focused and occur usually towards the end of the interview.

Using prompts: exploring mental toughness in Australian football

An example of using prompts is provided by Gucciardi et al. (2008) in their paper on mental toughness in Australian football. Semi-structured interviews were undertaken with 11 male football coaches. The interview schedule consisted of six questions, such as: 'What do you think mental toughness in Australian football is? Can you offer a definition, phrase or quote to describe it?' (p. 265). Questions were followed up by both clarification prompts such as 'What do you mean by...?' and elaboration prompts such as 'Can you give me an example of...?' This encouraged the clarity and richness of data.

As we suggest in Chapter 10, Spradley (1979) gives suggestions for interviews as well as observation. In interviewing he differentiates between grand-tour questions and mini-tour questions. One type looks at an overall scene, for instance questions on football fans' behaviours at games; the other on more specific issues: 'How do you feel when doing this particular exercise?' or 'tell me about a typical day on the football field'. Both types of question need to be followed up.

Patton (2002) adds other types of questions, which are more focused on the state of mind and the sensitivities of the interviewer. He distinguishes between:

1   Experience and behaviour questions such as: 'Tell me about your first visit to watch the team you support';
2   Opinion and value questions: these explore people's goals and expectations. An example is: 'To what extent is winning important to you as a sport participant?';
3   Feeling questions: these are about emotions and belong to the affective dimension. For example, 'How did you feel when you learned that you had not been selected for the national team?';
4   Knowledge questions (not often used in qualitative research). For example, 'What is the talent identification pathway in your sport?';
5   Sensory questions: these are used to explore what is heard, smelled or seen. For example, 'Can you describe the atmosphere at the opening ceremony of the Olympic Games in Beijing?'; and
6   Demographic questions: these are only used as fact finding at the beginning or end of the qualitative interview. For example, 'How many years have you been playing competitive sport?' Such experience questions are generally in addition to questions asked about the relevant characteristics of the participants, such as age.

In terms of the language in which questions are phrased, Schensul et al. (1999: 154) produce helpful guidelines:

- The questions should be easy to understand by the participants and be sensitive to their background.
- They should be short, clear and neutral.
- They should be phrased so that participants have the opportunity to talk rather than give short answers.
- They should only contain one single question, not two at the same time.
- They should not be factual and demand 'yes' or 'no' answers.

Interviewing skills

It is important in qualitative research to attend to participants' comfort, as the more relaxed they are the more likely it is that researchers will elicit useful data. In order to make participants feel comfortable, researchers must use the interpersonal skills that are needed in everyday social life, such as maintaining eye contact, adopting relaxed body language and showing an interest in what they say (O'Reilly, 2005). The need to strike a relaxed pose is, however, one of the stressful aspects of qualitative research (Mason, 2002). At no point must interviewers show negative judgement of participants; this is not only unethical, but it will also serve to make interviewees close up. Also important, particularly in the unstructured interview, where there is no interview guide, is the skill of asking relevant follow-up questions. This requires interviewers to 'think on their feet' and uses up a lot of emotional energy (Mason, 2002). In an early edition of their book (1995: 20), Rubin and Rubin argue that when participants are asked questions, in particular questions about their culture or a phenomenon with which they are familiar, it is like asking fish to describe the water in which they swim. An important interviewing skill, then, is to help participants to uncover that which is hidden to them, and to probe interesting points.

It has been suggested that pilot studies are not always used in qualitative research as it is developmental and researcher-sensitive, but we recommend a 'dry run' of an interview with a friend or acquaintance, so that researchers are prepared for the demands that the interview will place on them.

The relationship between interviewer and participants

It is important for qualitative researchers to establish rapport, defined by Spradley (1979) as a harmonious working relationship with interviewees: this requires emotional effort, time and awareness. The relationship between researcher and participant is based on respect and equality. This is why the term participant is used, which implies active involvement, and the more passive term 'subject' should be avoided. Researchers are, of course, in a position of some control and accountability, in that they set the research agenda and present, interpret and disseminate findings. In studies where the relationship between researcher and informant builds over time, trust and rapport develop because of 'prolonged engagement' in the field. For a successful one-off interview, trust in the researcher is an important ingredient, and has to be worked at. Pitts and Miller-Day (2007), however, argue that interviews 'have to balance both closeness and distance'. The research relationship is a bond between two partners who cannot become too close to each other as it is a professional relationship but need to get to know one other well in order to gain the best results from the research encounter.

Enhancing rapport: exploring self-handicapping in rock-climbing

Ferrand et al. (2006) explored the use of self-handicapping in rock climbing through semi-structured interviews with six elite French teenage rock-climbers. The authors identified a number of measures that enhanced the rapport between interviewer and interviewees. For example, first, all the interviews were conducted by a former competitive athlete familiar with both the elite context and the appropriate use of language. Second, the interviewer was trained in qualitative methods. Finally, issues related to confidentiality and informed consent were clearly outlined. All of these measures encouraged participants to be 'honest and open with their responses' (p. 273).

Practical aspects of interviewing

Before the start of the interview, the researcher should introduce themselves to the participant, give their credentials and state the broader aim of the research (the details of which can be given at the end of the interview. At the start of the interview, the researcher does not wish to lead the interviewees in a specific direction but rather allow them to be able to talk freely). The physical comfort of the interviewee should be attended to where possible: comfortable seating should be provided, a drink should be offered, and noise and interruptions should be minimised.

According to Seidman (2006), the optimum number of interviews is three for each individual because they extend both depth and breadth. However, many Masters students and especially undergraduates only have limited time for their research and often just carry out one single interview with each participant. The length of time for an interview depends on the participants, the topic of the interview and the methodological approach. Seidman suggests 90 minutes as an approximate time-span so that participants can know what to expect, but the interviews may be shorter or longer depending on the responses and interests of the participants and the researcher.

The researchers might use several different ways of keeping a record of the interview. They might make notes of the interviews, but this is the least satisfactory way of keeping a record – much may be missed; attention will not be focused on asking questions or following up on answers; and finally it may discomfort the participant. The most common recording method is to digitally record the interviews, which means that a literal text for analysis is available after transcription has taken place. The researcher can choose to make a video-recording of the interview, though this might unnerve participants and raise doubts over confidentiality and anonymity. Occasionally participants might not wish to be audio-recorded if they have concerns over disclosure of their identity and if the research topic is highly sensitive. Digitally recording the interview does not release the researcher from taking notes immediately after the interview to note down important issues that have arisen during the interview or for the researcher simply to comment, for methodological reasons, on the conduct of the interview. These are important memos that might be used in the findings and methodology chapters. Memory recall can be a problem so it is best to leave a gap between interviews so that notes can be made and, importantly, so that resources of energy can be regrouped. (We shall discuss transcription and other practical issues in Chapter 14.)

Potential problems in interviewing

Debates and tensions exist about the use of one-to-one and focus group interviews. Atkinson and Silverman (1997) criticise the interview society and 'the rhetoric of interviewing' where researchers assume that they have access to the feelings and inner thoughts of the participants, uncovering the personal and private. The authors question the over-use of interviewing and argue that researchers have a naïve and uncritical stance when hearing the words of participants and fail to analyse them appropriately. Kvale (1996: 292) suggests that much interview research might:

- centre on individuals
- not take social interactions into account
- neglect the social and material context
- not take account of emotions
- take place in a vacuum and not in the real world
- focus on verbal interaction and not include thoughts and experiences
- be atheoretical and trivial.

It is interesting that Kvale was an ardent defender of interviews in spite of this warning. The researcher's perspective on interviews need not be atheoretical or take place in a vacuum if they are tied to both lay and social theories and located in context.

Some writers, for instance Silverman (2007), decry the over-reliance of researchers on interviews. They argue instead for observation, listening to participants talk in interaction with others, and for the collection and analysis of 'naturally occurring data'. Silverman also argues that, when interviewing, researchers sometimes manufacture data 'rather than finding them in the field' (p. 37) and adds that data sources such as interviews and focus groups 'should only be used as a last resort'. Mindful researchers, however, do not make or manufacture data but listen carefully to the participants' words. People might be misunderstood, but misinterpretation is not the same as deliberate manufacture. Further, like Carspecken (2009), we feel that the subjective state of participants, their motives and intentions are valid areas for exploration.

Unfortunately students seldom use observation to complement unstructured or semi-structured interviews although it usually would enhance the research greatly. Observation generates data about social action and interaction, and offers a form of within-method triangulation which enhances validity (trustworthiness). Indeed, Deutscher (1966) mentioned many years ago the dilemma and potential contradiction between 'what people say and what they do' (see also Chapter 8). However, the tension between 'words and deeds' is in itself an interesting source of material for the researcher who is able to explore this inconsistency and give the study more depth.

The interviewer effect (in observation referred to as the 'observer effect') is the impact interviewers have on the participants by their presence. It may be due to the appearance and personality of the interviewer or the perception of the interviewer by the participants and their anxiety to appear in a positive light even when they are not conscious of it. Gender, class, membership of ethnic group and many other factors might have an effect on the interview, and researchers need to be aware of this. They need to monitor their own appearance and behaviour – for instance, by dressing and behaving appropriately for the people they interview and the setting they observe. Good relationships with the participants and prolonged contact will help to minimise the interviewer and observer effect. Interviewers might have conflicting perspectives and priorities from participants and they must avoid being judgemental when listening to the people with whom they are carrying out the research (the interviewer effect is less noticeable in online interviews).

Summary

- Through interviewing, researchers uncover the perspectives of the participants and illuminate the phenomenon under study
- The qualitative interview has depth, richness and flexibility – the participants have some measure of control over the direction, area and timing of the interview
- A variety of types of interview can be used by researchers
- The interviewer needs complex skills to conduct a good interview

7

Focus Groups

A focus group interview is an interview with a group of people, generally numbering between four and 12, sharing common experiences or characteristics, for the purpose of eliciting ideas, thoughts and perceptions about a specific topic. The hallmark of focus groups is the explicit use of group interaction to produce data and insights that would be less accessible without the interaction found in a group. As Weeden (2005) notes, focus groups are essentially group discussions. Interaction between group members enriches the data collected as a result of members clarifying, challenging and discussing individual and group attitudes towards a topic (Jennings, 2010). The type of group and the number of interviews are largely determined by the research question. Researchers might use pre-existing groups whose members have the same experience – for instance, fans of a particular sports team – or they can establish their own groups for which members are carefully and purposefully selected to achieve the functions of the particular type of research. An example of this could be a study of barriers to participation in physical activity, where the researcher might establish a single group consisting of varied socio-demographic characteristics, or a number of groups, each consisting of a different such characteristic in order to identify a wide range of barriers. Although focus group research can stand alone, focus group interviews are often complemented by other data sources, for example in the study by Hanton et al. (2008) of the relationships between experience and anxiety in sport, which used interviews as well as focus groups, or Johnston and Paulsen's (2011) research of the congruence between a sports club and its main sponsor, which used focus groups to inform a subsequent questionnaire.

The origin and purpose of focus groups

Focus groups have been used in the business community since the 1920s when market researchers in particular adopted the method in order to collect data about customers' thoughts and feelings about a product or an advertising campaign. Research findings were used for business development purposes. Merton and Kendall wrote the first text on focus groups in 1946, based on their use of the method during and shortly after the Second World War. The use of focus groups has since expanded beyond the world of market research; it is one of the tools available to qualitative researchers in all fields, and has been adopted in the areas of sport and physical activity to look at varied issues ranging from adolescent girls' perceptions of physical activity (Whitehead and Biddle, 2008), to the role of sport events in peace tourism (Schulenkorf and Edwards, 2010).

Using focus groups: attraction to charity sport events

Filo et al. (2008) carried out a study to explore the factors that attracted people to attend charity sport events, specifically those related to the Lance Armstrong Foundation. To explore people's experiences of the events, they chose to undertake a number of focus groups, noting that first they were more conducive to opinion formation and expression formation than other methods, and second that such group discussion was able to leverage perceptions that would have otherwise remained uncovered. Through four such focus groups, each consisting of between six and 11 participants, the authors were able to determine a number of important motives, such as the social aspect, the opportunity to meet new people, the opportunity to achieve a valued goal, the chance to 'give back' to a worthy cause and increased self-esteem.

Focus groups now tend to be more open and less directive, though they are still set up to explore a specific issue. As Morgan (1998) notes, the primary aim of a focus group should be to learn from participants and to be sensitive to their priorities, recognising that whilst 'it is *your* focus, it is *their* group'. A further defining feature of focus groups is the crucial role played by social interaction among participants (Smithson, 2000); the data do not derive from conversations between the researcher and a single participant as is the case in the individual interview. What distinguishes focus groups from interviews is that participants respond to both the interviewer and to each other. As such, it is important to note not just *what* is said, but *how* conversation proceeds. Focus groups offer access to individual beliefs as well as group norms, which are important in understanding the judgements reached by the group (Bloor et al., 2001; Warr, 2005). Focus group interaction may stimulate changes in opinions; it may lead to group conflict; it may provoke a development of ideas that would not arise in a one-to-one situation. On the other hand, as Hydén *and* Bülow (2005) claim, group members can express individual opinions that are unshaped by other members; they may not reach consensus. Jennings (2010) suggests that interactions can help participants reflect and develop or clarify their opinions. Alternatively, as could be argued within the study by Filo et al. (2008) cited above (see the case study 'Using focus groups: attraction to charity sport events'), there is also the danger that participants may be unwilling to disclose information they perceive as sensitive, in their case, for example motives of charity participation. Analysis must thus focus on the *group* and on *interaction* between focus group members, given that this is a differentiating feature of focus groups (Wibek et al., 2007).

Choosing the sample: size, number and composition

Size of the focus group

A focus group might range in size between four and 12 people: Morgan (1998) states that a small group is better for controversial or complex topics, while larger groups tend to be appropriate for less sensitive research topics. There are pros and cons to both: individuals have more of a voice in smaller groups whilst more ideas might be elicited by a larger group. Greenbaum (1998) however maintains that group dynamics suffer if the group is too small. Meanwhile, the larger the group, the more formalised and less free-flowing the discussion, and the harder is the moderator's task to ensure that all participants get a chance to speak (Jennings, 2010). Transcription also becomes more difficult and time-consuming. The number of members in a group must be thought through and justified in the methods section of the final written account of the research.

Focus groups and sample size: attitudes of young talented athletes towards doping and the effects of attentional focus on golf performance

Topics that are sensitive, for example those involving unethical or unlawful sporting behaviour, tend to benefit from fewer participants compared to more socially acceptable issues. Bloodworth and McNamee (2010), for example, held a number of groups ranging in size from between just two and five in their exploration of the attitudes of young talented athletes towards doping in their own sports – an approach that allowed them to gain richer data than interviews, 'which failed to elicit anything other than staunchly anti-doping attitudes' (p. 278). This is also an outcome that, we would suggest, would have been similar had a large focus group been undertaken, given the potential unwillingness of athletes to discuss such issues in front of a larger group of peers. In contrast, Bell and Hardy's (2009) examination of the effects of attentional focus on golf performance utilised three focus groups of 11 participants. Such a relatively uncontroversial subject, with no apparent issues, allows the use of a greater sample size,

(Continued)

> *(Continued)*
>
> and removes, to some extent, the issue of participants being unwilling to undertake discussion within a larger group through fear of revealing sensitive information. It is still the case, however, that a larger group, although potentially providing more information, may also lead to some participants being less willing to speak, with the option to 'hide away' being easier.

The number of groups

Careful consideration must be given to the number of groups to be facilitated by the researcher. According to Bryman (2008), this depends on the purpose of the study and on the amount of cross-comparisons required. Morgan advocates three to five focus groups, on the basis that this should lead to data saturation. Having said that, time-permitting, data collection should proceed until the group provides few meaningful new insights. As Bryman comments, once saturation has been achieved, collecting more data will be a waste of time.

Variety in the number of focus groups undertaken: four examples

There is considerable variation in the numbers of focus groups carried out within the literature. Often, when focus groups are used alongside other methods, then a single group may be used, as was the case with the study by Thomas et al. (2011) of defining sport confidence, where a single focus group was augmented with 16 interviews. For studies involving the focus groups as the sole method, multiple groups are the norm. Jones et al. (2009), for example, used four focus groups consisting of between six and eight people to explore the experiences of older adults of undertaking a 12-week pedometer-based intervention, a number that is fairly typical within the literature. Keegan et al. (2009) used a total of eight focus groups in their study of the roles played by coaches, parents and peers in influencing motivation for athletes aged 12 years and under, leading to a total of 220 pages of single-spaced transcribed text. At a more extreme level, Munroe-Chandler et al. (2007) carried out a total of 16 focus groups in their study of imagery in youth sport.

Composition

The purposive sampling technique is commonly used in focus group research whereby specific characteristics are sought. The criteria to be used for the selection of participants include demographic factors, gender, ethnic group membership and a common experience, interest or role (Morgan, 1998). If the interviewer wishes to interview a group of runners with an injury, she or he obviously recruits participants with this particular complaint. This does not mean that participants will share the same views about the topic, or that they have a similar background. Thus, a shared experience does not necessarily denote a homogeneous sample. Researchers may make use of pre-existing, naturally occurring groups in focus group research, such as fitness classes, antenatal swimming groups or sports teams. While they have similar experiences, they are nevertheless heterogeneous in other ways, which will lead to lively and interesting debate. The advantage of choosing a pre-existing group is that members are familiar and more comfortable with each other. This means that the 'warm-up' time is shorter, and that the researcher can focus on the topic immediately. On the other hand, participants may hesitate to reveal sensitive information to someone with whom they have an ongoing relationship. Conversely, the researcher could recruit participants to the group, who although share common experiences, have not met before. Indeed, Morgan (1998) suggests that strangers are more likely to think through and talk about taken-for-granted assumptions: important issues might be glossed over if participants are familiar with each other.

Gender, status and age of group members influence the quality and level of interaction (Stewart et al., 2007). Mixed gender groups tend to be more conforming because in social interaction men and women tend to 'perform' for each other. There tends to be greater diversity of ideas in single-sex groups. Such issues must be taken into account and the decision-making on sampling must be made clear.

Focus group composition: understanding exercise among African-American women

Although African-American women tend to be more sedentary than Caucasian women, there are still significant numbers who undertake regular physical activity. By exploring the reasons for such continued participation in physical activity, Young et al. (2001) aimed to contribute to the development of effective intervention strategies through undertaking focus group research. Noting that discussion is facilitated by having participants who are similar, four focus groups, each consisting of between six and 11 people, were carried out, with each group focusing on one of the four criteria (currently active women, sedentary women, women who had lost weight and maintained that loss, and those who had lost weight and had not maintained the loss). Each group was moderated by a trained moderator of a similar ethnic background to the participants. Through a series of open questions, probes and visual aids, participants were able to fully discuss the role of physical activity in their lives. This discussion was recorded, transcribed and key themes identified. A number of key issues relating to the interventions were determined. First, the lack of clarity of what 'physical activity' and 'exercise' actually meant to participants emerged. Second, the importance of social support in maintaining activity was ascertained. Finally, the emphasis upon short- rather than long-term goals emerged. Through the use of focus groups in an under-researched area, the voices of the participants allowed a greater understanding of the issues relevant to the target population. As a consequence, a more 'culturally relevant' intervention could be developed.

Conducting focus group interviews

Focus group interviews must be planned carefully. Participants should be contacted well in advance of the interview and reminded a few days before the date they are due to attend. Some authors advise the over-recruitment of participants, to allow for no-shows.

The location of the interview is of little importance, according to Morgan (1998), as long as the room is big enough to comfortably contain the participants. The seating arrangement usually advocated is a spatial arrangement of a circle or semi-circle so that participants can make eye contact and the recorder can be placed in a central position, where all participants can be heard and recorded. Participants' comfort should be attended to; this will also enhance the quality of the data (Mason, 2011). Thus care should be taken that seating is comfortable, that the room is well-aired and at the optimum temperature, and adequate refreshment must be supplied. Morgan (1999) also advocates that the facilitator develops good time-management skills because both interviewer and participants have limited time. Usually the duration of a focus group interview is between nine and 120 minutes, though of course this is dependent on many variables such as the sensitivity of the topic, participant age, health and availability and participant responsiveness.

To start the interview, the researcher allows a few minutes for warm-up, to put the group at ease; they also use this time to re-introduce the research topic. The creation of an open and non-threatening group climate is one of their initial important tasks. If the group feels at ease with and trusts the interviewer, the interaction will be open and productive, and participants will be comfortable about disclosing their attitudes and feelings. Before discussion begins, the researcher should reassure participants that there are no right or wrong answers. No judgement is made about them. Researchers should also emphasise that each participant is free to present their personal ideas during the discussion even if they differ from others in the group (Vicsek, 2007). To start the discussion, the researcher might use stimulus activities such as showing a film, telling a story or showing photographs (Kitzinger and Barbour, 1999). This might help to enhance participation and to create the basis for analysis across different groups, or as an ice breaker. Some researchers give paper and coloured pens to group members as an ice-breaker (particularly useful for research with children), or as a means to collect data itself, such as Perry and Hoffman's (2010) study of patterns of physical activity behaviour and beliefs about physical activity of American Indian children, where participants were asked to draw pictures of physical activities that they enjoyed.

Researchers must develop both a clear agenda and their own conversation-management skills so that discussion is focused on the topic and that time is not wasted in irrelevant conversation. They should plan the initial stimulus questions and prompts, but many writers, including Byrne (2004), advocate the use of open-ended, flexible questioning styles to allow for a more considered and bias-free response. As Vicsek (2007) observes, this places the content of the focus groups in the hands of the participants. This non-directive approach has particular importance in exploratory research. A 'funnel strategy' means that largely unstructured conversation is encouraged during the group; only towards the end does the moderator guide the discussion if there are any further topics or themes to be considered (Weeden, 2005). Indeed, much of the discussion evolves from the dynamics of group interaction – the defining feature of focus group research.

Conducting a focus group: using imagery in youth sport

Munroe-Chandler et al. (2007) were interested in the use of imagery by young athletes. To do this, they carried out a number of focus groups with young males and females of various ages between seven and 14. Athletes were contacted through various organisations, such as university sport camps or gymnastic camps, and both athlete and parents were asked to provide consent to take part in the study. Given the age range of participants, a younger moderator with experience of working with children was chosen. The focus group consisted of three parts. The first was a more open discussion of participants' sporting experiences, within which participants were also provided with a definition of imagery. The second part was more structured, and used a pre-existing conceptual framework to guide the discussion among participants. The final phase involved the moderator synthesising the key points that had emerged in the first two parts of the focus group, allowing the athletes to develop or clarify any key points as and when appropriate. Specific probes were also used where elaboration or explanation was needed. Given the age range of participants, it was considered important to keep the focus group short and with a limited number of questions, and, as such, all groups were kept to between 45 minutes and one hour.

The involvement of the interviewer

In educational research using the focus group method, the researcher is usually both interviewer and facilitator (or moderator). In market research, professional moderators are usually employed, but due to scarce funds and resources, they are rarely used in educational research.

Moderators of any focus group have a key role in ensuring the quality of the data obtained. Before the group commences, they will need to be able to explain clearly its structure and purpose in a way that promotes trust among participants, puts them at ease and enables interaction among group members. The researcher should have the particular qualities of the in-depth interviewer: flexibility, responsiveness, open-mindedness and skill in eliciting information. Researchers must also be able to stimulate discussion and to show an interest in what participants say. The leadership role of moderators demands abilities above that of the one-to-one interviewer, however. They must have the social and refereeing skills to guide group discussion and they must be able to exert control over participants and topic without directing the debate or coercing group members but be able to probe responses to develop key points in sufficient depth. Interviewers must be able to defuse but not suppress interpersonal hostility when it arises: this demands sensitive handling skills. They must also recognise that whilst polarisation of views may generate a difficult group climate, conflicts of opinion can produce valuable data (Parker and Tritter, 2006). This is a delicate balance that the moderator has to negotiate. Conversely, the skilful facilitator should help to avoid group conformity whereby the group tries to reach consensus on a topic (Morgan, 1998).

Furthermore, bias in the interviewer has to be controlled, necessitating self-reflection and attention to their own comportment. This means that gestures and facial expressions have to be monitored; any display of judgement must be quashed, and care must be taken to show that the researcher values the views of all participants. A special relationship with a specific individual, an affirmative nod at something of which the interviewer approves, or a lack of encouragement for unexpected or unwelcome answers, will skew the data (Holloway and Wheeler, 2010).

The role of the moderator: exploring training behaviours and athlete development

As well as the generic skills and attributes of the moderator highlighted within the text, it is often important that the moderator has some familiarity with the subject matter. Oliver et al. (2010), for example, carried out a series of four focus groups to investigate which training behaviours were viewed as important within team sports for athlete development. Each group was carried out by a moderator and an assistant moderator, each of which had relevant coaching experience, as well as holding recognised coaching qualifications. This was important as, according to the authors, it 'enhanced their ability to interact with participants, obtaining a deeper level of understanding and more easily facilitating discussion than would have been possible with researchers unfamiliar with the process and demands of training youth athletes' (p. 435).

Analysing focus group data

Focus groups can be analysed through the technique of thematic analysis (see Chapter 15 for a step-by-step account). Initially, and before transcription, the researcher repeatedly listens to the recordings of the interviews. A problem unique to focus group interviews is that individual voices may be hard to identify. It is important to be clear about who says what, because this can identify those individuals who try to dominate discussion or those who try to blend in or to be silent. This problem can be overcome through video record-ing, but this might inhibit participants, particularly when discussing a sensi-tive issue. The next step, that of transcription, is therefore time-consuming in focus group research. Krueger and Casey (2009) suggest that it can take from eight to 12 hours to transcribe a two-hour focus group.

The transcript must identify participants as focus group researchers need to be sensitive not only to individual comments but also to the dynamics of group interaction, noting conflict, diversity, consensus and so on. The researcher must remember that the data are to be seen within the context of the group setting. Thus, the unit for analysis necessarily becomes the 'group' rather than individu-als within the group, the rationale being that individuals within focus groups cannot simply be treated in the same way as individuals speaking in one-to-one interviews: data derived from the group members are not independent from the group itself. Lehoux et al. (2006) further state that the interactions of the modera-tor are also analysed. Kidd and Parshall (2000) argue that neither the individual nor the group is the sole unit of analysis. The important thing is to have an analytical approach that is sufficiently flexible to recognise when the individual or the group is driving the data at any given stage of the discussion.

Emergent themes from analysis need to be drawn from across a sample of groups, as opposed to across participants within focus groups. Therefore the analyst repeats the process of coding and categorising the interview tran-script with each focus group interview. The major themes arising from indi-vidual interviews are then connected with each other; topics in one interview will overlap with those of other focus groups. Where deviant cases are iden-tified, these must be accounted for. Once major themes have emerged, the relevant literature is discussed and is used as confirmation or a challenge to the researcher's findings (see Chapter 4).

Ethical issues

In focus groups, as in all other research, ethical issues must be considered. Confidentiality, in particular, could be problematic in group interviews as participants might fear that others will divulge the findings outside the research setting. Participants should therefore be reminded to keep group discussion confidential. Anonymity is also problematic; it cannot be guaran-teed, as members of the group might be able to identify other participants even if only first names or pseudonyms have been used. Trust, therefore, is also an important issue.

Researchers have an ethical duty to make sure that no harm comes to par-ticipants, and this must be borne in mind when conducting focus groups. Participants may make hurtful remarks to one another and may show disdain for others' opinions: all this can cause distress, and must be sensitively man-aged by the researcher.

Finally, incentives towards participation in focus group research must be declared: as Weeden (2005) claims, it is unusual for focus group participants to give up their time for no remuneration, but transparency is important and the impact of incentives must be considered.

Advantages and limitations of focus groups

Focus groups allow access to a range of perspectives on a topic and a range of life experiences. The social interaction permitted by the focus group also acts both to trigger participants' own thoughts and feelings and to develop new attitudes that would not have emerged without the presence of others. All participants, including the interviewer, have the opportunity to ask questions and to make comments, leading to the production of more ideas than would have emerged in individual interviews. A third advantage is that focus groups allow the researcher to collect a large amount of data very quickly.

However, the depth of the one-to-one interview is lost during a group discussion; the opportunities to probe in detail are not as available in a group situation for reasons of time and sensitivity. Furthermore, the researcher has to develop good moderating skills in order to ensure that the group isn't dominated by one or two individuals or that some members become too compliant (Creswell, 2007). There are practical difficulties too – it may be difficult to organise focus groups because of clashes in participant availability and the ease of finding a suitable location. Transcription is also much more challenging than in one-to-one interviews, and time must be allowed for this important stage.

Summary

- A focus group consists of a small number of people with common experiences, interests or characteristics
- Several focus groups with a small number of individuals are involved in each study; sample size and focus group number vary
- Whilst interviews are carefully planned, the interviewer must at the same time be flexible and non-judgemental
- The dynamic of the group situation is intended to stimulate ideas and elicit feelings about the focus of the study
- It is important that an open climate exists so that group members feel comfortable about sharing their thoughts and feelings
- The data can be analysed by thematic analysis
- Transcription is time-consuming

8

Participant Observation

The term 'participant observation' is a phrase originally coined by Lindeman in 1924 and can be defined as the exploration of a culture from the inside. Participant observation has its origins in anthropology and sociology, and is indeed a staple of anthropological research. From the early days of fieldwork, anthropologists became part of the culture they studied and examined the actions and interactions of people in their social context – 'in the field' as it is called in research language. It is probably the earliest of all forms of data collection, as early travellers in ancient times wrote down their observation of cultures they visited, often as participants in those cultures.

Participant observation is a method which researchers employ to explore and understand a group or culture. Indeed many sports researchers in particular participate in the setting they study. It is a systematic description of events and behaviour in the social setting under study, 'a written photograph' (Erlandson et al., 1993). A holistic view of the research setting is provided by observational studies in a number of research approaches. In particular, it forms an essential element of ethnography (see Chapter 10) but also in grounded theory (Chapter 9). Participation ranges from spending limited time in a group, to full and extended immersion in the group's activities (Spradley, 1980). Fully immersed researchers can move around in the location as they wish, without appearing unusual or intrusive, observing in detail, with access to spontaneous observation as well as opportunistic interviewing (Mason, 2002). Thus, participant observation involves more than *watching*. Indeed, DeWalt and DeWalt (2010) state that observation involves looking, interviewing, writing field-notes and, above all, patience. The researcher therefore needs to be both a careful observer and a good listener. Strauss and Corbin (1998) see observation as qualitative research *'par excellence'* as it provides a holistic understanding of the setting. Furthermore, triangulation through interview and documentary data also enhances validity.

The research setting

When researchers decide to observe sport and physical activity related behaviours, they do not set up artificial situations but look at people in their natural settings; settings which have relevance to the research question, rather than the more contrived settings often created for more experimental designs. Within the natural settings, events and behaviour are systematically recorded as they occur; they are not retrospective accounts as remembered by participants. Czech and Bullet's (2007) observation of the role of prayer for Christian athletes, for example, involved the prayer practices of the athletes being directly observed during their normal prayer group gatherings. Such research settings vary on a continuum from open to closed. Open settings are public and highly visible such as a park, a beach or a football ground. In closed settings, access is more difficult and has to be carefully negotiated. These might include personal offices, meetings or training sessions.

Participant observation in a closed setting: the reproduction of homosexually themed discourse in university rugby

McCormack and Anderson (2010) examined the types of sexually based language used by members of a university rugby club, and the intent and function of such language in reproducing or challenging homophobia in the sporting context. As such, this was an extreme example of a closed setting, with membership restricted to male students (who were almost exclusively white and middle class), with a particular aptitude and interest in rugby union. For a researcher to simply enter the setting was not feasible. To overcome this issue, McCormack and Anderson recruited and trained one of the team's players in data-collection methods. As a result, the player was able to participate in training, socialising and competition, and collect data that would otherwise have been unattainable to the research team.

Schensul et al. (1999) argue that the process of learning is through exposure to or involvement in the daily routine of participants. The researchers usually become an integral part of the setting they enter and, to some extent, members of the group they observe, although they may already be immersed in the setting and choose to research their own cultural group, as was the case with research by Adams et al. (2010) into the construction of masculinity within semi-professional football, where the primary author was an existing member of the team prior to the study. Immersion in a setting can take a long time, often years of living in a culture (DeWalt and DeWalt, 2010). Prolonged observation generates more in-depth knowledge of a group or subculture, especially because researchers who have gained entry and acceptance do not disturb the scene in the way that an occasional visit from an outsider might. The researchers as insiders can observe and ask questions, which outside spectators cannot. If they become deeply engaged and stay for a considerable time, participants will become used to them, and the observer effect will be minimal.

Observation is less disruptive and more unobtrusive than interviewing. However, the method does not just involve observing the situation, but also listening to the people involved. Participants can describe their experiences in interviews and conversations and reflect on events and actions, but researchers will not have to rely only on such accounts; through observing, they will be able to distinguish between 'words and deeds'. These are not always the same. There may be a gap between claimed and actual behaviour, which can be examined. It is possible that participants may be unaware of this gap; alternatively there may be a desire to impress the researcher, especially if the topic of research is sensitive.

Immersion within the physical education setting

The Sport Education Model (SEM) is a model of sport instruction that is designed to provide a motivational environment for students, by giving them greater autonomy within aspects such as leadership, instruction, assessing and performing within physical education classes. Perlman and Karp (2010) undertook a study to explore the experiences of both teachers and students who used this model of instruction. One aspect of their data collection was observation of student and teacher behaviours within lessons. One of the authors became immersed in the setting through not only observation of classes, but also being in the physical education office both before and after the lesson, travelling with students, dressing in professional attire and moving from field to field while games were played. This allowed critical incidents relating to the Sport Education Model to be collected through field-notes which described the settings and documented the relevant incidents. It allowed the authors to identify three themes relating to the SEM of social support, winning as a team and the enhancement of feelings of self-determination.

Some researchers will, of course, already be members of, and familiar with, the culture they examine, either through direct experience, or, in the case of many sporting activities, through more indirect media consumption of such activities. They will not therefore need a long introduction to the setting, but they might miss significant events or behaviours in the locale because of over-familiarity, or preconceptions about the activity. This needs to be guarded against. For those researching such a familiar setting, it will be necessary that they train themselves to see the setting with fresh eyes, so that they don't overlook important features which they take for granted (Gobo, 2008), or focus on ideas that reinforce prior ideas and expectations.

Types of observation

Though the stance of the researcher in the field has been the subject of some debate, Gold's (1958) identification of four types of (overlapping) observer involvement in the field is still used by most qualitative researchers:

1   The complete participant
2   The participant as observer
3   The observer as participant
4   The complete observer

The complete participant

The complete participant is part of the setting, a member of a group within it and takes an insider role that often involves covert observation. Many researchers argue that covert observation produces more trustworthy data as participants behave more naturally when they are unaware of being observed. In other words, the observer effect – the impact of the presence of the researcher on those being observed – is absent. In online research, often called 'netnography' (a term coined by Kozinets in 1998), researchers often conceal their presence and identity in order to simply observe the interactions that take place on an internet forum or blog. There is an ongoing debate among researchers as to the ethics of this stance – some arguing that this practice does not disturb the scene or harm participants, while others claim that it is a violation of privacy.

The researcher as complete participant: the 'twelve commandments' of jock culture

Sparkes et al. (2007) studied the 'twelve commandments', a series of practices that appropriate an idealised and internalised 'jock habitus' within a university campus. The study involved one of the researchers undertaking a variety of observational roles, moving from complete observer to complete participant. To undertake the complete participant role, the researcher joined both the women's football and badminton teams, took part in team trials, participated in competitions and league matches, and attended team 'socials', and was thus able to engage fully in all activities. For this approach it is essential that the complete participant is able to fully engage, and thus required a degree of sporting competence, without which such an approach would not have been possible.

Covert observation is usually considered unethical unless it takes place in public settings and individual participants cannot be identified. There might occasionally be situations in which researcher identity should not be disclosed in order to safeguard the researcher's safety or in research with people to whom access is difficult (Pope and Mays, 2006). Spaaij's (2008) observation of football hooligans, for example, initially took place in strategic locations, such as a particular location within a football ground, or in a pub, but at a distance away from the hooligans at the beginning, at least until opportunities to develop rapport were developed at a later stage.

In spite of the value of some of these studies, complete participation generates a number of ethical problems. First of all, one would have to question seriously whether covert observation of a closed setting, such as a training session, is ethical. After all, this is not a public, open situation such as a rugby match, where individuals can't be identified. Following publication of research findings, participants may feel betrayed when deception is uncovered (Kawulich, 2005). Some of these issues have already been addressed, and the ethics of any such study will need careful consideration. In the public domain, covert observation is permissible and may produce valuable data though care must be taken to protect anonymity as in all research.

The participant as observer

Here, researchers are already part of the research setting; they have gained entrance and are accepted by the participants. They have used their existing role to facilitate data collection, and are not seen as outsiders or spectators. Furthermore, participants are comfortable with the researcher and go about their routines and rituals in a natural way. Meanwhile, researchers can move around in the location as they wish without being obtrusive, and thus observe in more detail and depth. The advantage of this type of observation is the ease with which researcher–participant relationships can be forged or extended.

For ethical reasons, researchers must ask permission from the relevant gatekeeper to conduct their observational study and they must explain the observer role to participants. Given their existing role in the research setting, there will be a possible trade-off between the data revealed in the final research report and their duty to ensure confidentiality (Kawulich, 2005).

The participant as observer: exploring Masters sport participation

Lyons and Dionigi's (2007) examination of the sense of community associated with being a Masters sport participant involved one of the authors taking on the role of 'observer as participant' by becoming a volunteer during the Australian

(Continued)

(Continued)

Masters Games, a role that allowed her to observe and interact with the participants. This enabled her to get close enough to the participants to establish an 'insider's identity' (p. 380) without actually undertaking the activities of the group, but through having a role that provided an 'invaluable vantage point' for understanding the life-worlds of Masters participants. The study involved approximately four hours per day of observation for ten days, both of the actual sporting events, including pre- and post-event preparations and celebrations, and more informal non-sport contexts such as cafes, focusing on the general behaviours of the athletes and their interactions with others during the Games. This helped in the identification of four relevant themes, these being a shared sporting interest, a sense of comradeship in continued activity, providing a sense of purpose and a feeling of 'giving back' to their sport.

The observer as participant

An observer who participates in the research setting only by being in the location for the duration of the research is only marginally involved in the situation. In this case, researchers might observe a particular setting but not necessarily as a member of the group. They have to go through the process of gaining entry, of asking for permission to conduct their research from both gatekeepers and participants; their role as researcher is declared. The advantage of this type of observation is that the researcher is not called upon as a member of the workforce to perform work duties; they are freer to take notes and to dedicate themselves to the research task. On the other hand, observers are prevented from playing a 'real' role in the setting. They have only a peripheral role and their access to participants may be limited if acceptance isn't forthcoming (Kawulich, 2005).

The observer as participant: brand auras in sport sponsorship

Alexander (2009) explored how the association between a sport organisation (the Welsh Rugby Union) and a brand (Brains Beer) contributed to the aura surrounding that brand. To develop an understanding of this, the researcher became participant as observer, utilising a role which included forming relationships with key individuals associated with the relationship between the two organisations, participating in activities, and observing events and responses to those events on the day of international competition. This allowed Alexander to identify the key role of shared national identity and heritage, and the downplaying of commercial motives within the relationship as essential to the development of an 'authentic' aura.

Daymon and Holloway (2010) mention the observational technique of 'shadowing', which can be found in this category, whereby unique and privileged access to the research setting is granted to the researcher who follows a person through their daily routine. This imposes demands on both researcher and participant, however, as shadowing and simultaneously taking notes is an emotionally and physically tiring task. Meanwhile the shadowed member may find it frustrating to have to 'babysit' the researcher throughout the day. Nevertheless, the data collection opportunity offered by this role is invaluable and should be taken up.

The complete observer

Complete observers do not take part in the setting; rather they use a 'fly on the wall' approach. This role is sometimes known as silent observation; no role is played, and the scene isn't disturbed at all. Being a complete observer, when the observer does not participate, is only possible when the researchers have some distance from the setting; they observe through a window, in a corner or through a two-way mirror where they are not noticed and have no impact on the situation, or when they use static video cameras fixed on the ceiling. Though the setting is untainted by the observer's presence, the researcher has no access to participants to ask questions or to hold fleeting conversations.

Seale (2004) argues that the most appropriate stance positions the researcher at a distance from the setting so that over-rapport can be avoided, but close enough for a familiarisation that allows the researcher to grasp and represent the emic perspective. This might be a difficult balance to achieve, and, indeed, there is no clear distinction between some of these types of observation; they overlap. Lugosi (2006), for instance, claims that there is a continuum between overt and covert observation.

The researcher as complete observer: girls attitudes towards trampolining

McCabe and Palmer (2007) were interested in the views of girls towards participating in trampolining both as part of their PE lessons, and in an after-school trampoline club. The researchers initially used a strategy of researcher as complete observer, whereby no interaction with participants, or engagement with the trampolining took place at all – the role being simply to observe and record the activity. Whilst this approach had the advantage that the information could – as far as possible, given the effect of a stranger within the setting – be a truthful representation of the students' natural behaviour, the research team were aware that their access to more subtle or nuanced information was limited. Thus, a number of other observational strategies were also used, such as that of observer as participant.

Getting started

Creswell (2007) provides researchers with a series of useful steps that can be taken to start observational research:

1   The setting for the observation is selected in accordance with the research aim and permission for access is obtained from gatekeepers.
2   The researcher obtains informed consent from participants.
3   Decisions on time sampling and the duration of fieldwork will be made (though it might be changed during the research).
4   The researcher decides on and justifies the type of observation to be used.
5   The researcher keeps a field journal where observations are made and where they also note down their own feelings about the research.
6   The researcher disengages from the site and debriefs the participants while assuring anonymity. The latter step will not apply to the participant observer who will continue to be involved in the setting, though the researcher role will end.

Progression and process

When researchers first enter the field (or in the case of people who already work in the setting, when they first start collecting observational data), it may seem confusing and daunting because a connection may not easily be made between their research aim and what is being observed. Participant observers should enter the setting without wishing to limit the observation to particular processes or people; they should adopt an unstructured approach. This may seem a little chaotic and directionless at first. Occasionally certain foci crystallise early in the study, but usually observation progresses from the unstructured to the more focused until eventually specific actions and events become the main interest of the researcher.

Spradley (1980) claims that observers progress in three stages: they use *descriptive*, *focused* and finally *selective* observation. During descriptive observation, everything that goes on in the setting provides data and is recorded, including colours, smells and appearances of people. Indeed, DeWalt and DeWalt (2010) advise researchers to observe and record *everything* in the early stage. Unwanted data can be discarded. Indeed, the dross rate – the rate of information irrelevant for the specific research – is high in observational research.

As time goes by, certain important areas or aspects of the setting become more obvious, and the researcher focuses on these because they contribute to the achievement of the research aim. Eventually observation becomes highly selective, centring on very specific issues only. Once researchers have collected the initial observational data, they start analysing them so that the collection and analysis of data interact and go in parallel. This way the observation can become progressively focused on emerging and interesting themes that are important to the research. Thus researchers adopt the strategy of progressive focusing.

To help researchers to get started in their observational role, a number of writers have provided helpful checklists. These are useful in the beginning when novice researchers are unsure about data collection which can appear to be directionless and daunting, but as time proceeds, researchers will develop more confidence in their ability to practise selective sampling.

Spradley (1980) offers a checklist of focal points for researchers in the early stage of observation, which have been adapted below to the SPA context:

Space: This refers to the location in which the research takes place, for example a gym, its layout, and its general features.

Actor: The actors are the participants in the setting, so in this instance, this could refer to the users or employees of the gym – who they are, and any relevant details of interest to the researcher.

Activity: The activity is a general overview of what is happening; for example, the activity might be an exercise class, or general cardiovascular training.

Objects: This refers to the material objects present in the setting, for example the equipment, the layout of the gym, mirrors on the wall, posters, signs and so on.

Act: An act is a single action within the activity; for example, this may be the way in which participants enter the class, and locate themselves in a particular position.

Events: Events are activities and happenings related to the act, so this might refer to participants' interactions whilst choosing their location.

Time: This is the time-frame and sequencing of events, i.e. what is happening and in what order.

Goal: The goal is what participants are aiming to accomplish, for example to secure a particular location within the space.

Feeling: This is what people feel and how they express their emotions, for example, observations of joy or anger depending upon whether the goal has been achieved.

Whitehead (2006) has expanded on what he describes as Spradley's useful criteria. Students in need of structure and guidance on collecting observational data should record the following:

1   A description of the site and the immediate vicinity
2   Objects in the setting, for example furniture
3   A profile of the people in the setting (age, height, gender, race, etc.)

4   Precise time and date
5   Divergence between individual and group behaviour – what do people do, how do they seem?
6   Interaction – how do people communicate, are some characters more dominant than others?
7   Language – what is said, who says it, how is it said?
8   Non-verbal behaviour
9   Expressive culture (music, dance, art, etc.)

Marshall and Rossman (2006) argue that observation means systematic exploration of events and actions, but as Abrams (2000) notes, researchers must also record and dwell on critical incidents and dramatic events. Though it is important not to overlook regular mundane activities that are revealing of cultural norms, it is vital to record critical incidents, which fall outside routine activity.

Keeping a record

Taking field-notes is an important task. Observations are translated into written records which researchers make while observing or immediately afterwards. Writing might be difficult at the time of observation, not only because participants might be made to feel uncomfortable if the researcher takes notes in their presence, but also when it is physically impossible for the researcher. An example of this second instance occurred with Palmer's (1996) participant observation study of elite cyclists, with the author being physically active training and racing throughout the period of the observation, and physically exhausted at the end of the activity. If note-taking is not possible during observation, researchers need to write them soon afterwards, or, as with Palmer's study, at the very least to record them verbally and transcribe them as soon as possible afterwards. Mulhall (2003: 311) suggests that 'recording events as they happen' means that the memory of the researcher is fresh and details are not lost. In the first instance, field-notes consist of jotting down quick notes which become expanded at a later stage. It is important to record impressions as soon as possible after the observation period. These are described by Whitehead as sharp mental notes that are expanded later. A daily discipline of writing is needed, and it is important to remember to record date, time and location as well as pseudonyms to protect confidentiality (Schensul et al., 1999). A map of the location can be drawn and it might be helpful if researchers create diagrams and charts of actions and interactions in the setting. These can be included in the final report.

Given technological advances of recent years, there is the option for researchers to use cameras and video equipment to catch movements and expressions of participants more accurately. High-definition recording is now available to researchers at minimal cost, and this can be considered, although video cameras could intimidate or disturb the participants and change their behaviour. There are also situations where recording behaviour would obviously be inappropriate, for example children's play within an open setting. If a recording is made, it can be viewed over and over again so 'nothing is lost' (Abrams, 2000: 58). This also means, of course, that the recordings must be kept secure and confidential, and they cannot be shown to colleagues or friends (for student projects, only to supervisors with permission of the participants).

The researcher's own reflections and feelings are also recorded in field-notes. However, it is advised by many, including Wolcott (2009), that these are kept separate from the observational data. These reflections and field-notes should be recorded at the time of the study, or as soon as possible after, and include anything that may impact upon the observer's experience within the field, and anything that may relate to the data collection.

Using documentary sources of data

Documents collected while in the field are further useful sources of data as they contain added knowledge about the group being studied. They might consist of photographs, digital recordings, leaflets, reports, memos, minutes of meetings and newsletters. The researcher treats them like transcriptions of interviews or detailed descriptions of observations; that is, they are coded and categorised. They act as sensitising devices and make researchers aware of important issues in the community.

Many of these texts exist before researchers start their work, others are initiated and organised by the researchers themselves. Historical documents, archives and media materials exist independently from researchers while personal diaries might be written through their intervention or instigation. There are two different forms of diary data: *solicited* and *unsolicited*. The former are written at the request of the researcher, and will often be guided, for example, by a set of open-ended questions designed to encourage participants to focus on specific activities or occurrences. Unsolicited diaries are spontaneously maintained accounts, or 'documents of life' (Allport, 1943: xii), kept by participants at the behest of researchers – the personal and informal records people keep, which are not easily accessed.

Scott (1990) further differentiates between types of document by referring to them as *closed, restricted, open-archival* and *open-published*. Access to closed documents is limited to a few people, namely their authors and those who commissioned them. As far as restricted documents are concerned, researchers can only gain access with permission of insiders under particular conditions.

Using documents to support observation: the practical knowledge of a sport coach

Sport coaches often possess the requisite theoretical knowledge to under-take coaching activities, yet their practical knowledge, or the ability actually to use theoretical understanding is often more limited. Dorgo (2009) was interested in 'the practical knowledge of an expert strength and condition-ing coach', and used several methods to explore this, including both obser-vation and participant observation of the coach in action. To augment his observational data, he used various documents, including training plans, handouts and educational booklets provided to athletes. The use of such documents allowed the researcher to support emerging themes from the observation, as well as creating new ones. In addition, the documents also offered a historical understanding of the practical knowledge of the coach. This allowed Dorgo to suggest that most aspects of practical knowledge were actually developed through field experience, real-life practices and other professionals, rather than through education and training.

Permission for access is needed from the living authors of diaries and keepers of other confidential documents. Open-archival documents are available to any person, subject to administrative conditions and opening hours of libraries. Published documents, of course, can be accessed by anybody at any time. The benefit is that there is no reactivity or observer effect when using documen-tary data.

Images are increasingly becoming part of qualitative inquiry, and can form a useful part of participant observation. Loizos (2000) advises researchers to log images with written details of location, actors and dates, to get permission from participants to reproduce their image, and crucially to only use films and other images when they really enhance the research as they may be expensive to buy or disturbing to participants to record them.

Problematic issues

Observation, through familiarity with the culture under study, generates much information about settings and situations. However, there are also some problems and disadvantages particularly for researchers who have time constraints; indeed interviewing is popular because it is not as demanding of the researcher's time. The main disadvantage of conducting an observational study is that it is so time-consuming. Traditionally observers would spend at least a year in the field collecting data, though this is not feasible for many researchers, particularly for undergraduate students and applied research. Additionally, it is often recommended that researchers maximise observation opportunities and choose different times of day and days of week (e.g. DeWalt and DeWalt, 2010). This requires a great commitment of time and energy.

It is difficult to record the data during observation as scribbled notes take time and might cause reactivity from the people who are being observed. It is also difficult to take notes on a scene in which one is participating whether in a professional or a social role. Often researchers have to base their recollections on memory rather than notes, and memories decrease over time. This means that notes which are not recorded in the location need to be written immediately after the observation.

Ethical issues remain paramount. The researcher must try to fade into the setting, show sensitivity and not be too obvious so that there is little observer effect. On the other hand, the presence and intentions of the researcher need be disclosed to all participants. Researchers must be discreet enough that participants behave naturally, but they should also disclose their identity as researchers so that participants don't feel compromised.

Observation might change the situation, as people act differently in the presence of observers, although they often forget being observed in long-term research. The latter, however, takes more time than is available in student projects (unless the researcher is already a part of the setting and is already therefore accepted) and therefore it is more often used by postgraduates and experienced researchers who have a longer timespan for their research.

Summary

- There are different types of observation
- Observation can pose ethical problems for the researcher
- Researchers need to record their observations in a systematic way
- Observational research is tiring and time-consuming
- Documents such as diaries, historical writing or guidelines are popular sources of data and complement observations

PART III

CHOOSING THE
RESEARCH APPROACH

9

Grounded Theory

Grounded theory (GT) – an approach which generates theory directly from the data – is one of the earliest methods of collecting and analysing data in qualitative research. Within the last decade, researchers in the sports and physical activity arena have popularised this approach (Weed, 2009).

Students sometimes mistakenly believe that GT offers an easy way of carrying out qualitative research, when it is, in fact, one of the more difficult because of theoretical sampling and constant comparison. The completed study is called a grounded theory (for instance, 'a grounded theory of substance abuse in sport') depending on which phenomenon has been investigated. The main purpose of GT is the development of theory directly and systematically from the data. Most researchers in GT adopt a qualitative approach though quantitative elements could be included (see later in this chapter). Of course, students are not always able to develop a completely new or original grounded theory; instead they may make modifications to an established theory. Modifying theory is a legitimate task of a grounded theorist.

The origins of grounded theory

In the 1960s two researchers and sociologists, Anselm Strauss and Barney Glaser, collaborated on several research projects and developed a way of data collection and analysis which they called grounded theory (Glaser and Strauss, 1967). Glaser was originally a quantitative researcher, while Strauss developed his research approach within the qualitative tradition of the Chicago School of Sociology. The intellectual origins of these writers are important as they brought to GT both the rigour and systematic way of quantitative research, and the story-telling and flexible approach of qualitative inquiry. The approach (some, including Strauss, would neither call it a method nor a methodology) had its origin in sociology, particularly in symbolic interactionism, although its use has extended to diverse social sciences such as psychology, business and health studies as well as other interdisciplinary areas. Initially GT was a response from Glaser and Strauss to the positivist stance of other researchers at that time, but they were not purely focusing on qualitative research – in its early days GT included both qualitative and quantitative strategies – indeed Glaser still argues that quantitative elements can be used. Apart from their foundational text in 1967 (and its applications in healthcare), Glaser and Strauss, together and separately wrote several other books, including *Theoretical Sensitivity* (Glaser, 1978) and *Qualitative Analysis for Social Scientists* (Strauss, 1987). Strauss and Corbin, the latter a nurse researcher, modified the initial approach in the two editions of *Basics of Qualitative Research* (Strauss and Corbin, 1990, 1998). They experienced sharp criticism from Glaser (1992) who maintained that their version was not faithful to the original approach. This was followed by a third edition (Corbin and Strauss, 2008), which we find wordier and less clear. There is now a variety of versions of GT, the best known of which is the constructivist grounded theory of Charmaz (2006). Charmaz focuses on the process of knowledge generation and meaning making of people who construct their own social world.

Symbolic interactionism

Glaser and Strauss initially stressed the basis of GT in symbolic interactionism (SI), which was developed by G.H. Mead, C.H. Cooley and Herbert Blumer (who coined the term).

SI focused on the self and its interaction with others, especially on the social roles people inhabit. Symbolic interactionism explains how individuals see themselves as others do, interpret others' perspectives and attempt to fit their own behaviour to that of those they interact with (Blumer, 1969). Actions and behaviour are based on shared meanings. Cooley (1922) speaks of the 'looking glass self'– a self as reflected in the perspectives of others.

George Herbert Mead (1934), the founding father of SI, views the self as a social phenomenon. He discusses the social self of individuals in relation to others' expectations and perspectives. People not only model their roles on the important figures in their lives – 'their significant others' – but also learn to behave in reaction to others' actions, focusing on the 'generalized other'. He compares this to a baseball game in which each player knows the position and role of the other and acts or reacts according to what others do. GT focuses mainly on interaction and processes and hence embodies the ideas of symbolic interactionism. An example is given by Stegelin (2003) who shows how team interdependence and group cohesion are elements of an 'efficacy theory' which she developed, while Wheeler (2012) shows how the significance of the family and the interaction of its members influences children's participation in sport. Glaser later suggests that SI is not essential to grounded theory.

The main elements of grounded theory

GT differs from other qualitative approaches in that it is explanatory rather than descriptive. While the latter do not seek to find cause and effect, GT researchers seek an explanation for a phenomenon; the theory which emerges should have 'explanatory power'. The questions researchers ask of the data will include the following:

- What happens here in this setting?
- When does it happen?
- What are the consequences of what is occurring?
- What are the conditions under which it occurs?
- Why does it occur?

The following sections identify the key elements of a grounded theory study.

Constant comparison and interaction of data collection and analysis

Glaser and Strauss call their strategy the constant comparative method as the incoming data are constantly compared with other data. The process is iterative, going from one piece of datum to the other, formulating concepts and going back to the data themselves. They are checked for similarities and relationships as well as differences. This means that data collection and analysis proceed simultaneously and interact. The incoming data from observations, interviews and other data sources generate ideas during the analysis which can guide the researcher to collect further data. The process goes on throughout the research, and also involves a dialogue with the literature. Students, in their eagerness to see progress, often collect all their data at once and then attempt to analyse these. In GT this is inappropriate.

> **Using constant comparison: the psychosocial factors associated with success in football**
>
> The study by Holt and Dunn (2004) explored the psychosocial factors associated with success in football. Players and coaches were interviewed with subsequent data analysis based on Strauss and Corbin's (2008) approach. This involves progressive analysis from the initial description of the interview data through conceptual ordering to the final theorising. Differences and similarities between the two groups of participants (Canadian and English) were assessed using the constant comparative method. Subsequently, the entire data set was analysed to develop the final theoretical integration. Through this, Holt and Dunn were able to identify an overall theory to explain achievement in football that involved four psychosocial competencies: discipline, commitment, resilience and social support.

Theoretical sampling

The constant comparative method involves theoretical sampling. The *initial* sample is small and, as in all qualitative inquiry, the researcher searches for people who are appropriate to be interviewed or observed, i.e. those who have knowledge of the phenomenon to be studied. Further sampling depends on the data collected. Collection and analysis generate concepts, and these determine the decision of the researcher as to where to go next. Theoretical sampling is sampling on the basis of concepts that arise in the research, 'rather than pre-determined before the beginning of the research, [it] evolves during the process' (Strauss and Corbin, 1998: 202). Participants might be added to further the understanding of concepts that arise. For instance, on interviewing participants in a study of the uptake of sport psychology, a concept such as prejudice may arise, and this has to be followed up by the recruitment of further participants with the knowledge to advance this concept or the researcher returning to re-interview prior participants. The purpose of theoretical sampling is to develop and refine concepts, not to have a larger sample of participants to justify the research though the study may end up with more participants. Different types of situations and settings might also be sampled in this process.

Using theoretical sampling: the social experiences of black sports men attending a predominantly white university

Melendez (2008) studied the social experiences of black sports men attending a predominantly white university. The initial sample consisted of six black first- and second-year undergraduates; however, as the study progressed and analysis was undertaken, the sample was broadened to include the perspectives of third-and final-year student players as well as white players, coaches and administrators. This allowed a deeper understanding of the various social and developmental issues that emerged from early analysis. Melendez was able to identify the relationships between the key stressors which emerged largely as a consequence of participants feeling misunderstood or rejected by the white university environment. These feelings linked to both their status as athletes and to their race.

Theoretical sensitivity

This is a term used by Glaser (1978), which has gained prominence in GT research. As Strauss (1987) suggested, the researcher does not start the study as a 'tabula rasa' – a blank slate. Although researchers set aside preconceived assumptions, they have ideas from their experience and reading that might make them sensitive to particular issues or concepts. Theoretical sensitivity does not only mean illuminating emerging concepts in the light of prior experience and the literature relevant from the field but also from years of working in the field or ideas which arise during the research. The literature in particular enhances awareness in that researchers gain a sense of significant ideas from the relevant studies which have earlier been carried out in the field of study. Sensitivity enhances awareness of researchers when working with the data. By being sensitive, they can develop insight into phenomena and interpret the meanings of ideas from the data. This skill needs development, but it can only be acquired over time by reading articles on qualitative research.

Theoretical sensitivity in grounded theory

Holt and Tamminem (2010) discuss the idea of theoretical sensitivity in grounded theory research in sport psychology, noting that such literature is generally strong in clarifying the role of theory within their studies, focusing specifically on the study by Holt et al. (2008) on parental involvement in sport. As with many grounded theory studies, reference was made to theory at the beginning of the study but, rather than testing such theory, the authors explicitly stated that theory was used to provide conceptual context and sensitise researchers to the theoretical context rather than adopt a 'tabula rasa' approach. The key issue is that such use of theory must be clearly articulated within such a study.

Saturation

Theoretical saturation occurs only when no new ideas important for *the developing theory* arise. Students sometimes misunderstand the meaning of the concept 'saturation', and believe it to be a stage when no new information or concepts are obtained through data collection and analysis, or when a concept arises which is mentioned by all participants and described in similar ways; for instance, Groom et al. (2011) showed that the data collection was complete after the twelfth interview when no new concepts or categories arose during the research which fitted the phenomenon under study.

Saturation is difficult to achieve and students might be careful to claim that they have obtained it. So researchers are advised to be careful before stating that they have arrived at saturation point where no new ideas of significance for the emerging theory arise. Also each study nears saturation at a different point in the process of research.

Achieving saturation: the maintenance of physical activity amongst African-American women

The study by Harley et al. (2009) examined how physical activity could be maintained amongst African-American women. Initially, 30 women were

(Continued)

(Continued)

screened for the study and, of those, 17 were deemed eligible as research participants. The final sample size of 15 was determined using theoretical saturation, based upon the depth of data, and the scarcity of new and relevant information emerging from analysis.

The process of GT: data collection and analysis

Like other qualitative approaches, GT is rooted in:

• The personal or professional interest of researchers
• Their prior experiences
• Their reading
• A gap in the knowledge of the field.

Data sources are many and varied, but observations and participant interviews are the most common. Diaries and other documents such as letters or historical papers might also be used, while at some stage relevant literature for the developing concepts becomes a resource for the researcher. Indeed, Glaser (1978) believes that 'everything is data'.

As we suggested, there is interplay between data collection and analysis, and ideas that arise are followed up and guide the grounded theorist through the whole of the process until theory has been developed. Throughout, the focus become more specific and centred on particular concepts or ideas that seem to become especially important – a process called 'progressive focusing'. For instance, a student might come across the expression 'trying my best' in an interview, and this idea is prevalent in several interviews. The researcher can then follow up by focusing on this, clarifying and sharpening these ideas rather than having broader-based questions. Charmaz (2006) suggests that researchers become more directed by their data over time.

Interviews in other types of qualitative research and grounded theory differ only in the strategies which have been explained – theoretical sampling and progressive focusing – though other approaches have sometimes included these too.

Coding and categorising

The distinct processes in GT are coding and categorising. Combined with constant comparison, coding for category development goes on throughout the research. Coding means identifying, labelling or naming concepts during the data analysis (note that the term 'code' has a specific meaning in GT – it is part of the process of analysis). Strauss (1987) mentioned three types of coding:

- Open coding
- Axial coding (not used by Glaserians)
- Selective coding

Open coding means breaking down the data; the researcher examines the data line-by-line or sentence-by-sentence (one paragraph at a time) to gain provisional categories with their properties and dimensions; for instance, the line 'I have always feared my brother's achievement in running and never believed I could reach the same standard' *might* generate the initial *in vivo* code (a label or words that the participants themselves use) 'fear of brother's achievement'. In vivo coding is often the first step in coding. However, the researcher might transform this into a more abstract idea or category, such as 'comparison with significant others'. Codes which link are clustered together and collapsed or reduced to overarching ideas or categories. For instance, the codes 'fear of falling', 'anxiety over achieving the goal' and 'being last in the race' might be reduced or collapsed to the category 'fear of failure'.

Axial coding, a term initially employed by Strauss (1987) and carried out by researchers who take the Straussian route of GT, is coding that demonstrates the relationships between concepts (Corbin and Strauss, 2008) while Glaser uses neither the term nor the process. In axial coding the researcher thinks about the 'axis' of relationships around a category, the 'where, when, why, who, how and with what consequences' (Charmaz, 2006: 60); for instance, when speaking of the category 'feeling pain' (the axis), one might think of the causal condition: over-training, the action of 'taking a break', the consequence of this is 'pain relief' (more about this later). Memoing or memo-writing parallels open and axial coding.

Selective coding starts only when the researcher has found the core category – the storyline – which relates to all others in important ways. The integration of categories is the last step in the analysis process. Bringer et al. (2002) developed a core category labelled *role conflict and role ambiguity* in a study of coaches' and athletes' sexual relationships which interlinked all other main categories.

Coding and categorising: the professional socialisation experiences of certified athletic trainers

Pitney (2002) explored the professional socialisation experiences of certified athletic trainers using a grounded theory approach. Data from interviews with 15 participants were coded using open, axial and selective procedures. The open coding allowed two concepts to be generated: an informal induction process into the role; and the creation of networks for learning. The axial coding allowed connections between these concepts to be examined, and the context that influenced the overall process to be understood. The selective coding allowed the overarching explanatory theory to be identified, which was the importance of the informal learning processes to the socialisation of the athletic trainers.

Theoretical coding is similar to selective coding in that it shows that categories are related to each other and can be integrated into a theory. It helps to relate the concepts to each other and the core category, and demonstrates concepts, their interrelationships and the underlying pattern in the research (Glaser, 2004). Glaser confirms throughout his work that there are terms indicating causal relationships which should ᵔᵔ taken into account for each category when coding theoretically. These are causes, context, covariance, contingencies, conditions and consequences.

- *Causes* are reasons for or explanations for the occurrence of a category
- *Context* is the setting and factors surrounding the phenomenon
- *Covariance* occurs between the given category and others (i.e. a category changes with change in another)
- Certain *conditions* affect the development of a category
- *Contingency* means that the given category has an impact on another category
- *Consequences* are the outcomes or functions of a given category

Students can take either the Straussian or the Glaserian route, but they should describe and explain what they do and justify their actions. Most of our students now use Charmaz, who explains GT processes and strategies very well, and her less complex and less wordy approach is easier to understand.

Induction, deduction and abduction

As we have stated, qualitative research does not start with hypotheses and is initially at least, inductive. Inductive reasoning is a process in which researchers start from individual incidents or cases, they go from the unique to the general (Holloway and Wheeler, 2010). GT also starts this way; however, as stated before, during the research process, researchers might develop working propositions (or working hypotheses) or conceptualisations that are provisional, and which they then hope to examine and check empirically by returning to the data. The latter is deductive reasoning where researchers draw a conclusion from general ideas (the working hypothesis). GT thus shows an interaction between induction and deduction. As Strauss and Corbin (1998) state, researchers validate interpretations through constant comparison. Glaser denies that there is a deductive element in GT research, though one might point out that GT is not only inductive as constant comparison and theoretical sampling are used which means that working propositions are examined and followed up in a further process that tends to be deductive. Charmaz (2006) speaks of abductive reasoning where researchers form possible hypotheses and examine the data empirically for each possibility to find the most plausible explanation. Researchers treat ideas as provisional until they have been examined over time and are re-confirmed by the data from which they emerged.

Memo-writing and diagrams

Like all qualitative researchers should, grounded theorists keep research diaries into which they transfer their field-notes and pen items of general interest. The grounded theorist has one more task to undertake, that of writing memos. According to Strauss (1987) different types of memos might be used. These are, for instance:

- Operational and technical memos (related to research design)
- Discovery memos (related to the emergence of new ideas)
- Memos of speculation and conjecture
- Theoretical memos (development of theoretical ideas and theory)

Corbin and Strauss (2008) differentiate between field-notes and memos which should be written up separately. While field-notes contain ideas from the field and analytic remarks, Strauss and Corbin (1998: 110) define memos as a record 'of analysis, thoughts, interpretations, questions and directions for further data collection'. Hence memos are complex and have more depth and conceptualisation; memo-writing is part of the analysis process. Memos assist in the building of theory, developing provisional categories and working hypotheses. In the course of the research, memos become more complex and theoretical. As Charmaz (2006) notes, early memos initially record what is going on in the data and present early attempts at interpretation and elaboration of meanings. They help to develop concepts and uncover patterns in the incoming data. Later memos might reveal changes in the emerging theory. Glaser (2004) claims that although memo-writing slows down the process of analysis, it also is of assistance because it forces researchers to be reflective and thoughtful. Excerpts from memos might even become part of the research account. Grounded theorists might also use diagrams in an attempt to illustrate clear links between concepts and categories. These visualisations of the research will also become more complex as the research proceeds.

The presentation of memos needs consideration; just like field-notes and field diaries they must be dated and, if possible, titled. This is important for the audit trail and for their use during the writing up stage.

Using memos: the development of expertise in cricket

Weissensteiner et al. (2009) studied the development of expertise in cricket through interviews with 14 elite cricketers. As well as coding the data from each interview, the researchers were careful to document their own observations, ideas, questions and decisions that emerged throughout the collection and analysis of data. This helped to ensure the trustworthiness of the overall analytical procedure.

The core category and storyline

From the processes of coding, categorising and comparing, the researcher generates or discovers the core category. This links categories and conceptualisations; indeed it is the main storyline. The linking of all categories around a core is called selective coding. This means that the researcher uncovers the essence of the study and integrates all the elements of the emergent theory. We summarise Glaser (1978) who in the early days of GT suggested that the core category:

- has to be central;
- occurs frequently;
- needs more time to become saturated; and
- can be a process, condition or a consequence.

Strauss (1987) added to this that the core category needs to be part of a pattern and naturally provides a connection to other categories. It can only be fully developed on completion of the research. The congruence of the core category with the storyline is obvious. The storyline shows what the research is all about and provides a general sense of the essence of the research. It also demonstrates the development from description to conceptualisation. In a study on the perceptions of exercise among school-aged children with asthma, for instance, Shaw (2010) named the core category *Ongoing Creation of Perceptions of Exercise*. This, she claims, is the main story of the participants' experiences, found frequently in the data and linking all other categories.

Using the literature

Although grounded theorists have read widely in their broader field of study, not all the literature need be examined from the very beginning. Nevertheless, some foundational concepts related to the study should be reviewed at the start. This is no different from other qualitative approaches. If a very detailed literature precedes the research, researchers might be directed to focus on particular ideas rather than allowing them to develop from the data. The literature will, however, create awareness of concepts, as long as an open mind and flexibility permit new ideas to emerge. Indeed Glaser (2004) suggests only the general literature in the substantive area of the study should be reviewed, and that an extensive reading of the literature in the very beginning of the research might be inappropriate; the detailed, relevant literature should become part of the data at a later stage. We do remind researchers, however, that they need to have some idea of the literature on the topic, otherwise they might go over old ground or, as in popular jargon, 're-invent the wheel'.

During the process of the research when data are being gathered, analysed and initial findings discovered, the specific literature linked to these is used to develop a contextual framework. Researchers use the literature to confirm or challenge (disconfirm) their own data – they create a dialogue between the data and the literature. In grounded theory this is of particular importance as theoretical sampling demands that not only can the sample of participants be increased, but new ideas from the literature can also be sampled.

The developing theory

Theory develops from conceptualisations. In GT, theory can be understood as an explanation – or a supposition – which is rooted in evidence from the data. Glaser and Strauss differentiate between types of grounded theories, namely *formal* and *substantive* theory. For instance, were we to suggest that 'identity construction is difficult if it is not rooted in socialisation by significant others', we might have built a formal theory at a general level, which is generated from many varied situations and not tied to time and place. A substantive theory, on the other hand, is tied to specifics, such as 'football fans discover a fan identity if they are part of a football club supporters group which follows the club around the country'.

Students and other researchers thus usually develop substantive theories in an empirical and smaller, more limited, area of research.

Developing substantive theory: the use of music to manipulate emotional state in youth tennis

Bishop et al. (2007) examined how young tennis players used music to manipulate their emotional state. Analysis of interviews with 14 participants led to a theory to explain the use of music. Five key determinants of use in the model produced by Bishop et al. were found. Four were classified as extrinsic: extra-musical associations (such as associating music positively with past memories); peer and family influences; film soundtracks; and identification with the artist. The one intrinsic motivation that was discovered related to the acoustic properties of the music. The authors were able to determine that the extrinsic sources were stronger determinants of emotional state than the intrinsic factor.

This substantive theory cannot always be applied in a general way but might only have validity in a particular context, location and time. Most expert grounded theorists demand that the theory must:

- have explanatory power;
- show links between categories;
- demonstrate a process over time; and
- be grounded in reality.

The original text also demands 'fit, workability and relevance and modifiability'. Fit needs to be established to show how the theory fits with the data and the categories generated from analysis; workability means that the theory must work and needs to be plausible; relevance is tied to the significance of the theory and its 'grab' as the originators themselves say; and modifiability means that the theory can be changed when new incoming data point to the need for adaptation. The theory does not magically 'emerge' but the researcher has to actively build and uncover it.

Researchers can see here the complexities of GT, and we would not advise undergraduates to use GT unless they are already experienced qualitative researchers.

Problems in grounded theory

Several experts on qualitative research have identified problems and contradictions within GT. Charmaz (2006), in particular, criticises a trend of decontextualisation, whereby GT might become divorced from its context of time, location and culture, especially when the studies are small. Students tend to forget context sometimes because they wish to develop a theory that is transferable beyond the case studied.

Seldén (2005) criticises theoretical sensitivity, remarking that conceptualisation is an outcome of the experience and the reading of researchers and does not derive directly from the data. However, the literature and experience are linked to (or as some, such as Glaser, believe, are even part of) the data, and all are legitimate sources for the development of concepts. Charmaz (2006) deplores 'premature closure' (a term coined by Glaser), where researchers complete their analysis too early and do not aim for saturation. Another problem lies in the initial fracturing of data by coding and categorising; students, in particular, need to be theoretically sensitive so that they keep in mind the whole, the pattern, the holistic sense of the research. Only then can a theory be generated.

It is interesting that researchers have often modified GT too much as they use just some of its elements in their studies. In this case, of course, the study is not truly 'a grounded theory' but research which applies some of the principles of GT. Analytic or conceptual description (which is inherent in much qualitative inquiry) or research that employs thematic analysis cannot be called GT, nor can any study which has not developed a theory or at least major theoretical ideas. Grounded theorists claim to be interpreters of the data and do not stop when they have described and reported the experiences of participants. Weed (2009) strongly criticises studies which proclaim GT status but have only made use of some of its constituents and not of others. Students need to stay true to the principles of grounded theory, but they can modify the strategies they adopt as long as they justify this and make it explicit. GT has often been used in combination with other approaches, but there is a danger that the unique features of each approach might be lost and the study becomes inconsistent (Holloway and Todres, 2003).

Concluding remarks

From its origins in 1967, grounded theory has been developed, modified and changed until it becomes an approach with several branches. We shall not take sides in the debate between Glaser and Strauss, as researchers need to make up their own mind after examining each approach. It is necessary, however, that they justify and explain what they have done in their own grounded theory and on whom they based their specific way of researching. Although writing a number of books together, Glaser and Strauss diverged from each other and developed GT in different ways. Glaser in 1992 and in many subsequent writings maintains that Strauss does not write grounded theory but 'full conceptual description'. Indeed Glaser's approach seems more purist (he calls it 'classic' grounded theory), while Strauss and Corbin are concerned about mentoring novices in the approach and give detailed, sometimes formulaic instructions to help them. (The debate between them cannot be discussed here at length as it generates complex issues within GT.)

Charmaz (2006) developed her own version of GT – constructivist grounded theory. It appears that she believes the debate between the originators of GT to be futile as it seems inflexible. The approach, she suggests, should be flexible and developmental, neither rigid nor prescriptive. She calls her version of GT constructivist, as 'the interpretation of a phenomenon is in itself a construction' (p. 187), and advances GT by stating that theories are not discovered but 'constructed'. We believe that Charmaz has produced a workable version of GT.

Summary

- GT is a theory developed directly from the incoming data.
- GT has 'explanatory power'.
- The researcher collects data through in-depth interviews, participant observation and other data sources.
- Data collection and analysis interact. Researchers code and categorise the data.
- All data, incidents or concepts are compared.
- Sampling can be extended depending on emerging concepts (theoretical sampling).
- A dialogue between the literature and the categories takes place in the discussion.

10

Ethnography

Ethnography refers to the description of a group, culture or community. Angrosino (2007: 14) defines it as: 'the art and science of describing a human group – its institutions, interpersonal behaviours, material productions and beliefs'. It is traditionally the approach associated with anthropology, a term which derives from the Greek, and means the study of people. The goal of anthropology is to describe and explain social behaviour, with the principle of studying behaviour in a natural setting (Brewer, 2000). Ethnographic data collection takes place mainly through observations, interviews and the examination of documents (see relevant chapters). This illuminates and provides insight into the participants' social world. The term ethnography refers to both a process – the methods and strategies of research – and to a product – the written story as the outcome of the research. People 'do' ethnography: they study a culture, observe its members' behaviour and listen to them. But they also 'produce' *an ethnography*, a written text (or, unusually, a performance such as a play or dance for instance) which is the ethnographic account. Ethnography can be qualitative or quantitative or combine both methods, but here we have focused on qualitative ethnography.

Ethnography refers to both the research in unfamiliar cultures and to the study of subcultures within the researcher's own society. A good example of the latter is the study by Whyte (1943) who investigated the urban gang subculture in an American city. *Street Corner Society* became a classic, and other sociologists used this work as a model for their own writing. Many of the early sport-related ethnographies focused upon aspects of physical education; however, there is now an increasing wealth of ethnographic literature in sport and physical activity that explores a varied range of themes.

Undertaking ethnographic research: 'we' and 'them' in Norwegian surfing culture

Langseth (2011) undertook ethnographic research to examine the construction of surfing identities within Norway, to determine who, according to the

---

participants, were 'real' surfers, and how they constructed such ideas of who 'we' and 'them' were. Through a variety of methods, including interviews, observation, participant observation and analysis of documents, Langseth explored first how four forms of symbolic capital (skills, subcultural knowledge, commitment and local affiliation) were acquired by participants. Second, the ethnography examined how the presence of surfers lacking these four forms of capital led to the creation of 'out-groups'. Through his use of ethnography, and the focus on the group from the group's own perspective, Langseth was able to determine their particular norms and values, and was thus able to show how the Norwegian surf subculture has become characterised by what he refers to as 'partial social closure', whereby membership was increasingly guarded by insiders, 'protected' by those four forms of capital.

Adopting an ethnographic approach to a familiar culture helps researchers not to take assumptions about their own society or cultural group for granted. This type of ethnography has been described as 'anthropology at home'. An advantage is that there is no alien tongue to master and the culture of interest is partially known at the outset of study. This is not necessarily an advantage, as a common problem of conducting anthropology at home is 'making the familiar strange' (Spindler and Spindler, 1982: 123–24). It is difficult to achieve an outsider's perspective on a familiar setting, as the outsider can usually see things that an insider might miss.

'Anthropology at home': the formation of networks in the health club

An example of researchers exploring their own culture is provided by Crossley (2008), who, after an extended period of attending a health club, chose to undertake a study that examined how social networks within the club were formed, and the extent to which such networks provided sources of social capital for members. An initial and informal six-year period of observation at the club led to a more formal 18-month period of participant observation. Observations were made at a variety of settings, such as in changing rooms, in the gym and studio, and the relaxation area. This was augmented by casual conversations, rather than interviews. This allowed Crossley to identify the processes of network formation and their functions, such as counselling, information-sharing and exchange of services, as well as the 'dark side' of networking, such as the creation of tightly bonded groups and the identification of outsiders, who may negatively experience the effect of participating alongside cohesive groups.

As this chapter will show, ethnography has been much used by researchers into sport and physical activity, the majority on home terrain. For many ethnographers in the area of sport and physical activity, the goal of research is not just to understand behaviour but also to influence practice for the better.

Fieldwork

Ethnography requires researchers to become immersed in the 'field' with extended periods of fieldwork in order to become accepted within the research setting. The term fieldwork is used by anthropologists to describe data collection outside laboratories and in the field, that is the research setting. The researchers' physical presence in the field allows them to gain first-hand experience of the group under study and to be spontaneous and instrumental in terms of when and what type of data are collected. However, as Derrida (1976) observed, the mere presence of a spectator is a violation, and may colour the behaviour of those observed. Prolonged involvement helps to counter this as it allows participants to become used to the researcher and thus behave naturally, rather than putting on a performance; as an insider, the researcher becomes familiar with the setting and with participants. People are therefore studied in everyday naturally occurring settings, interacting as they would normally do, with minimal interference and influence from the researcher (Brewer, 2000). Researchers may already be immersed in the setting, for example Stewart's (2008) doctoral study on the norms, values and culture of boxing, which built upon the author's many years experience as a competitive boxer. Alternatively they may be conversant with the activity, but need to gain access to that activity in a new setting; for example the study of Andrews et al. (2005) into the 'geography of fitness' required one of the authors to join an existing group of bodybuilders. Finally, they may need to gain entry as a 'complete outsider'; for example Ollis et al. (2006) focused on talent identification and expertise in rugby refereeing, but the researchers had no previous knowledge of either rugby or refereeing.

> ### Barriers to inclusion and accessibility: an ethnography of a tennis club
>
> Tennis clubs within the United Kingdom have, historically, been seen to be exclusive, largely due to the specific norms, values and 'rules of engagement' that create an exclusive community, which outsiders may find difficult to access. Within a context of declining participation, the Lawn Tennis Association (LTA), through its policy of 'Club Vision', attempted to address the issue of social exclusion by requiring clubs to demonstrate greater openness, and greater opportunity for inclusion. This is an agenda that encountered resistance among clubs wishing to maintain exclusivity. To explore the issues surrounding this, Lake (2011) undertook an ethnographic study of what he

described as a 'typical' suburban tennis club. Accessing the club through two gatekeepers, Lake spent ten months immersed within the research setting, modelling his appearance and behaviour on existing members, taking part in all aspects of the club, including activities such as social events. Field-notes were written after each session, and at the end of the study, a number of interviews were conducted. Further data were collected from the documents and artefacts such as the club website, clubhouse plaques and photos, and informal conversations with members. Through this immersion, Lake was able to explore issues such as: the use of complex club rules by existing members; the lack of appropriate socialisation for new members on and off the court; the impact of peer pressure on existing members' behaviour towards new members; and the difficulty that new members faced in being accepted within the club. As such, Lake's ethnographic study provided an illuminating example of the barriers to inclusion and accessibility within tennis clubs.

Anthropologists advise spending a year with a group: time enables relationships to develop, and permits the observation of detail and processes, rather than a static image captured at certain points (O'Reilly, 2005). Furthermore, cultural patterns have an incubation period, which takes time to develop and to study. To illustrate, Jones (2000) conducted a study of football fandom, becoming immersed over a period of two years in the subculture of the fans of Luton Town football club. However, a shorter period of immersion in the setting has become acceptable because a long immersion is not always possible in an MSc or MA.

Keeping an open mind

There is a focus in ethnography as in most other qualitative research approaches. The researcher does not usually begin the research process with a theory, but with curiosity (Brewer, 2000). The aim of the research is to discover that which is not already known outside the culture. In the anthropological research tradition, researchers suspend prior assumptions. It should be the aim of researchers not to impose their worldview on participants through a highly structured interview or questionnaire, but to understand social reality and emotional associations from the insider or emic point of view. Thus the researcher's data have primacy and drive ongoing data collection.

Capturing the insider view

Ethnography prioritises the perspective of the members of the social group being studied. Indeed, according to Wolcott (2009), ethnographers start by 'experiencing' the social world of participants before systematic inquiry and examination can begin. The emic (insider) view is presented through *thick description*, a term used by the anthropologist Geertz (1973), which has its origin in the writing of the philosopher Ryle. This is description that makes explicit the detailed patterns of cultural and social relationships and puts them in context at the same time as including emotions and the meaning that these have for the participants (Denzin, 1997). As such, it privileges the internal world of participants. Ethnography rejects the idea that the researcher's view has primacy. As Harris (1976: 36) states: 'the way to get inside of people's heads is to talk with them, to ask questions about what they think and feel'.

Though it is crucial that ethnographers present data from the emic perspective, they must subsequently seek to *interpret* behaviour, combining the view of the insider (the emic) with that of the outsider (the etic) to describe the social setting (Fetterman, 2010). Thick description must therefore be theoretical and analytical, in contrast with thin description, which is superficial and does not explore the underlying meanings of cultural members. Etic meanings stress the ideas of ethnographers themselves – their abstract and theoretical view when they distance themselves from the cultural setting and try to make sense of it. Harris (1976) explains that etics are scientific accounts by the researcher, based on that which is directly observable. The researcher's job is to translate the words of informants into the language of their discipline, in this case SPA – moving back and forth from informants' meanings to interpretation. The researcher must seek a balance between the raw data which represent the insider (emic) view and the outsider (or etic) view.

A focus on culture

Ethnography differs from other approaches through its emphasis on culture. Culture is used as the central organising concept of anthropology (Spradley, 1979), and ethnography, which similarly derives from the Greek, means *the writing of culture*. In the nineteenth century, anthropologists adopted the term 'culture' to designate a distinctive way of life, with an emphasis on lived experience, communication patterns and shared practices (Williams, 1981). Hofstede (2001) states that culture is a phenomenon collectively generated by people who share the same social environment and are mentally programmed in a way that distinguishes them from other social groups. Although the term culture is most often used to categorise a nation, it has also been used to apply to any collective or community whose membership is self-defined and changeable. Barker (2011) points out that subcultures represent divergent though often overlapping life-worlds, with group membership often determined by people's particular location and power within a culture. It is important not to see culture as a monolithic concept; the way people behave and think depends on their location in that culture.

Ethnography refers to the description and interpretation of a culture or social group; its aim is to understand social reality by focusing on ordinary, everyday behaviour and prioritising the meanings that participants attach to their cultural environment (Holloway and Todres, 2003). The researchers' responsibility is to describe the patterns of beliefs and behaviour and the unique processes in the subculture or culture they study. After reading the ethnographic account, the reader should have a clear picture of the group's cultural life.

Ethnographic methods

There is a specific research approach associated with ethnography: ethnographic data collection occurs mainly through observations and interviews which fall under the umbrella of *participant observation*. This is possibly the earliest form of data collection, where early anthropologists and sociologists, such as Malinowski and Mead, became part of the culture they studied and, over time, examined the actions and interactions of people 'in the field'. Participant observation means that researchers are immersed in the setting; they interact with participants, observe what is going on and are able to ask questions about it (Hammersley and Atkinson, 2007). Though researchers collect data by the standard methods of observation and interviewing, they also rely on documents such as letters, emails, reports, contributions to online fora, diaries and taped oral histories of people in a particular group or connected to it. Wolcott (1994) calls these strategies 'experiencing' (observation), 'enquiring' (interviewing) and 'examining' (studying documents). Using these methods acts as a way to triangulate data (see Chapter 16).

Observation

Observation involves collecting data from the culture under study, as observers who become or are already part of the culture take note of everything they see and hear and talk to members of the culture to gain their interpretations. There are three steps in fieldwork. In the first stage, researchers observe and study the culture in which they are interested and write notes on their observations. This initial phase in the field consists of a time for exploration as researchers learn about an area of study and become familiar with it. This is not difficult if they are already part of the community; acceptance need not be earned. Second, researchers start focusing on particular issues, and they question participants on their initial observations. As time goes on, and preliminary analysis has been undertaken, a more instinctive approach is adopted. Selective sampling takes place (Spradley, 1980), which is shaped by the emergent themes from ongoing data analysis. Therefore data collection becomes more focused and less time-consuming as the field research proceeds. In the third stage, researchers realise that saturation has occurred, and they start the process of disengagement (see Chapter 8).

Ethnographic interviews

Observations are the starting point for in-depth interviews. Researchers may not understand what they see, and ask the members of the group or culture to explain it to them. Participants share information on and their interpretations of events, rules and roles with the interviewer. Some interviews are formal and structured, but often researchers ask questions on the spur of the moment. Researchers must make the most of opportunistic conversations. Often ethnographers uncover discrepancies between words and actions – what people do and what they say – a problem originally discussed by Deutscher (1970). On the other hand, there may be congruence between the spoken work and behaviour. If any discrepancies exist, they must be explained and interpreted.

Unstructured interviews are the most common type of interview in ethnography. These are seen as the best way to access experiences, emotions and perceptions, allowing those being studied to express themselves in their own words and in which the participants are in control of pace and wording. The ethnographic interview is responsive to situations and informants, and for this reason, each interview will tend to be unique. Indeed, the flexibility and spontaneity associated with ethnographic data collection means that the researcher can explore many avenues. Fieldwork can and often will lead researchers in unexpected directions, as it will be directed by the interests and preoccupations of the participant.

In order to make participants feel comfortable, researchers must use the interpersonal skills that are needed in everyday social life, such as maintaining eye contact, adopting relaxed body language, showing an interest and asking relevant follow-up questions (O'Reilly, 2005). It is important in the ethnographic interview to ask questions that are open-ended, to get interviewees talking about a broad topic area, whilst remembering that the interviewee guides the content. Spradley (1979) recommends the use of grand-tour or experience questions in the opening ethnographic interview, followed by focused mini-tour or example questions, depending on the interviewee's response (see Table 10.1 below for an illustration adapted to the context of research into the experiences of elite athletes).

Table 10.1   Interview question types

Grand-tour question	
An open, descriptive question that can keep an informant talking for hours.	Can I ask you how you tend to feel during your training?
Mini-tour question	
Stimulated by response to grand-tour questions, deals with a smaller unit of experience, woven throughout the interview.	You said that you feel nervous before competing – can you explain why?
Example question	
Used to gather further information on a topic raised by the informant.	Can you give me an example of maltreatment? (Only asked in response to allusion to difficulty.)
Experience question	
Open-ended and best used after asking numerous grand- and mini-tour questions.	What was it like when you went to your first training camp?

Source: adapted from Spradley (1979)

Sample and setting

Ethnography, like other qualitative approaches, might involve case study research, which focuses on the particular – a specific case, group or organisation. Spradley (1980) recommends the following criteria in choice of research setting: simplicity, accessibility, unobtrusiveness and permissibleness. There is a continuum between large- and small-scale studies, between macro- and micro-ethnographies. A macro-ethnography examines a larger culture with its institutions, communities and value systems, whilst micro-studies consist of research in small units or focus on activities within small settings. Most students choose a micro-ethnographic study as it makes fewer demands on their time than macro-ethnography. A large-scale study means a long period of time in the setting and is often the work of several researchers. Both types of ethnography demand a detailed picture of the community under study as well as similar strategies for data collection and analysis. The type of project depends, of course, on the focus of the investigation and the researcher's own interests.

Ethnographies range from large-scale, complex analyses of social settings, to small, focused studies.

Choosing the setting: sport television production processes and cohesion in a university sports team

Silk et al. (2000) carried out a major ethnographic study of the television production process involved in the 1995 Canada Cup of Soccer through varying levels of observation status, from observer to participant observer, at a range of sites. The study explored a variety of key issues related to the way in which industry-held values enabled and constrained certain practices within the labour process involved in the production of televised sport. Observations were made on the conditions and means and 'moment of production itself, looking specifically at the practices on which the broadcast drew and the ways in which these were reworked at the production site'. Preliminary findings were used as a base for further ethnographic data collection at the sport network's head office. From the observations, interviews and document analyses it became clear that there was a network-held belief system of the 'right way to cover soccer', which could be traced to an institutionally held, 'legitimate' set of values and beliefs – an industry practice – which served to shape the labour processes of the production team.

This can be contrasted with, for example, Holt and Sparkes' (2001) ethnographic study of cohesiveness in a university football team. Their study aimed to identify the factors that contributed to a cohesive team, and focused on a much smaller unit of analysis (university football team as opposed to a sport production network), focusing on a much more specific analysis (factors affecting cohesion in a specific team, rather than the role of industry values, and their impact upon sports production).

As in other types of qualitative research, ethnographers generally use purposive sampling which is criterion-based and non-probabilistic (Daymon and Holloway, 2011). This means that sampling issues are straightforward, as the sample includes those involved in the scene and those who have knowledge of the culture under study. Central to ethnography is the use of *key informants* with whom ethnographers work to produce a cultural description (Gobo, 2008). Key informants own special and expert knowledge about the history and subculture of a group, about interaction processes in it and cultural rules, rituals and language. Researchers should choose their informants carefully to make sure that they are suitable and representative of the group under study. Thus in Granskog's (2003) exploration of the socialisation of athletes into triathlon events, for example, key informants were female triathletes, whilst Atkinson (2008) targeted triathletes in his ethnography of pain and suffering among participants in Canadian triathlon events. In both cases, informants could offer the researcher access into the triathlete subculture.

Spradley (1979) advises ethnographers to elicit the 'tacit' knowledge of cultural members – the concepts and assumptions that they have but of which they are unaware. Conversely, Fetterman warns against prior assumptions which key informants might have. If they are highly knowledgeable they might impose their own ideas on the study and the researcher must try to guard against prioritising these over the observed reality. As noted before, any discrepancy between what is observed and what informants say must be recorded and scrutinised, and the motives of informants critically questioned. Giulianotti's study of Scottish football hooliganism, for example, resulted in a situation where:

> Aberdeen and Hibs casuals put it to me in forceful terms that each mob is number one in Scotland – the hardest and, to a lesser extent, the trendiest. Recent fights between the two have been inconclusive, inflicting more talk than injuries on each other ... One Hibs boy suggested, 'If you don't say we're number one, I'm gonna ... do ya, and that's a promise'. (1995: 10)

Ethnography and cross gender issues: researching the world of the wives of professional athletes

Ortiz's (2005) ethnographic study of sport marriages, and particularly the social world of the wives of professional athletes, raised a number of interesting questions about the role of the ethnographer within such studies. Although it might be easy to assume that in such an instance, a male researcher within a female world could be dismissed as inappropriate, being unable to gain access or data, Ortiz found that, through adopting an 'acceptable type of masculinity' (p. 266), such status actually led to a number of advantages. The key element in gaining trust and acceptance was to adopt an alternative masculinity to the strong hegemonic hyper-masculinity common in professional sports, focusing instead on a non-threatening 'muted masculinity' (p. 267), through careful presentation of appearance, speech and behaviour, to present a masculinity that was an alternative to that experienced by, and disliked by, the athletes' wives. Ortiz became seen as someone who was non-threatening and 'safe to confide in' (p. 274), as well as being professional, knowledgeable about the private world of athlete's wives and non-judgemental about that world. This allowed participants to relax, and trust and rapport to be developed. Thus, through minimising aspects of masculinity that were seen as negative, Ortiz was able to successfully enter the social world.

Key informants are important for ethnography. Researchers have therefore to work hard to establish rapport – a good working relationship between researcher and informant – which requires effort and awareness. This represents one of the key challenges of ethnography, especially in a lengthy ethnography, as discussed by Sands (2002), for example, who highlights the need to develop, and most importantly maintain, relationships with group members.

Also important in sampling decisions are issues of time and context. If full immersion is not possible, it is advised to arrange to observe the community at different times of the day and on different days of the week. It is also important that different contexts within the setting are observed. Guidelines for data collection are provided in Part I, although these guidelines cannot be seen as complete or all inclusive.

The ethnographic record

From the beginning of their research, ethnographers record what goes on 'in the field'. This includes noting down early impressions as well as accurate and detailed descriptions of events and behaviour in context. Spradley (1979) lists four different types of field-notes in ethnography:

- The condensed account
- The expanded account
- The fieldwork journal
- Analysis and interpretation notes

Condensed accounts are short descriptions made in the field during data collection while expanded accounts extend the descriptions and fill in detail. Ethnographers write short notes during fieldwork, often as unobtrusively as possible so as not to disturb the informants' flow of talk and action. Indeed, the term 'ethnographer's bladder' has been coined to refer to the use by ethnographers of toilet facilities during fieldwork where they can make notes in private (see, for example, Weed's (2006) ethnographic account of watching the Football World Cup in the pub for a brief discussion of the efficacy of this approach). Ethnographers extend the short account as soon as possible after observation (or interview if they were unable to record). It is important to unload the observation experience as soon as possible to avoid the problems of memory recall (Hammersley and Atkinson, 2007). Though it may be challenging to find time to write up an expanded account, the researcher may otherwise not be able to recall observations in their entirety. A discipline of daily writing and systematic recording tactics are vital.

The ethnographer's task is not one of only recording observed events, but also of introspection and thought, as ethnography is a subjective construct of both observation and analysis, as Hammersley and Atkinson maintain. In the field journal, ethnographers note their own biases, reactions and problems during fieldwork. The main 'instrument' of research is the researcher; therefore a reflexive account of the research process is vital. By keeping a diary, researchers are able to subject their research activities to rigorous analysis and to develop analytic thinking. However, researchers must clearly distinguish personal opinions and feelings from the data they have collected (Aspers, 2004). These notes will be worked into the final research report, reflecting the interplay between the data collected, the literature and the researcher's own insights.

Analysis and interpretation

Wolcott (1994) states that an ethnography consists of cultural description, analysis and interpretation. Ethnographers describe what they see and hear while studying a culture; they identify its main features and uncover relationships between them through analysis; they interpret the findings by asking for meaning and inferring it from the data.

Ethnographic analysis can be defined as the process of bringing order to data, organising undifferentiated comments and observations into patterns, categories and descriptive units, and looking for relationships between them (Fetterman, 2010). The process of analysis involves several steps (see also Chapter 15):

1 Ordering and organising vast amounts of data;
2 Breaking the material into manageable – and meaningful – sections through the process of coding;
3 Grouping similar codes together and finding a coherent label for the research category formed;
4 Comparing and contrasting categories;
5 Searching for relationships and grouping categories together so that major categories are formed;

6   Introducing the literature, connecting with other researchers' work;
7   Interpreting, searching for meaning.

The second step in analysis, that of coding, is a time-consuming task, as it involves reading and rereading through notes and transcripts and repeatedly listening to recordings. Coding stops the researcher from getting lost in the data (Mason, 2002), which are organised and broken down into manageable chunks. Thus paragraphs, sentences or even groups of words are each given a descriptive label which reduces or collapses the mass of data obtained. A code is a word used to represent a phenomenon the researcher notices in the text. It must be distinct so that it is obviously different from another code, and there must be a low level of inference (it must be close to concrete description). For example, *self-presentational behaviour* may be a single code.

When codes have been identified, researchers need to look for the main theme, i.e. the core category, a cluster of codes with similar traits, asking themselves questions such as: Is it central? Does it recur? Is it meaningful? Does it have implications for theory? Once the researcher has coded the first interview, the second and third interview transcripts are then coded and compared with the first. Commonalities and similar codes are sorted and grouped together. This happens for each interview (or observation). The researcher then tries to find the ideas that link the categories, and describes and summarises them. From this stage onwards, diagrams are helpful because they present the links and patterns graphically. This is the most common form of analysis in ethnographic research but others also exist. Angrosino (2007: 69) states that there is no single formula that is accepted by all ethnographic researchers, and some analyse their data differently.

As ethnography produces great amounts of data, analysis is therefore highly demanding, and sufficient time must be reserved. Furthermore in ethnography, analysis is not a distinct stage of research, but takes place throughout and after the fieldwork has been completed. It is an interactive process, used to guide ongoing interviews and observation. Researchers listen to their recordings, read the transcripts and field-notes from observation and note down significant elements. Thus the data are scanned and organised from the very beginning of the study. If gaps and inadequacies occur, they can be filled by collecting more data. While this work goes on, researchers choose to focus on particular aspects which they examine more closely than others.

The process of analysis is followed by the act of interpretation, which is a creative enterprise involving skill and imagination (Geertz, 1973). It is also based on the subjective judgement of the researcher. Researchers undertake interpretation during and after analysis, making inferences, providing meaning and giving explanations for findings. Though interpretation involves some speculation, it must be directly grounded in the data. To aid interpretation, the researchers generally engage in a dialogue between their research categories and the relevant and related literature, comparing and contrasting others' work with their own, modifying or generating theory. Thus emerging ideas that derive from analysis are compared and contrasted with established theories.

Writing ethnography

As noted before, the term ethnography refers to both methodology and product. Ethnography as written product is a picture or story of a cultural group. Indeed van Maanen (1988) refers to ethnography as a tale. Thus the presentation of ethnography requires much care, and ethnographers need to cultivate their skills of writing (Atkinson et al., 2007).

There are different choices available to the ethnographer when writing up their findings, and researchers should read a variety of examples in order to familiarise themselves with these options and to make the most suitable choice. Hammersley (1992) tells us that the most common mode of writing ethnography is realistic or naturalistic whereby the reader feels they are observing the scene described. This involves the adoption of an institutional voice, the third person; the ethnography reads as objective reality. There is often an assumption of good faith that a similarly placed and well-trained participant observer would see and hear the same things as the researcher saw and heard (van Maanen, 2011.

However, there is radical scepticism in the research community about the claim of any author to faithfully reconstruct social reality (Brewer, 2000), thus confessional accounts of field research are common companions of realist tales whereby realism' (van Maanen 2011) is mediated by acknowledgement of the subjectivity inherent in research. Confessional tales involve personal language to describe the research strategies adopted as well as to describe the researcher's own biases and feelings during the research process. In any ethnographic study, reflexivity is important – this means adopting a critical attitude to the research and to the researcher's contribution to it. Marcus (1998: 198) describes this as the context-related nature of ethnography, the 'situatedness and partiality of all claims to knowledge'. Researchers are part of the world that they study. How the data are collected, analysed and interpreted depends on the researchers' locations and stance which need to be uncovered to establish trustworthiness. Thus whilst 'silent authorship' is common in research reports – which Charmaz and Mitchell (1996) consider a myth – many ethnographers use the first person throughout their writing to show their personal involvement in the field and consequent influence on the collection and analysis of data.

Van Maanen (2011) identifies a third option for writing, that of the impressionist tale, which presents the culture under study in a creative and imaginative way. This might involve giving names to informants, creating a plotline, building a sense of tension. Thus the ethnography reads like a work of fiction and grips the reader more effectively than traditional modes of writing. The idea of data as a work of art is taken further by performative social scientists who collect and/or present data through artistic media such as film or poetry; for example Markula's work used dance as a medium to create 'sensations of concepts' (2006: 361).

When writing ethnography, an important consideration is one of voice. To give informants their voice (a much discussed concept), polyvocality is advocated (Denzin and Lincoln, 1998), achieved through the use of quotations (as is true of other qualitative approaches). Brewer claims that these are the stuff of ethnography, bringing a sense of immediacy and involvement in the field. This also fulfils the author's moral commitment to give voice to the Other, who should not be misrepresented through extensive paraphrasing (Hollway and Jefferson, 2000). However, quotations should not be overused; they should *illustrate* not replace analysis (Brewer, 2000).

Finally, the engagement of the researcher in a *dialogue* with the literature is reflected in the fact that reference to the literature is made throughout the research report. The literature does not drive data collection; rather it is used where possible to illuminate findings. (The role of the literature is covered in Chapter 4.)

Problems in conducting ethnographic research

There are a number of problems with ethnographic research. First, it is difficult to examine one's own group and become a 'cultural stranger' who questions the assumptions of the familiar culture whose rules and norms have been internalised. Gobo (2008) warns that this might present practical and epistemological problems.

Second, ethnography – like all qualitative research – is demanding in terms of time and emotional energy, and it is important that researchers are prepared for the tiring aspect of both fieldwork and analysis.

Students often write up their research, making statements that seem to be applicable to a whole range of similar situations. An ethnography, like other qualitative research, cannot simply be generalised. Findings from one subculture or one setting are not automatically applicable to other settings. However, Wolcott (1994) asserts that there is always a possibility for transferability, and often the readers can themselves make that leap. The researcher can compare with other specific situations similar to the case studied and can achieve typicality.

Finally, ethnographers are often too descriptive, presenting raw data without sufficiently analysing or interpreting them. There must be evidence in the research report of analysis and interpretation that are grounded in the data. As stated earlier, the emic must be interwoven with the etic.

Summary

The main features of ethnography as a research method are as follows:

- Ethnographers immerse themselves in the culture or subculture they study and try to see the world from the cultural members' point of view
- Data are collected during fieldwork through participant observation and interviews with key informants as well as through documents
- Researchers observe the rules and rituals in the culture and try to understand the meaning and interpretation that informants give to them
- They compare these with their own etic view and explore the differences between the two
- Field-notes are written throughout the fieldwork about events and behaviour in the setting
- Ethnographers describe, analyse and interpret the culture and the local, emic perspective of its members while making their own etic interpretations

11

Phenomenology

Phenomenology is an umbrella term encompassing both a philosophical movement and a research approach operationalised in different ways. It originated as an approach to philosophy; it was only later on that it developed as a method of inquiry: 'phenomenology is first and foremost philosophy' (Caelli, 2001: 275–6). Phenomenology as a philosophical research tradition emerged in the early part of the twentieth century. Edmund Husserl (1859–1938) is credited as the founder of this tradition (Giorgi and Giorgi, 2008), though he built on earlier philosophers such as Brentano who examined human consciousness and the notion of intentionality.

Phenomenological research focuses on people's perceptions and experiences of the world in which they live – the life-world (Lebenswelt) – and what this means to them. Phenomenology is concerned with the way things appear to people in experience. The reality in which we live is an experiential one, and it is experienced through practical engagements with things and others in the world (Eatough and Smith, 2006). The world is then a subjectively lived experience, rather than an object to be studied. Indeed, Husserl's (2012) call 'to the things themselves' (*zu den Sachen selbst*) expresses the phenomenological intention to describe how the world is experienced. The goal of phenomenology is to get to the truth of matters, to describe a phenomenon as it manifests itself to consciousness, to the experiencer (Moran, 2000). A phenomenological investigation is concerned, states Langdridge (2007), with using first-person accounts of life experiences to arrive at an understanding of the meaning and essence of the experience. The project of identifying essences represents a move from the exploration of individual experience to the identification of a universal structure. This move from the individual to the universal is known as the eidetic reduction.

Giorgi and Giorgi (2008) succinctly define phenomenology as 'a study of consciousness' as it is experienced by human beings. What the phenomenological researcher aims to do is provide a rich textured description of lived experience with a focus on the way things appear to us in our consciousness (Finlay, 2008). Indeed, the term 'phenomenology' derives from the Greek word phainomenon, meaning 'appearance'. The promise of phenomenology is that people can be understood from 'inside' their subjective experience; this is essential for a comprehensive understanding of human behaviour. The partici- pant's subjective perspective is the starting point of the analysis (Aspers, 2004). Whereas other approaches also attempt to see things through the eyes of the people they study, phenomenology goes further because it provides a means to set aside the researcher's own preconceived ideas, which is called bracketing (also see Chapter 4), in order to understand a phenomenon from the world in which participants exist, that is from the inside perspective. As Moran (2000) states, explanations are not to be imposed before the phenomenon has been understood from within. Moran is interested in the phenomenology of the body which has implications for sport and exercise. Phenomenology is particu- larly useful in the arena of sport and physical activity because of its emphasis on the body and embodiment. Allen-Collinson and Hockey (2007) argue that the concepts of the 'lived body' and embodiment need to be brought back into sport; they argue for a 'phenomenology of the sporting body' addressed at an empirical rather than an abstract theoretical level. In 2009, Allen-Collinson stated that there exists indeed only a small body of work in her field, and there seems great potential for growth in this approach to researching sport and physical activity.

Descriptive and interpretive phenomenology

Phenomenological researchers today face a rich diversity of empirical approaches from which to choose. Just as there are many variants of phenom- enological philosophy, there are many ways it has been operationalised in research (Moran, 2000). Since the major phenomenological philosophers differ among themselves, it should not be surprising that different strategies emerge when phenomenological thought is applied to method (Giorgi and Giorgi, 2008). Each approach carries different ways of conducting phenomenological research, with different aims and different methods of gathering and analysing data. The integrity of any approach, however, has to be preserved, and in phenomenology this is particularly important because of its distinctive under- lying philosophy. Phenomenological research is generally divided into two main types which have some common but also several distinctive features: *descriptive phenomenology* and *interpretive or hermeneutic phenomenology*. Either approach can be used, depending on the stance of the researcher.

Descriptive phenomenology stays close to Husserl and has been translated into an empirical research approach by Amedeo Giorgi. Giorgi and Giorgi state that Husserl's philosophy could not be used as scientific practice; it required modification to enable researchers to apply it as a method. Giorgi's project was to develop a rigorous descriptive empirical phenomenology inspired by Husserlian ideas aiming to study 'essences of phenomena as they appear in consciousness' (Finlay, 2008). Giorgi (1985) states that social scientists should describe what presents itself without adding or subtracting from it. His advice is to acknowledge the evidence and not go beyond the data, although he believes that description can never be complete. The major aim of a descriptive phenomenological research approach is to generate a description of a phenomenon of everyday experience, to identify its essential structure. For example, in the study by Bruner et al. (2008), the research aim was to describe the transitioning experience of young athletes entering elite sport.

Hermeneutic inquiry, on the other hand, prioritises understanding over description and is interpretive. Interpretive or hermeneutic phenomenology stays close to Heidegger, Gadamer (Heidegger's student) and Ricoeur. Heidegger (who was an assistant to Husserl for a while) developed phenomenology into interpretive philosophy and this became the basis for hermeneutical methods of inquiry. The focus is on understanding existence, thus Heidegger's phenomenology moved the phenomenological project beyond description to interpretation. To illustrate, in Gellweiler's (2011) hermeneutic study, the aim was to interpret and understand the experiences of sport event volunteers. Indeed, Heidegger argues that all description involves interpretation. According to Todres and Wheeler (2001), the value of hermeneutics is that it incorporates reflexivity into research findings, allowing researchers to ask meaningful and relevant questions. Van Manen is one of the present-day hermeneutic researchers whose work is particularly known in the field of education. Sometimes phenomenological research is carried out by health professionals, such as the study by physiotherapists on their lived experience of rehabilitating elite athletes (McKenna et al., 2002).

A weakness of hermeneutic phenomenology is, according to Giorgi and Giorgi (2008), the lack of guidelines for students practising the method. Van Manen (1998) proposes six steps for researchers, but they are by no means prescriptive, or indeed easy to implement. As Langdridge (2007) argues, there is reluctance among interpretive phenomenologists to formalise method, which can be frustrating for novice researchers. This formalisation is sometimes observed, however, for example in Gellweiler's (2011) doctoral study of sport event volunteers, which used a hermeneutic approach.

In the view of Todres and Holloway (2006) the distinctions between descriptive and hermeneutic phenomenology have been over-emphasised. Both types of phenomenology share the following features: eliciting 'life-world' descriptions, the use of 'bracketing' or sensitising as a reflective analytic method and arriving at 'essences' or 'fusion of horizons' to characterise the experienced phenomena. Nevertheless, students must be clear about the approach used and the underlying philosophy associated with each approach. Giorgi (1997) cautions that the proper understanding of the phenomenological method requires, as a minimum, the understanding of the philosophical under-pinnings of the method chosen.

Eliciting life-world descriptions

At the core of phenomenological study is the notion of the life-world (*Lebenswelt* in German), also known as 'lived experience'. According to Husserl this is the basis of all philosophy and human science research. Both descriptive and hermeneutic phenomenologists use the term life-world rather than the term 'data'; both recognise the subjective nature of reality that the researcher must try to access in order to capture the essence of the phenomenon under study. They do not study an objectively existing reality but a phenomenologically experienced world (Aspers, 2004). Thus researchers focus on everyday lived experience. Moran calls this the ordinary world of experience; experience before it has become thought through and described; the world as it appears to consciousness. Husserl stated that this is the world in which we are always already living and which furnishes the ground for all cognitive performance (Moran, 2000: 12). Right from the beginning, Husserl stressed the principle of 'presuppositionlessness', which discards abstract theorising in favour of care-ful attention to the phenomenon itself. Distancing himself from arid and abstract discussions of philosophical problems, Husserl stressed the impor-tance of capturing life as it is lived in all its richness. This marked a radical departure from the theoretical attitude previously adopted by many philoso-phers, which is removed and remote from everyday experience. Indeed, for Todres and Wheeler (2001), this is one of the key strengths of phenomenology; it grounds research and stays away from theoretical abstraction.

Phenomenological research begins with gathering examples of everyday expe-riences, describing them and reflecting on them. These might include 'compet-ing in elite sport', 'being a football fan', 'living with a disability caused by a sporting accident', or 'recovering from a sports injury'. Husserl argues that each person lives in 'the natural attitude', in which their everyday surroundings are taken for granted. According to Husserl, this lived world is pre-reflective – it takes place before we think about it, 'before it has been formulated in judge-ments and expressed in outward linguistic form' (Moran, 2000: 12). It is this attitude that people hold while living in the life-world that phenomenologists need to try to access in order to capture its essence. The challenge for phenom-enological researchers is two-fold: how to help participants express their world as directly as possible; and how to convey these experiences in such a way that the lived world – the life-world – is revealed and that its essence is captured. As Finlay (2008) states, the description of the lived experience is the route to the phenomenon, though it is acknowledged that the language used to recapture the phenomenon can never do justice to the reality of the experience as lived.

Exploring the life-worlds of student athletes coping with stress

Kimball and Freysinger (2003), in their study of the relationship between stress and participation in sport by student athletes, identified three key questions that would be answered with the elicitation of life-world descriptions:

- Why or how is leisure activity (in their case, college sport) a means of coping with stress?
- Is leisure activity a source of stress?
- Why, or how, is leisure activity a source of stress, either positive or negative?

According to the authors, previous research on the topic is limited because it doesn't use the life-world experiences of participants to explore the meanings and experience of such stress. By eliciting detail on such life-worlds, Kimball and Freysinger were able to present a rich picture of the experiences of stress by sport participants.

The use of bracketing and sensitising

The process of bracketing (a mathematical term) involves suspending beliefs and prior assumptions about a phenomenon in order to properly examine what is present – 'in order to grasp the essence of things' (Aspers, 2004: 3). For Husserl, this was at the centre of his understanding of the practice of phenomenology. Husserl called this suspension of preconceptions 'the phenomenological reduction' which aims for open-mindedness in researchers. In such 'openness', something new can be discovered that is not tainted by previous theory or taken-for-granted assumptions. Giorgi (1997) argues that this does not mean that one empties oneself of all past knowledge, but that one puts this knowledge aside. Both descriptive and hermeneutic phenomenologists would agree that the possibility of 'seeing something' freshly, differently or from a new perspective is a crucial dimension of phenomenology's discovery-oriented approach. Finlay (2008) states that bracketing means the researcher is prepared to be surprised, awed and generally open to whatever may be revealed.

Example of bracketing

Alyson Jones (2010), who studied depression in female collegiate athletes, carried out a 'bracketing interview' at the start of her masters research. She claimed that, as a result, she became aware of her assumptions and biases. As a result of the bracketing interview, she suggests that her research was more rigorous than if such bracketing had not taken place. It also gave her an understanding of the participants' feelings on being interviewed.

This reflexivity and openness needs to be maintained throughout the entire research process, not just at the start. It is clear, however, that researchers cannot exclude all assumptions during their study.

While descriptive phenomenology uses the term 'bracketing', hermeneutic phenomenology is more likely to use the term 'sensitising'. Hermeneutic phenomenological researchers use existing preconceptions as a way of 'sensitising' themselves to what is missing or different. Hermeneutic phenomenologists do not believe that researchers can be very successful in suspending their preconceptions. Rather, they should use their preconceptions positively, making them more explicit so that readers of the research can understand the strengths and limitations of the interpretations that the researcher makes. As Heidegger (2010[1927]) stated, researchers are inseparable from the world they investigate; hence researchers should locate the phenomenon under study in its historical and cultural context.

It has been suggested that researchers adopting a phenomenological approach should read very little relevant literature about the research topic before starting in order not to be influenced by preconceptions. However, the research questions do need to be informed by what has already been done, and what the gaps in the literature are. 'Bracketing' is not about pretending that prior knowledge does not exist, but about looking freshly at the area of study, and questioning the assumptions that may be in the literature. This bracketing process is often misunderstood and misrepresented as being an effort to be objective and unbiased. Instead, the researcher aims to be open to seeing the world differently. The process involves putting aside how things supposedly are, focusing instead on how they are experienced (Finlay, 2008). Letting the data 'speak' involves a certain self-discipline. For example, in an interview situation where interviewers have some life experience of the topic under research, which may often be the case in sport where many researchers have prior experience as participants, coaches, or fans, they must take care not to influence the interview in the direction of what they feel and think about the phenomenon. Also, when analysing the interview, they must avoid imposing the ideas from their own experience onto the analysis.

Setting aside assumptions: exploring the body self-compassion of young adult women

Berry et al. (2010) explored the body self-compassion (taking a non-judgemental attitude towards one's own perceived imperfections or limitations) of young adult women who identified themselves as exercisers. Prior to undertaking interviews with five women (between the ages of 23 and 29), the authors suggest that the primary requirement was to bracket previous knowledge about self-compassion to identify and thus be able to set aside prior assumptions. This would ensure that they could be fully present to the actual phenomenon described by participants. Accordingly, the first author who had responsibility for data collections and analysis engaged in a self-reflective process which involved writing about how she felt about her own body through the lens of self-compassion. This facilitated a more self-critical approach to the research and allowed the first author to identify her guiding assumptions prior to the collection of data.

The findings of phenomenological research

The purpose of phenomenology is to find insights that apply more generally beyond the cases that were studied in order to emphasise what we may have in common as people. Indeed, van Manen (1998) describes phenomenological research as a search for what it means to be human. Husserl called such common themes 'essences', and they are also known as 'essential structures'. Thus phenomenological research generates findings that go beyond individual cases. The findings of a good phenomenological study can resonate at a feeling level and richly describe experiences that people can either identify with or, alternatively, learn about.

When phenomenologists present their findings, they aim to show how a number of common themes are related. The essential structure of the phenomenon is often written as a story: it has a general plot that brings the essential themes together in an understandable way. Husserl was interested in finding qualitative features that define what a phenomenon is most generally. For example, one defining feature of many different examples of competitiveness may be the quality of wanting to outshine others in order to bolster self-esteem. When formulating essences from a number of cases of an experience, one notices and tries to put into words what is common, but also, what varies or is different between cases studied. So, the findings of phenomenological research should make sense of both the unique details, as well as the commonalities between the experiences studied.

Hermeneutic phenomenologists are also interested in communicating the meaning and significance of experience but express this differently. Meaning is 'pointed out' in multiple ways and relies on personal insight as well as relevant theories. Gadamer (1975), a hermeneutic phenomenologist, used the term 'fusion of horizons' to show how different people's understandings could come together, thus achieving broad shared insights that, nevertheless, tolerate some freedom in how readers interpret the significance of findings for their own lives or situations. By this, he was pointing out that the validity of phenomenological findings is not based on their ability to correspond perfectly to all cases, but rather that they have sufficient coherence to be meaningfully applied in similar situations. Clearly, one seldom finds common themes that are universal across all cultures and circumstances. Rather, one finds common themes that are typical within a context such as a particular culture or time in history.

Exploring themes of coping in professional cricket

Holt's (2003) descriptive phenomenological study of coping in professional cricket found that the dominant coping strategies employed were evaluation and planning (such as learning about new opponents); the use of proactive psychological studies (such as confidence-building) and reactive psychological skills (such as resilience and self-talk). Holt suggested that the findings offered by his study would serve to lay a potential foundation for teaching such skills to younger or more inexperienced athletes. Thus the findings carried meaning beyond the sample of participants who were investigated.

Sampling

Phenomenological researchers choose participants who can give examples of relevant experiences that they have personally lived through. It is thus not enough that they have opinions about the topic; they must be able and willing to give descriptions of their own personal experiences. This kind of sampling is called *purposive sampling* (see Chapter 5), in that the selection of participants is made on the basis of a particular purpose. In the case of phenomenological research, such purpose is that the research participants included in the study can provide good personal accounts of the experience under study. One can study lived experience in retrospect because it still has meaning for the person even though the event may have taken place a while ago. However, the richness of the account is often better when it is closer to the experience in time.

The primary method of sampling in descriptive phenomenology is *maximum variation sampling* where the researcher seeks out participants who have a common experience but who might vary on a wide variety of demographic characteristics (Langdridge, 2007). The principle is that with such variation it should become possible to determine the invariant aspects of the essential structure.

Using maximum variation sampling
to explore the meaning of Kalarippayattu

McDonald's (2007) three-year study exploring the meaning of Kalarippayattu (the martial art of Kerala) involved a sample of 41 participants. The sample varied geographically across five Kalaris (training schools) spread through Kerala: interviews were carried out with both men and women of all levels of ability and experience; participant ages varied between 17 and 40; participants were of varied education level and religion; and their nationality varied across the sample.

Phenomenological research can generate valuable transferable insights based on an in-depth analysis of only one case study, but value may be increased by studying a number of cases. According to Todres and Holloway (2006), phenomenological research has achieved the most profound insights through the use of six to 12 cases as 'windows' to, and illustrations of, a phenomenon. An appropriate sample size might be five or six participants because of the depth and richness of the interview data. There is danger in choosing a sample that is too large – depth may be sacrificed to breadth. Indeed, a number of journal reviewers have commented that, in such cases, depth and thoughtfulness in the analysis are sacrificed. The analysis is also very time-consuming. The following show how small a sample might be appropriate for phenomenological research. Occasionally only one participant is involved.

Sample sizes in phenomenological studies

The literature shows some considerable variation in the final sample sizes for phenomenological studies:

- Berry et al. (2010) in their study of body self-compassion interviewed five participants.
- The study by Bruner et al. (2008) of transition experiences of young athletes entering elite sports used a sample of eight participants.
- Willig's (2008) study of the meanings and experiences of extreme sports was based upon interviews with eight extreme sport participants.
- Darker et al. (2007), in their study of walking as exercise, involved a snowball sample of ten.
- In their study of the experiences of breast cancer survivors who took up dragon boating, McDonough et al. (2008) interviewed 14 participants.

Phenomenological interviews

A phenomenological interview that gathers life-world descriptions of experiences is an unstructured, open-ended interview that begins with a request that an interviewee describe a relevant experience as fully as possible. Essentially, the researcher is likely to have very little in the way of an interview guide in unstructured interviews, and will have to rely on the use of prompts and probes to facilitate conversation. What is sought is a concrete detailed description of the participant's experience, as faithful as possible to the actual event (Giorgi, 1997). Phenomenologists will tend to pose open questions designed to elicit rich accounts of the lived experience. For instance, in a study of what it means to be a fan, a football fan might be asked: 'Can you describe a typical day at a football match?' A study of the phenomenon of maltreatment of athletes might start with the researcher's question: 'Please describe a situation in which maltreatment occurred.' During the rest of the interview the researcher will focus on clarifying the phenomenon. The interviewer helps the interviewee to 'tell the story' as fully and concretely as possible, eliciting examples of the experience and what it was like for the participant. The interview is open-ended, but the interviewer at times may become more focused on attempting to clarify in greater depth the nature of the phenomenon being studied. This requires both sensitivity and attentiveness on the part of the researcher. The interaction approximates a therapeutic interview in that the researcher is open and non-judgemental, but it is not interventionist in the way that a client–counsellor situation would be.

Phrasing phenomenological questions

Phenomenological questions seek detailed description of the participant's experience, which should be as faithful as possible to the actual event (Giorgi, 1997). The phrasing of the questions is important in terms of eliciting such information, hence phenomenologists will tend to pose open questions designed to elicit rich accounts of the lived experience, for example:

- Please describe as much as you remember about what happened when you were selected for the squad.
- What were your thoughts and feelings about it?
- You were in this room, and you were alone – what was that like?
- Please describe for me a situation in which you sustained an injury.
- What was that like?
- And then what happened?
- Tell me the story of learning to swim.
- Is there any more you would like to tell me before we end?

Eliciting the experience of breast cancer survivors who took up dragon boating

In their study of the experiences of breast cancer survivors who took up dragon boating, McDonough et al. (2008) implemented a two-stage design. In their first round of interviews, their main questions were focused on participation motivation, body image and social support. Example questions are as follows: What are your reasons for participating in the programme? Can you describe to me your social support network?

In the second stage, interviews focused upon their experiences of the sporting activity itself, and an opening question asked participants to describe any physical goals or any physical changes experienced, followed by a number of open questions to elicit rich, detailed information from participants.

Analysis in descriptive and hermeneutic phenomenology

The goal of analysis is to present an exhaustive, analytic description of the phenomenon under study and to capture its essence. After gathering life-world descriptions of personal experiences, each account is transcribed by the researcher and thus becomes a 'text' that is ready for analysis. Various researchers have developed approaches to data analysis and interpretation depending on the school of phenomenology to which they belong. Colaizzi advocates seven, Giorgi four and Van Kaam six steps but many of these are similar or overlap, and they are seldom rigidly applied. In selecting a school of phenomenology, the researcher will be guided by the approach to the most appropriate procedural steps in data analysis. It is a decision for student and supervisor (novice or expert researcher) to select the approach best suited for the phenomenon under investigation and to utilise the appropriate literature to guide the research methodology and analysis. In this chapter, we will cover two methods of analysis. The first shows the student how to analyse data from a descriptive phenomenological study, and the second is the technique used by followers of IPA, an interpretive approach to conducting phenomenology. Both offer clear guidelines for analysing data, unlike researchers such as van Manen who resist providing rules for analysis, even flexible ones. Interpretive phenomenologists take a less systematic approach than that offered by Giorgi and Smith, and are more concerned with the insightful art of writing. Van Manen (1998) states that insight emerges through the way researchers interpret experiences in the act of writing. Narrative writing is used as a method in itself for reflection in order to integrate the different strands of meanings that may be implicit in people's descriptions.

Giorgi's steps for analysis are as follows (see Giorgi and Giorgi, 2008):

1 The phenomenological approach is holistic and so it is expected that the researcher reads through all of the data before beginning their analysis. The entire description is read to get a sense of the whole – the Gestalt – before proceeding further.

2 Since phenomenology is interested in meanings, the next step of the analysis, once the Gestalt has been grasped, is to differentiate between 'meaning units'. What drives the analysis is the search for meanings. These units are formed by a slower rereading of the text; each time there is a transition in meaning, a mark (usually a slash) is made by the researcher to distinguish sections (sentences, groups of words or whole paragraphs). The end of this step is a series of meaning units still expressed in the participants' own words, which the researcher labels in everyday language.

3 When the meaning units have been labelled, the researcher transforms the everyday language used to label them into the language of the discipline of the study. Giorgi states that the life-world is pre-theoretical and pre-scientific; therefore its expression must be examined and redescribed from the perspective of the chosen discipline. Some of the units will have no disciplinary significance and may be ignored (Langdridge, 2007).

4   Once the meaning units have been transformed using the 'proper disciplinary perspective' (Giorgi, 1997) the essential structure of the concrete lived experience is presented. Langdridge states that a structure is written for each participant; this is a synthesis of the meaning units. Following the creation of these structures, common properties are identified and one general structure, or essence, is produced, which is illustrated with quotations. As Giorgi and Giorgi (2008) note, the researcher has to determine which constituents are essential to account for the lived experience reported. It may be that researchers will find more than one essential structure, and this is perfectly acceptable. It is important to observe that the structure refers not only to the key constituents but also to the relationships among them. The essence offered by the researcher shows how the phenomenon under investigation coheres or converges. Any variations have to be accounted for. The essence, or fundamental meaning, is then presented to the community of scholars as a durable research finding (Giorgi, 1997).

Although the researcher discovers structures of experience in the themes generated by individuals, they look at the phenomenon rather than focusing on individual narratives. This does not mean that there is no interest in individuals, but the search is for the overall structure or essence of experience. Philosophical essences are, according to Giorgi (1997), usually universal. Students are advised to look at Chapter 6 in Langdridge's book (2007) for an example of analysis. It will also be useful to look at the example provided by Giorgi and Giorgi (2008).

Analysing data: threats and aggression directed at football referees

For an example of analysis, we advise students to consult the study by Friman et al. (2004) of threats and aggression directed at football referees, which detailed the identification of 187 meaning units, collapsed into 30 categories. Four main themes were finally generated: perceived sources of threats and aggression; reactions to threats; managing stressful situations; and motivations to referee.

Colaizzi's (1978) seven-stage process offers a similar approach to Giorgi's data analysis which takes some elements from Husserl and Heidegger and some from his own research experience.

Analysing data: participation in extreme sports

Willig's (2008) descriptive phenomenological study of participation in extreme sports used Colaizzi's analysis technique to identify the themes of research. These are the stages described in her paper:

1 Individual transcripts were analysed, involving identification of relevant statements or phrases
2 The themes invoked by the statements were grouped together
3 One general statement per theme was created to capture the essence of the theme
4 A number of constitutive themes and general statements were generated
5 Themes were integrated to capture the overall essence of the phenomenon
6 A final descriptive statement was created based on the themes developed in step 4

The themes developed were: context, challenge, suffering, other people, mastery and skill, contrasts, being in the present, compulsion and pleasure.

Students are advised to consult Colaizzi's (1978) chapter if they are interested in finding out more.

Finlay argues that each type of analysis and style of presenting findings simultaneously reveals and conceals; all analysis is incomplete and partial. However, as Todres (2002) states, any good analysis will tell us something that connects with universal human qualities so that the reader can relate personally to the themes; it will tell a story with which readers can empathise in imaginative ways; it contributes to new understanding. Indeed, the rigour of the research is judged on the extent to which the account is evocative and resonates with the reader (Todres and Holloway, 2006).

To achieve resonance, researchers need to be aware of the importance of creativity and pay attention to writing style. Researchers need both scientific and communicative skills; they should be able to do 'good' and rigorous research as well as communicate the findings and meanings in a language that captures the richness of the life-world of the participants. Thus communicating the meaning and significance of an experienced phenomenon is both a qualitative and literary effort. Reflexive writing and aesthetic presentation are essential and integral to phenomenological research. As van Manen (1998) observes, to write phenomenologically is to write poetically.

As in other forms of qualitative research, the findings of phenomenological research are considered in dialogue with the literature and current research in order to offer critique, possible applications and further directions for research.

Interpretative phenomenological analysis (IPA)

A well-known approach to phenomenological inquiry is interpretive phenomenological analysis (IPA). IPA is unique in that it provides clear flexible guidelines for students and researchers. Developed by Jonathan Smith in the 1990s, this method stresses the interpretation of data; it is intellectually connected to hermeneutics (Smith and Osborn, 2008). Due to the accessibility and clarity of the guidelines for collection and analysis of data, it is very popular among students, although researchers who prefer a purist approach to phenomenology sometimes see IPA as a generic qualitative method. It differs considerably from other types of phenomenological research in its conception and data analysis. There is, of course, some overlap between IPA and other phenomenological perspectives, but IPA is also close to grounded theory in that there is a search for patterns across individual cases and for connections across themes. Like hermeneutics, IPA seeks interpretation (see Smith et al., 2009: Chapter 5). IPA researchers tend to prefer semi-structured interviews, but email dialogues and even observation have also been used (though the latter is rare or non-existent in other types of phenomenological research), and unstructured interviews are also possible.

Thematic analysis is the usual analytical method used in IPA. The following stages are identified by Smith and Osborn (2008; we recommend that students read this useful chapter on IPA):

1   Read and reread the transcript, adding comments on what is interesting and significant on the left-hand side of the page (not all of the transcript needs to be annotated).
2   Emerging themes are noted on the right-hand side of the page. Initial notes are transformed into language that aims to capture the essential quality of what was found in the text. The themes are expressed at a higher level of abstraction but at the same time they are grounded in the participants' words.
3   The researcher makes a separate list of themes and tries to identify common links and to group common themes together.
4   Undertaking (3) will have identified clusters of themes, which represent the superordinate themes. A table of themes is created next, each of which will be illustrated later on through participant quotations.

The above process is followed for each transcript until a final table of themes is created, which form the body of the research report (though a single transcript can be written up as a case study). This requires the researcher to prioritise the data and to reduce the number of themes generated. A final research account is produced which respects convergences and divergences in the data. In simple terms, it should recognise ways in which accounts are similar and different.

Interpretative phenomenological analysis: experiences of walking

Darker et al. (2007) aimed in their study to provide a rich and detailed account of participants' walking experiences. The authors used IPA for the following reasons: it is a well-established method, allowing for an eclectic, idiographic and hermeneutic approach to inquiry; it has broad theoretical underpinnings; it can be used to understand and make sense of other individuals' activities based on a detailed series of directed procedure; and it is 'conceptually rich and offers contextually grounded understanding' (p. 2174). Their findings showed that participants valued walking not as exercise but as a means of transport, companionship and psychological benefits such as reduced anxiety.

Appropriate areas for phenomenological research include topics that are important to life experience such as happiness, fear and anxiety or what it means to be a fan, an athlete or a coach. Potential topics include the experience of having a sport-related injury, losing a major competition or being left out of a squad.

Limitations

The central strength of a phenomenological approach is that it provides both philosophical and methodological support in attempting to capture and express the meaning of significant human experiences in a rigorous manner. The narrative product of such studies seeks to express insights in such a way that it may evoke a sense of recognition and understanding in readers. The central limitations of a phenomenological approach are four-fold:

1   The use of observation is problematic in phenomenological research. Because phenomenology wants to get the inner perspectives of people from their own point of view, it is reluctant to judge behaviour from an external perspective. Critics of phenomenology have noted that descriptions of the world from an 'insider' perspective may be inadequate as an account of human behaviour. Such critics would say that it is not people themselves that can best explain their behaviour, as their behaviour may be caused by forces that are more appropriately analysed in other ways with reference to social, political or chemical analyses.

2   Descriptions of life-worlds depend on full and rich verbal accounts by people who are articulate. This raises challenges for phenomenological methodology, for example when studying children. There are some ways forward in this regard, such as using photographs or drawings as prompts for people to talk about a particular topic.

3   It can be elitist in that there is an artistic-literary capability required of the researcher when reflecting and writing. The 'method' does not guarantee the quality of the narrative coherence achieved in the writing of the final stages of the research product. This can be said to some degree of all research, but phenomenology is on the literary side of the scientific-literary continuum.

4   Unfortunately, some phenomenological researchers, especially novices, neglect the philosophical origin of the method. Without a clear grasp of the philosophy of phenomenology, students will find it difficult to apply their chosen research approach. This is not easy because researchers have to understand the underlying philosophies before carrying out a study and decide which type of phenomenological approach to use.

Summary

- Phenomenology is primarily a philosophy but is sometimes applied as a research approach.
- Phenomenology is a discrete qualitative research approach that is embedded in the philosophical traditions of the early part of the twentieth century.
- Descriptive phenomenological researchers find and describe essential and universal structures, while researchers who take the hermeneutic approach attempt to interpret the meaning of the phenomenon in context.
- Phenomenologists describe and interpret human experience in ways that apply more generally beyond the particular cases studied.
- The phenomenological researcher uses descriptions and/or interpretations of everyday human experiences (the life-world) as sources of data.
- When undertaking descriptive phenomenology the researcher seeks to bracket any preconceptions and attempts to arrive at the essence of experienced phenomena. By contrast, hermeneutic phenomenology uses interpretation and personal or theoretical sensitising to highlight important themes.
- Researchers who use phenomenological methods have formulated various methods of data analysis.
- Phenomenologists seek to enhance understanding in readers by presenting plots or stories in a narratively coherent way.

12

Narrative Research

Human beings are natural storytellers and live their lives through stories. In narrative research – sometimes called narrative inquiry or narrative analysis – researchers elicit stories of experiences and events from people in order to gain access to their feelings and thoughts and to the way they make sense of and interpret their experiences. In everyday language use, narratives are stories which people tell each other. These stories are not necessarily the re-telling of facts but accounts of people's perceptions of occurrences; they are 'oral versions of personal experience' as Labov and Waletzky (1967: 12) call them. Narrative accounts are then analysed by the researcher.

The concept of narrative has its roots in the classical tradition of Aristotle's 'Poetics', according to Bruner (2002), and we know that the ancient Greeks and Romans were storytellers. The term is also used in literature where storytelling can be imaginative and inventive, but in research, stories reflect the perceptions and perspectives of participants – the 'truth' as they see it (this is discussed later in this chapter). Polkinghorne (1988) tells us that in the modern era, the term 'narrative' has been popular in linguistics, hermeneutics and in literary criticism. According to Bruner, the Russian folklorist Propp was one of the first people of the twentieth century to stress the importance of stories. The concept 'narrative turn' has its origin in French structuralist theories from the 1960s but in the social sciences it refers to the recent attention given to people's stories. Narrative inquiry is an umbrella term, it may take an ethnographic or, more usually, a phenomenological form, but it can also stand alone, and we refer to it as a separate approach in this chapter. Narrative research can be either qualitative or quantitative as Elliot (2005) suggests, but it is better in its qualitative form, because it is less fractured, more holistic and fits with the essential character of stories. Indeed, all qualitative research abounds with stories, those of participants and those of researchers. Meaning is better captured in qualitative research: Polkinghorne (1988: 11) states that 'narrative is a scheme by means of which human beings give meaning to their experiences of temporality and personal actions'.

Career transitions in professional golf: a narrative analysis

Carless and Douglas (2009) examine how the stories an athlete tells throughout their life in sport have a significant influence upon the creation and maintenance of his or her identity. They explored the career stories of two female professional golfers, stories that focused on their participation and subsequent withdrawal from the sport. The authors claim that narrative analysis has particular strengths in gaining insights into the concept of sporting identities, noting that storytelling is a particularly strong means by which to gain such understanding. They suggest that 'through studying people's stories it is possible to gain insights into the ways in which identity and sense of self are created, maintained or challenged over time' (p. 52). By viewing withdrawal from professional sport as a long-term, rather than an instantaneous, process, narrative interviews, both formal and informal, were undertaken over a six-year period. Beginning with a 'grand tour' question, participants were invited to provide an account of their life as a professional golfer. Follow up interviews were undertaken focusing on the stories of each golfer that were relevant at that moment in time, continuing after each had withdrawn from professional golf. The two participants demonstrated contrasting stories. Christiana (pseudonyms were assigned to both participants) suffered more negative emotions, viewing life without professional sport as empty; she had little anticipation of future possibilities and opportunities. This was contrasted with Kandy, however, who demonstrated a discovery narrative, one that showed optimism and excitement about future possibilities. Kandy demonstrated a dialogical narrative, with stories emerging from a variety of perspectives. This narrative allowed her to see the possibilities of life after golf. Christiana, however, demonstrated a monological narrative, told from a single viewpoint – that of professional golfer. This was a narrative that, after withdrawal, could not be maintained, carrying consequent emotional trauma.

The term narrative is popular in literature, where stories are fictitious or imaginative; however, the stories of participants in research show their 'true' genuine perceptions of events, though it must be recognised that they might be imagined or falsely remembered. Educationists such as Labov and Waletzky (1967) who were two of the foundational researchers in this field, and Clandinin and Connelly (2004, 2007), have seen their work published. Psychologists such as Cortazzi (1993), Polkinghorne (1988), Bruner (1986) and Riessman (1993, 2008) have written about and carried out narrative research, and it is an approach widely used in the arena of health and healthcare. Although narrative inquiry has been very popular in social science, in sport and exercise it is still in its relative infancy (Smith and Sparkes, 2009). Lately, however, its value has been seen by writers and researchers in this area, and much of it is being generated by Sparkes and his colleagues (Sparkes, 2002). Of course, in research, stories can be elicited for the purposes of a specific inquiry or they might occur naturally and then be analysed by the researcher.

> ## Cultural influences on sporting participation: a narrative account of an Islamic, female, Paralympian powerlifter
>
> Ethnicity, culture and disability are all, potentially, constraining influences over participation in sport. Whilst many studies explore them in isolation, Roy's (2001) narrative study focused upon the experiences of Paralympian powerlifting by an Islamic female Malaysian. Narrative interviews allowed the author to identify the interrelated nature of ethnicity, culture and disability, all three of which were key factors influencing participation. From an extended narrative interview, Roy was able to describe their impacts upon the life story of 'Saba', and through her story, to identify the strategies used to negotiate such barriers, for example through 'disassociation' and focusing upon performance.

Stories and their structure

In ordinary use, the terms 'story' and 'narrative' do not differ, but in academic texts and research a distinction is sometimes made, with the concept of narrative being a broader genre and more all-embracing. Frank (1995) sees narrative as 'general structures', which make possible the individual 'stories people tell'. However, the distinction between narrative and story might make narrative research rather complex, and therefore Polkinghorne (1988) suggests that story and narrative might be seen as synonymous. Riessman (2008) also states that she uses the terms story and narrative in the same way. For the purpose of this chapter we accept this idea and use these terms interchangeably. Most stories have a beginning, a middle and an end, but Jovchelovitch and Bauer (2000) state that stories have two dimensions. Sequential stories have a chronological dimension, while others are non-chronological, coherent stories in which the plot consists of a number of smaller tales woven together.

Every story has a plot (or theme), a pattern of events, descriptions of cause and effect that integrate into a meaningful story, and sometimes subplots which enrich the plot. The plot isn't straightforward, of course, as researchers well know; the story might be told in a chaotic, iterative and non-linear manner. Character, problem and explanation are integrated in the plot. Cortazzi (1993) identifies three characteristic elements in a plot which are temporality, causation and human interest. Temporality is a concept in narrative that has its origin in the books of Paul Ricoeur (1984). Time is experienced through the link between past, present and future, and this link is present in all stories; for example, 'A while ago I used to go running; then I became injured and took up swimming, and I now intend to win swimming competitions.'

Emplotment, or plotting, refers to the construction and development of a story, which enables the listener or reader to understand the important issues and storyline; it is the structure through which sense is made of events and the way in which things are connected (Czarniawska, 2004). Each story also has characters who inhabit the plot. In research the central character is usually the participant who tells the story. Paley and Eva (2005) maintain that other elements are included in the configuration of a plot:

- The plot contains a central character
- This character meets a problem
- A link exists between character and explanation
- The plot and its configuration finds an emotional response in the listener

Events, characters and plot thus interact.

Types of story

The researcher, particularly the student researcher, must know the constitution, function and type of stories that exist to be able to fully analyse them. Many competing and overlapping story types exist. Richardson (1990) describes some of these types:

1 Everyday stories
2 Autobiographical stories
3 Biographical stories
4 Cultural stories
5 Collective stories

Everyday stories

Participants tell the researchers what they usually do and how they spend their day going about their normal business of living.

> Example
> After taking tea to my wife in bed, I sit down and read the sports pages in the paper as that is what I am interested in. Usually I go to a football match on a Saturday, and I take my little boy who is becoming very interested.

Autobiographical and biographical stories

Participants tell the story of an event they experienced themselves; in a sense all stories which they narrate are autobiographical. The authors of autobiographical stories link the past to the present and future. They link disparate events in the telling (Polkinghorne, 1988) and give the researcher the feeling of the whole. There are also existing autobiographical and biographical accounts of great sporting heroes such as Steve Redgrave, for instance, and researchers can read and analyse these. Though some of these accounts might not have been produced for the purpose of research, they might nevertheless be useful for analysis of the life of the person who is being studied. Andrew Sparkes and Brett Smith (e.g. Smith and Sparkes 2005, 2011), and many others, have a whole host of work that relates to auto/biographies.

Autobiographical stories: Australian elite and sub-elite swimming subcultures

McMahon and Penney's (2011) study of the experiences of elite and sub-elite Australian swimmers used, as one of its approaches to data collection, one of the author's (McMahon) own experiences. These stories were sometimes prompted by looking at videos of her past performances, for example at the Commonwealth Games, which allowed her to re-live the event, and the experiences that she had, leading to 'emotional recall'. Through McMahon's autobiographical stories, she was able to connect her own experiences to the culture within which they took place. Specifically, it allowed her to explore her 'vulnerable self' in relation to the elite swimming culture. Her stories were then shared with three other participants, who were encouraged also to share their own vulnerable selves.

Cultural stories

Cultural stories are tales from a culture or subculture, for instance the cricket or running culture. Through their immersion in a particular cultural setting, participants can reveal to the researcher, who is outside the cultural group, the group's cultural norms and mores. For example, Kavanagh (2012) offered a restitution narrative account of life following spinal cord injury. Her portrait of the subsequent sporting life of a Paralympian wheelchair tennis player contrasts with the more familiar chaos narratives that dominate the literature and serve to reinforce disablist views that prevail in modern society.

Collective stories

Participants tell stories that show how they are connected to a group or a community of people who have had the same or similar experience. For instance, people who have gone through a disastrous event at a football match narrate what happened to their friends and colleagues or community on the day to create a picture of the event.

The functions of people's stories

People tell stories for a number of reasons. Here are just some:

- They want to give a full account of their experience and perceptions of it
- They wish to interpret and make sense of their experiences
- They tell their stories to others in their group or community to reaffirm a shared culture
- They want to assert and confirm their identities

There are various other reasons for storytelling, but in sports and physical activity studies these might be seen to be the major functions.

Riessman (2008) argues that there are a number of reasons why participants remember an event or experience through stories. Narrative research provides the storyteller with an opportunity to talk of past experiences, to order, understand and explain them. Furthermore, people also justify their actions and behaviour through stories. For instance, when gymnasts talk of their experiences, their activities and their suffering of pain, they might tell the researcher that pain is a 'necessary evil' to achieve their main objectives of success in their chosen sport.

The focus on narrative identity, another concept based in the work of Ricoeur, is one of the most important elements in sport research. Through telling their stories, individuals not only construct but also confirm their identities. They talk of the roles they play in interaction with others. For instance, runners might tell stories of belonging to a club, thereby confirming their collective identity, or stories of winning a race, which consolidate their self-identity.

Collecting data

Narrative data are generated from participants in one-to-one meetings with the researcher. Researchers use narrative interviews to gain a full story from participants in which they can tell their experience in an uninterrupted flow; thus giving the participants more power to guide the research. Riessman (1993) refers to certain types of interview which 'fracture the text', but narrative interviewing preserves the holistic nature of the story. Semi-structured interviews interrupt the participants, and we advise students not to use these in narrative research. In narrative interviews researchers let the storyteller talk fluently, without interruption (see Chapter 6). Questions are only used as stimuli to provide a trigger for the participants' tales.

Here are some examples of initial trigger questions:

Examples of trigger questions for narrative interviews

Tell me about your interest in football.

You are a runner – can you tell me about your experiences?

You teach sports studies – what motivated you to take up that profession?

Can you tell me about any negative experiences you have had while involved in competitive sport?

Subsequently, of course, one might occasionally need to spur participants on to follow up their ideas. Narrative interviews require minimum intervention in our view and only a few trigger questions are needed on the key areas which the researcher wishes to explore. The participants should be in control and tell the story in an uninterrupted way, while the interviewer listens, however long it takes for them to tell the story. When the participant stops and 'dries up', the researcher can gently move the interview forward. At the end of the story, the researcher might follow up some ideas of importance to the research. The interviewer does not force the story; too much probing destroys its coherence. Of course, although people are natural storytellers, some are better than others and the more articulate might tell a better tale.

The biographic narrative interpretive method (BNIM), developed by Wengraf (2001) and his colleagues, needs mentioning here as a popular recent way of researching people's stories. This has been used in particular in research projects focused on oral and life histories. It uses in-depth interviews with a minimum of two interviews for each participant.

Narrative analysis

Narrative analysis is often used as a term for narrative research or inquiry, but here it will be used in the sense of data analysis, namely the analysis of stories. Analysis usually is, as said before, the way in which researchers organise and systematise and scrutinise the data. There are no general or standard strategies to analyse story data, but many forms of analysis exist. Riessman (1993, 2008) and others, such as Lieblich et al. (1998), describe a number of procedures to analyse narrative data. Some of these do not do justice to stories as they 'fracture the text' as Riessman calls it, though they are structured and systematic; others keep the Gestalt of the story – its whole or essence. Holistic and thematic analyses are straightforward (see next sections), and most researchers choose these. The initial stages for all narrative research are similar.

The main data source is the narrative interview. Usually the first step in the analysis is the transcription of the data. This stage of data analysis is important to gain an overview of the stories. Although numerous articles and books on narrative research are published, few contain a description of how to do the analysis. It is left to the researcher to choose one of many. Some even develop their own type of analysis, but we would not recommend this to students.

Holistic analysis

In holistic analysis, as Lieblich et al. (1998) call it, researchers identify the main statements – the essentials of the experience which reflects and represents the narrators' accounts, even though it might not be told in order or sequence. The meaning of the story is of prime importance, thus the researcher seeks to make essential statements that contain the meaning of the experience. As in some other approaches to qualitative inquiry, researchers seek patterns from a number of stories. The story is not taken apart but kept together for interpretation. In this, researchers interpret and theorise from the whole story and its meaning, rather than breaking it into categories. Emden (1998) developed another way of analysing the story data holistically and 'crystallising the data'. She advises researchers to:

1   Read the story carefully a number of times.
2   Delete the questions of the researcher.
3   Delete the words that are not important to understand the essence of the story in each sentence.
4   Reread the text for meaning;
5   Repeat steps 3 and 4 and re-check the main text.
6   Identify subplots of the stories from the ideas in the text.
7   Create a coherent narrative – a storyline – from the stories of the participants; and
8   Attempt a member-check.

One might, however, have some reservations about the last step: the member-check (for further discussion, see Chapter 15).

Thematic analysis

Students and other novice researchers often favour thematic analysis; Riessman suggests that it is the most straightforward and we often recommend this type to our students. The attention focuses on the contents – on 'what' is in the story, rather than 'how' it is told, 'to whom' and for what reasons (Riessman, 2008: 54). Some of the steps in thematic analysis are common to a number of approaches. The obvious first step is familiarisation through transcription and careful reading of each story. The second step consists of coding. The stories are read for interesting and important ideas which are given names (labels, codes). While working through this stage, analysts tend to discern patterns. The codes which belong together are collated and form themes – broader and overarching ideas or categories. Of course, at the end, themes need review and refinement and to be given a label.

Structural analysis

Structural analysis was developed by Labov and Waletzky (1967) whose work investigated the structure and composition of adolescent narratives through structural coding. Structural analysis draws attention to form – 'how' the story is told – and is tied to the text of the story, so language and linguistic elements become more important. Labov and Waletzky break the story into various sections according to the text. These main narrative elements are as follows. (Note that these have been adapted from Elliot (2005: 42) and Riessman (2008: 84).)

1 *Abstract*: the summary of the story matter.
2 *Orientation*: the time, place, situation and participants.
3 *The complicating action*: the sequence of events, i.e. the plot with its inherent crisis.
4 *Evaluation*: the appraisal of the story and its meaning for the storyteller.
5 *Resolution*: the outcome of the plot.
6 *Coda*: the return to the present time.

An illustration

The **abstract** summarises the main points of the story and gives the storyline, for instance: *This is the story about attempts to improve my health and do physical exercise.*

Orientation shows the time, the location and the people involved: *It was on a bright summer's day during the vacation when my friends and I went to the gym…*

The **complicating action** lists the crisis points, the problems and the behaviour of the various participants: *I felt very strange all of the sudden, and I must have fainted. My friend had rushed to my help and they called the doctor…*

The **evaluation** is what the storyteller thinks of the actions and problems: *It really was very hot in the gym, and everybody felt nauseous…We had to get some air in there…*

The **resolution** is the outcome of the specific plot: *And so they got me into the ambulance and took me to the hospital where I recovered very quickly…*

The **coda** is the end of the specific story and takes us back to the present time: *So we always try to air the gym on warm summer days and open all the windows, or we don't go in hot weather…*

Of course the process is repeated throughout the plots and subplots. Many, though not all, narratives contain these traits but not all in the same sequence. An example of structural analysis is that of Smith and Sparkes (2008) exploring the life story of a young rugby player who had experienced spinal cord injury. Their analysis 'focuses on the formal plot and organisation of the story to tease out the distinct structures that hold it together' (p. 220).

Dialogic/performance analysis

The third approach to analysis is labelled by Riessman as dialogic/performance analysis. This takes a much broader approach to narrative as it is an analysis of interaction and interactive talk. Riessman argues that storytelling is a process of interaction. This shows similarity to conversation or discourse analysis and contains components of other approaches – an emphasis on the whole, but including elements such as gesture and mime. Goffman (1969) speaks of the 'presentation of self', meaning that individuals present themselves to others as they see themselves and want to be seen.

Smith and Sparkes (2009) note that within sport and exercise psychology a performative analysis has rarely been used. Noting that narrative analysis is about how things are said as much as what is said, a means to explore the idea of 'how' is through performative analysis. The authors go on to outline some of the questions that a researcher may ask within this approach, for example:

1   Why was the narrative developed in that way, and told in that order?
2   How does he or she locate themselves in relation to the audience?
3   How does he or she locate characters to one another and in relation to him or herself?
4   What was the response of the listener and how did this influence the development and interpretation of the narrative?

Students might find this type of analysis difficult, and therefore we would recommend that it be adopted only by doctoral students who have more time to acquaint themselves with the approach.

Visual analysis

The last of Riessman's examples of analytic procedures is visual analysis which does not rely on language, discourse or other forms of oral or written stories, but on paintings, photographs, films, collages and videos which she calls 'visual presentations of experience' (2008: 142). This is not a new form of telling stories, as it is based in the traditions of film or painting, but it *is* more recent in research. A story can be told with the aid of images, which become part of the data, though verbal explanations and interpretations must accompany them in a research report. Examples of images are media representations of, for example, sport performances; these can be used by researchers who describe, analyse and interpret them. Some of these images already exist, but they can alternatively be created expressly for research purposes. This type of analysis is increasingly known as performative social science.

Using visual methods: measuring physical activity in ethnic minority women

Keller et al. (2008) acknowledge the challenges of measuring physical activity in ethnic minority women through verbal expression. They identify a number of specific issues, such as the difficulty in capturing the variability in women's activity, for example including household-related activity, and in recognising ethnic and cultural differences in the perception and meaning of physical activity. They observe that self-reported measures often lack accuracy particularly in terms of under-estimating the time spent in physical activity. The authors suggest the use of visual methods in creating a narrative of activity. First, they elicited 'stories of life that relate to perceptions, experiences and behaviour' (p. 432), which provided tangible rich data that 'speaks to the truth' (ibid.). Prior to interview, participants took photographs that documented their physical activities, which were explored through the narrative interview. The visual images were helpful in identifying patterns of behaviour of which participants were unaware.

The distinctive nature of narrative research

It should be remembered that the researcher's final account – the dissertation or thesis – is also a narrative; indeed, the full account of individual stories is constituted by the participants, and by the researcher who interprets the narrative accounts. Researchers can supplement the written text or research report with relevant visual and audio pieces. These are sometimes more lively and interesting than a straightforward conventional research report, but they need to be done well and have direct relevance to the research to have impact and credibility. It should be remembered when writing up that the stories of events or experiences are affected by culture and location in time and space, thus they do not exist in a vacuum but are only understandable in context, and this should be reflected in the final account.

How then does narrative research differ from other types of qualitative research? According to the writers of *Five Ways of Doing Qualitative Analysis* (Wertz et al., 2011) the approaches to qualitative research have much in common, in particular their emphasis on the social context. Narrative research is distinctive in that it always deals with stories, be they naturally occurring or constructed for the purpose of the research, and they can be visual, oral or written. Data are best treated as a whole rather than broken into small pieces. Narrative research is holistic, interpretive and centred (although not always) on content rather than structure.

A critique of narrative research

Studies of narrative and narrative identity which have become so popular in recent years have been criticised for a number of reasons. Much of this critique also applies to interview research and autoethnography. Atkinson and Delamont (2006), for instance, deplore the 'celebratory' character of narrative which neglects rigorous analysis. They claim that researchers often uncritically accept narratives and lack reflection, and narrative should not have precedence over other forms of qualitative research. Indeed, the story is of a remembered event, experience, motivation or action, hence it cannot be necessarily verified, though it is the 'truth' in the perception of the participants. Atkinson (1997: 339) suggests that 'narratives seem to float in a social vacuum. The voices echo in an otherwise empty world. There is an extraordinary absence of social context, social action, and social interaction.' He also claims that narratives are 'not single solutions to problems'.

Truth is another problem with storytelling. If stories are a way of understanding experience by both participants and researchers alike, one might examine these stories for 'truth'. As the tales are rooted in the participants' memory and perceptions, researchers find difficulty determining the truth. Of course, there is not just one absolute truth in narratives – they are subjective and selective. The truth is that which the people in the study perceive and construct. They do lie occasionally, but even a storied 'untruth' or over-dramatised story might be significant for the researcher's interpretations.

Summary

- Narratives are stories of experience and events as perceived and constructed by individuals; stories, which have plots, characters, problems and explanations, are rarely simple or linear.
- The different types of narrative analysis depend on the choice of the researcher; they all are appropriate and legitimate.
- Stories are always unique to the participant, but they are located in the socio-cultural context.

13

Mixed Methods Research

Mixed methods research (MMR) is not a new phenomenon. Indeed, as early as 1991, Morse (2003) discusses qualitative–quantitative triangulation in terms of simultaneous or sequential uses of methods. However, in recent years, MMR has become very popular. This is reflected in the launch of a journal dedicated to the topic and to the research methods text by Tashakkori and Teddlie (2003) which offers theoretical and practical guidance.

As Bergman (2011) observes, there is dispute over what constitutes mixed methods research. Most agree that MMR is a combination of qualitative and quantitative methods, though some argue that MMR can also take the form of a study which uses more than one qualitative method, for example observation and interviews. However, Brannen (2005) argues that this is multi-method not mixed methods research. For the sake of simplicity, we will adopt the definition put forward by Tashakkori and Teddlie (2003): MMR is the practice of collecting, analysing and integrating qualitative and quantitative data in a single study with the aim of gaining a more holistic understanding of a phenomenon.

Pragmatism is thus at the root of MMR. According to Bryman (2007), much research is driven by pragmatic or technical needs, and this is particularly so in MMR. Indeed, the choice of the research question will determine the adoption of MMR and the nature of the design including data collection, analysis and interpretation. In other words, researchers will adopt MMR if they feel that this is the only route to the data they need. Therefore the rationale for adopting MMR must be clear. Furthermore, awareness of the time involved is needed, as expertise is called for in both qualitative and quantitative research including knowledge of their underlying bases and assumptions. As Bryman (2008) notes, however, researchers often put to one side epistemological and ontological issues when conducting MMR. Questions in qualitative and quantitative research are asked from a different standpoint and ideology.

The benefit of conducting MMR is that findings from different methods complement each other. As Mayoh et al. (2011) observe, quantitative methods offer breadth, whilst qualitative methods offer depth. It is believed that a combination of methods is more enlightening and helps to understand a complex research problem or answer a question that cannot be answered in a mono-method study. Each of the methods adds strength to offset the other's disadvantages. As Jones (1997) claims, the weaknesses of either type of method are counterbalanced by MMR. Bryman advises that data sets need to be 'mutually illuminating' (2007: 8); thus, in writing up, he advocates that the researcher ensures that findings from each method are related and that the end product is more than the sum of its qualitative and quantitative parts.

MMR can also develop theoretical ideas which span both the macro and the micro world, namely that of interaction, life experience, etc. to the cultural and global level. As Mason (2006) suggests, these perspectives are in continuous interplay. Quantitative research is linked to commonalities, trends and generalities, while the inductive logic of qualitative methods answers 'how' and 'why' questions on a smaller scale. The points that are made foster a more questioning approach to research design and make the research more flexible and reflexive; they also demonstrate the validity of different approaches. For this reason, researchers often feel that they will find more favour with funding agencies if they adopt MMR.

Some writers suggest that MMR, however useful, is difficult because qualitative and quantitative researchers have their own distinctive view of the world and see their research from different epistemological positions; and these perspectives are sometimes seen as incompatible. Bergman (2011) states that qualitative and quantitative research belong to different paradigms; they are underpinned by different philosophies; they answer different research questions; they differ in data collection and analysis methods. Indeed it is often claimed that MMR cannot bridge incompatible positions. Most researchers now take a pragmatic view of mixed methods research. Indeed one of the strengths of MMR is that it may improve the researcher's knowledge base and it 'may dislodge ossified positions' (Bryman, 2007: 275). Researchers tend to acknowledge that by adopting mixed methods, they can broaden their horizon and realise that there are different ways of seeing the world, ways that generate innovation and creativity. Indeed, Mason (2006) states that MMR can help researchers to think 'outside the box'. Some, like Johnson and Onwuegbuzie (2004) and Teddlie and Tashakkori (2009), even call MMR a third paradigm, though there are disputes about this assertion.

Researchers who use mixed methods often see either one or the other method as dominant, though occasionally they carry the same weight. This may be influenced by the worldview researchers hold which forms their ontological and epistemological perspectives. One might argue that to stay within the worldview of qualitative research, the researcher only employs a quantitative method to enhance and enrich the study.

Adopting mixed methods research

The following steps, which we have adapted from Wilkins and Woodgate (2008), may be followed by the mixed methods researcher, and an account of these should find their way into the methodology section of the research report:

1 Researchers reflect whether MMR is appropriate for their study. This is the case if mono-method research will not answer the research question, solve the problem, or suffice for an understanding of the phenomenon under study.
2 The researcher needs to justify the approach.
3 The researcher chooses a specific design and decides on the priority of qualitative or quantitative procedures, or whether they should have equal weight. This is influenced by the research question.
4 The sample is selected according to the methods used, probability sampling in quantitative research, and purposeful or criterion sampling for the qualitative method.
5 Data are collected according to the design of the study, whether it is concurrent or sequential.
6 The researcher analyses the data according to the specific analytic technique needed for both qualitative and quantitative procedures.
7 Interpretation of qualitative and quantitative data takes place. The findings generated by each method may be compared or one set of findings may be used for enrichment or expansion.
8 The validity or trustworthiness of the findings is established. Triangulation is already built in, but an audit trail will be necessary (included in the methodology), and a reflexive stance will need to be taken towards the qualitative aspect of the research.
9 The researcher reports the findings and disseminates them.

Designing mixed methods research

Bergman (2011) states that research design is driven by the logic of inquiry. Researchers need to decide whether the design is to be primarily inductive aimed at discovery, or primarily deductive aimed at hypotheses testing. This will also influence the validity criteria used by the researcher. Second, researchers need to consider which method is dominant as well as the ordering of methods. According to Morse (2003b), MMR can be classified as either simultaneous or sequential designs. The most popular form is sequential whereby qualitative research is used first and a questionnaire is used second for the testing of dimensions identified in the exploratory aspect of the study. To this, Creswell and Plano Clark (2011: 109–13) add the 'transformative design'. When researchers use sequential procedures, they first employ one of the methods, then the other – this strategy enhances and expands the findings. With simultaneous procedures, qualitative and quantitative research is carried out at the same time, and the researcher interprets the information concurrently. When employing transformative procedures, a 'theoretical lens' is used which provides a framework for the study. This complex transformative design is used when researchers wish to make the voices of participants heard clearly – usually those of powerless or marginal groups – in order to help change their lives. It often becomes advocacy research.

Creswell and Plano Clark (2011) delineate several types of MMR; these are echoed by Terrell (2011):

1   Sequential explanatory
2   Sequential exploratory
3   Sequential transformative
4   Concurrent triangulation
5   Concurrent nested
6   Concurrent transformative

We shall discuss those strategies that are most often employed.

When researchers use a *sequential explanatory* design they first collect and analyse quantitative data, then collect and analyse qualitative data. Usually they give more weight to quantitative strategies (QUANT–qual) in this type of design. By adding qualitative data they wish to enrich the study and gain more depth, expanding and enhancing the quantitative part of the research by asking in-depth questions in interviews or observing the participants. Integration of the findings of both occurs during the interpretation stage.

Sequential explanatory research: affective responses to exercise

Rose and Parfitt (2007) explored affective responses to exercise at various intensities. An initial quantitative procedure was carried out to measure participant emotions, arousal and perceived exertion. Questionnaires were administered after participants had exercised at various intensities. Findings demonstrated that during exercise, affective responses were least positive at the higher intensity exercise level, and more positive at lower intensities. However, the authors noted that 'the quantitative results do not elucidate the underlying cause of the reported affective states or explain why there was individual variability' (p. 297). The qualitative phase allowed a number of factors to emerge, which mediated such affective responses. These were perceptions of ability, personal interpretation of the intensity of exercise, feelings of control and perceived outcomes from the exercise. The mixed methods approach allowed not only the affective response to exercise to be measured but it also provided explanation for the individual differences that emerged and insight into the cognitive factors influencing responses.

The *sequential exploratory* design gives priority to qualitative methods of data collection and analysis (QUAL–quant). The quantitative procedures test the working propositions, hypotheses or theories of the qualitative part of the research. Researchers are able to demonstrate the distributions in a particular group or population and generalise to different samples and for larger groups.

Sequential exploratory research: comparing nations' elite sport systems

De Bosscher et al. (2010) aimed to develop a method for comparing nations' elite sport systems. To achieve this, a sequential exploratory design was adopted. Phase one involved a qualitative exploration of the factors influencing international success in sport, using content analysis of secondary sources alongside interviews with coaches, athletes and performance directors. This allowed nine key 'pillars' (p. 574) to be identified, broadly categorised into two domains: inputs, such as financial support, and throughputs, such as the processes by which the inputs are managed. The second stage of the study used these pillars to measure the determinants of competiveness quantitatively through the development of two research instruments: an overall sport policy questionnaire and an elite sport climate survey. The study extended previous work in both the development of a theoretical model from the qualitative phase and comparative measurements of how countries manage their elite sport success.

Sequential transformative strategy might give equal weight to qualitative and quantitative data or prioritises one or the other. Usually the study is guided by a specific research question linked to advocacy or giving voice to marginalised or powerless people as we said before. Data can be integrated in the analysis or interpretation stage. This type of MMR is rarely used in sport and exercise research.

Adopting a sequential transformative strategy: the relationship between serious leisure cyclists and other road-users

Dickinson and Robbins (2009) refer to cyclists as a marginalised sub-group of society. O'Connor and Brown (2007) explored the relationship between serious leisure cyclists and other road-users with particular reference to issues of safety and motivations to cycle. A primary qualitative approach using focus group interviews allowed the authors to generate data on three subjects: context, relationships and the problems of cycling on shared roads. These themes informed questionnaire design that aimed to explore the extent of respondents' agreement with the key themes emerging from qualitative analysis. The study allowed the researchers to identify the need for policy-makers to consider the claims of cyclists over public roads in order to contribute to the legitimisation of cycling and to reflect on the relationships between motorists and cyclists. This should allow the development of contextually sensitive strategies for the provision of cycling.

In these and other types of sequential MMR, the researcher has separate questions whose answers are produced sequentially; findings from one method can inform the questions for the next. Terrell (2011), however, suggests that the weakness of some of these strategies is that they are time-consuming.

In the *concurrent triangulation design*, mixed strategies are used concurrently. The purpose of this strategy is to validate and confirm the data found by either method with the second approach. This is a strategy that is often employed by researchers who are not completely happy with just using approaches sequentially, usually quantitative researchers who argue for triangulation to assess validity (see also Chapter 15). This design is possibly most often used in MMR but it is difficult to compare the findings of one examination of a phenomenon with another (see also triangulation within method in Chapter 15).

Using concurrent triangulation: decision-making by sport coaches

Vergeer and Lyle (2007) examined the concept of decision-making by sport coaches. The authors recognised that previous work had generally used either qualitative or quantitative methods and aimed to evaluate how mixing methods could benefit the study of decision-making. Coaches (n = 64) were first asked to rate the likelihood of their decision to allow an injured athlete to compete in a number of scenarios related to an athlete's injury. The authors also interviewed the same sample to identify the reasoning behind their decisions. The quantitative analysis allowed the identification of two clusters of coaches: 1) the cautious coach; 2) the more flexible coach. Meanwhile the qualitative analysis allowed three components of the decision-making process to be identified: 1) limiting the activity; 2) sharing the decision process, for example discussion with parents; 3) identifying arguments that might affect the likelihood of competing, such as the risk to the athlete of non-participation. According to the authors, a concurrent design had a number of advantages, in particular being able to link the qualitative phase directly with the scenarios measured quantitatively; for example the coaches were required to provide immediate insights into the deliberations they made during the scenarios.

In the *concurrent nested* strategy, researchers 'embed' one of the methods in the other. The dominant design forms the framework for the study. It is suggested that the nested method can enrich the other, and that is the primary purpose of this design. It needs great skill from the researcher, however, to integrate the two models and make them coherent.

Adopting a concurrent nested approach: the perceptions, opinions and behaviours of mixed martial arts spectators

MacIntosh and Crow (2011) explored the perceptions, opinions and behaviours of mixed martial arts spectators using a concurrent nested approach, where the dominant methods was a quantitative survey that aimed to measure spectator motivations as well as basic demographic information. Questionnaires (n = 108) were administered during an amateur mixed martial arts event. This was supported by an observational phase of data collection, involving student volunteers' observations of the surrounding environment and spectator behaviour prior to, during and after the event. Document analysis was conducted using programmes, cards and promotional materials from sponsors. The authors suggested that 'this approach assisted in exploring a real-life context and helped to provide an account of a reality that might not have been easily perceptible otherwise through one method alone' (p. 167)

A further strategy is suggested by Mayoh et al. (2011) who advocate *complementarity* in research design. This allows the researcher to produce complementary views of the same phenomenon. It requires the setting of different questions for different stages of the research, reflecting the acknowledgement of and respect for paradigmatic differences. It is understood that qualitative and quantitative methods will address different topics within the same research project, and researchers are advised to clearly label the phenomenon to be examined by each method.

The problems inherent in mixed methods research

Although MMR is very popular, it has its critics. One problematic issue is the writing up of MMR. This cannot be done in a conventional way as the nature of evidence in either qualitative or quantitative methods is different and requires a different form of presentation. Bazeley (2004: 9) advises that researchers should 'progressively unveil evidence on a path to a common conclusion' if they want to avoid the generation of two different studies in the investigation of one phenomenon. However, Bryman (2007) found in his interview study with 20 MMR practitioners that findings are often not integrated – thus this is a common problem. Indeed he found a lack of integration of findings in 82 per cent of articles published between 1994 and 2003. Bryman states that more attention needs to be given to writing up mixed methods research, questioning that if they are not integrated, maybe the researcher is not making the most of the data.

The audit trail – the description of the aims and stages of the research – needs even more clarity than that of a mono-method research study. From the very beginning of the study researchers have to declare which type of mixed methods design they wish to adopt. Important elements of the study such as its justification, sequencing of methods, its priorities of one over the other and the way in which they have to be combined need detailed and clear explanations.

Bergman (2011) states that validity in MMR is problematic as a limited sample in the qualitative stage means that the dimensions tested in the quantitative stage of the research are not derived from a representative group.

A lack of knowledge of both qualitative and quantitative research can also cause problems. One solution offered by Bryman (2007) is to create a team with differing skills; however, this is not an option for students. Besides, Bergman (2011) argues that a mixed team rarely leads to a successful application of MMR as too many compromises have to be made.

Summary

- There is a growing use and acceptance of mixed methods research (MMR)
- MMR is often driven by pragmatic reasons
- Researchers may benefit from the complementary strengths of qualitative and quantitative approaches
- A number of types of MMR exist: sequential explanatory, sequential exploratory, sequential transformative, concurrent triangulation, concurrent nested and concurrent transformative
- There are a number of potential problems with MMR of which the researcher must be aware

PART IV

ANALYSING AND REPORTING QUALITATIVE DATA

14

Data Analysis

Analysis can be defined as the process of bringing order to data, organising undifferentiated comments and observations into patterns, categories and descriptive units, and looking for relationships between them (Brewer, 2000). Qualitative data analysis (QDA) consists of exploring, managing and interpreting the data collected over time, starting with the raw data and transforming them during a reflective process. It is a complex task which demands time and patience. In several approaches, data collection and analysis interact (for instance, always in GT and often in ethnography); in others collection and analysis are sequential (for instance, phenomenology and narrative research). Researchers need to know this from the start. Indeed, most qualitative research approaches have their own procedures for analysing the data. Grounded theory and phenomenology in particular have unique strategies of data analysis (and collection), and narrative research uses several different approaches. There is, however, much overlap between the way data are transcribed, organised and managed.

A generic approach to analysis also exists, usually known as thematic analysis, and in this chapter we shall give an overview of this. Novice researchers, particularly undergraduates, feel overwhelmed by the complexities of using a specific approach with a philosophical and epistemological basis, such as phenomenology. They often wish to adopt a generic approach, using straightforward techniques and strategies such as interviews or observation independent of a specific approach. The philosophical and epistemological underpinnings of such a generic approach to data collection and analysis are not as demanding of students as would be the case if, for instance, a phenomenological or ethnographic approach were adopted. At Masters and certainly at PhD level it is expected that students would adopt a less generic approach, requiring them to become familiar with a specific approach.

Analysis in generic research is sometimes known as *thematic analysis*, but as Braun and Clarke (2006) suggest, thematic analysis can be both a tool for analysis used in specific approaches (for instance, some forms of narrative research, grounded theory or IPA), or it may stand on its own. The authors state that there is no agreement about this. If students carry out thematic analysis they need to recognise the importance of making this explicit and justifying it.

Qualitative data refer to information that the researcher has collected through interviews and observations as well as through documentary research. The data come in the form of interview transcripts, field-notes, audio and video recordings and other images such as drawings or photographs, as well as documents and diaries. These are often called 'raw data', but the data to be analysed have already gone through an initial process of interpretation, because researchers choose some and omit other data; they make inferences right from the beginning when they decide which data to prioritise. Thus a process of selection is under way from the start of data collection.

There are four steps in thematic analysis:

- Data management: find a system for organising, ordering and storing the data;
- Transcription: transcribe interviews and type up field-notes;
- Familiarisation: listen to and read or view the material collected repeatedly;
- Reduction: code and categorise the data so that you can build themes.

Managing the data

Organising, sorting and examining the data are important steps in qualitative data analysis. A general overview helps researchers to become familiar with the structure and content of the data. They sort, number and label all data material, including memos and field-notes, for ease of access. In observational work, field-notes will be made on a regular basis; these will be expanded once the researcher has more time, but usually on the same day. A careful management system will have to be in place from the start so that the researcher doesn't get lost in a mass of data. Details of participants need to be noted, numbered and anonymised, keeping them separate from real names.

The more important stages are listening to recordings, reading field-notes, (if appropriate looking at video-recordings) and reflecting. These processes make the researcher theoretically sensitive. Breaking down and segmenting the data initially and then sorting them according to importance becomes another step in the analysis. The process of sorting data is not neutral but depends on the judgement of researchers. Students in particular are advised to devise a clear labelling system for files electronically stored from the beginning, to avoid the common trap of losing track of where data are stored. A discrete label should be given to files and folders so that they are easy to navigate. A back-up system must always be created, and it should be updated regularly.

Transcribing and writing memos

Transcription

One of the first steps in data analysis is the transcription of data. Field-notes in their expanded form represent a transcript in their own right, as do documentary sources and images. Hammersley (2010: 556) suggests that 'data are theory-laden' from the beginning of their collection, full of assumptions made by researchers when hearing or observing participants and listening to recordings or reading field-notes. Researchers usually transform audio-data, such as recorded interview or focus group data, into written text. Researchers occasionally transcribe by hand but more often they type the scripts on the computer. Each transcript needs a face sheet in which the researcher records factual elements.

Example of face sheet for interview transcript

Place of interview:

Date:

Name of interviewer:

Pseudonym of participant and details such as (approx) age and gender:

Number of memo and field-notes linked to interview:

Transcripts will usually have wide margins of about half a page for notes and initial analysis; the typing will be double-spaced and each line numbered (there are details of line numbering on the Taylor and Gibbs (2010) website). Verbatim transcriptions should indicate timing, such as pauses between words. Indeed some researchers transcribe every facet of the spoken text such as laughter or coughs as well as including non-verbal elements such as gestures or facial expressions. There are some common notation symbols for transcription, but researchers sometimes use their own throughout. The research approach adopted dictates that which is necessary; some approaches, such as phenomenology or grounded theory, do not need micro-transcription while it seems useful for conversation and discourse analysis. Having said that, most research reports will be enriched by an indication of delivery, behaviour and tone.

Transcription is often seen as 'a process of construction' (Hammersley, 2010: 556) rather than a simple reproduction of what was said, because the researcher not only reports but also makes inferences. Hammersley warns, however, that data are not 'made up' or invented, hence the transcript has to remain faithful to the data and capture the essence of what was said and done.

As interview transcription takes time, between four and six hours for an hour-long interview, researchers sometimes engage a typist for faster work. However, transcription works best if researchers do it themselves, because they gain an opportunity to familiarise themselves and become intimate with the data. Transcribers need training and explanations about ethical guidelines as well as a reminder to transcribe exactly what they hear. They should never alter or omit words. There are a number of transcription conventions, the best known of which is that of Gail Jefferson who in the 1970s and 80s invented a system that uses symbols for non-verbal action. Conversation and discourse analysts often use this, but for some approaches this type of transcript would be inappropriate as minute details might detract from the overall meaning of the interview, such as in phenomenology or grounded theory. Some researchers have their own system of transcription. Selective transcription may sometimes be carried out whereby researchers omit some of the less important elements of the transcription, particularly after having transcribed several recordings. We would not advise this, however, as such early analysis may lead to the erroneous omission of important data whose significance only becomes apparent during analysis.

To facilitate the processing transcriptions researchers might use a transcription machine. There are also foot pedals, transcription software and/or headphones available (Burke et al., 2010), but for Masters or undergraduate students it is easier just to transcribe from the recording itself by listening to it. Students commonly use a digital recorder to record the interview. This is a detachable device with a USB that connects with a PC, allowing the researcher to transfer the recording to their computer. The recording can be transcribed straight onto a document.

Writing memos and field-notes

Interview data are not the only data to be transcribed and considered. Researchers need also to organise and expand on notes and memos, which they will have written during the whole of the research process. These need to dating and numbering so that a progression in the researcher's train of thought can be observed. Like field-notes, these analytical memos need to be contextualised – the context often becomes part of the writing. Novice researchers often forget the ideas they had during data collection and analysis; hence it is important that they remember to write analytic memos and notes from the start. Different types of memos exist; they are theoretical and analytic and should be kept separate from the data.

Whilst analytic memos remind the researchers of the thoughts and feelings they had when collecting and analysing the data, more importantly, they help in the reflection on theoretical ideas and concepts that arise during analysis. Relationships between concepts can be noted in memos. Researchers can relate these analytical notes to the initial field-notes and memos, and set up links to other ideas which might lead to further analysis. Strauss (1987: 18) suggests that these memos lead to 'greater scope and conceptual density' as well as helping the researcher to plan for the writing-up phase. They also assist in checking the progress of the research and in upgrading its quality.

The memos and notes describe what researchers reflect on during the process of analysis – why and how their thinking is important to the study. To show the decision trail throughout the research, these analytical notes sometimes become part of the research report, though usually they serve as reminders to be followed up when the researchers engage in dialogue with the relevant literature. As noted in Chapter 4, the researcher is guided on much of the literature to consult by the themes that have emerged from data analysis. Gibbs (2007: 31–32) gives examples of how memos can be used in the analysis process.

Using memos: athletes' experiences of poor coaching and coach–athlete relationships

Gearity (2011) explored athletes' experiences of poor coaching through interviewing 16 current or former athletes. Each interview was transcribed before the next interview took place. Initial analysis was also undertaken at this stage so that the interviewer could get a sense of emergent themes, which might influence ongoing data collection. Memos were written, recording the researcher's early impressions and analytic insights. These helped in the final analysis, providing detail of the researcher's thoughts and ideas at the time of the data collection.

Bringer et al. (2006) interviewed three coaches who had either engaged in sexual relations with athletes or who had experienced allegations of abuse, to develop an understanding of the concepts of sexual exploitation in sport. The authors used seven different types of memo to support their analysis:

a The meaning and analytical thinking underpinning each code;
b Thoughts about the evolving theory;
c Notes about procedures;
d Visual representations of the relationships between categories;
e Details of news articles that influenced the coaches' responses;
f Technical notes about the use of CADQAS;
g Notes taken at meetings with officials from the national governing body where the emerging results were discussed.

Concept mapping also assists in the analysis process (Stake, 2010). This is a way of using diagrams or flowcharts to establish a picture of the links and relationships between concepts and gives an overview of the developing thoughts of the researcher. Through such linkages, patterns can be more easily established. A graphic illustration of the main research themes can often find its way into a research report, possibly at the start of the 'Findings' section, to give the reader an overview of the major findings.

Data reduction and conceptualisation: codes, categories and themes

The terms category, theme and construct are sometimes used interchangeably in qualitative research. For the purpose of this chapter we shall try to differentiate between them.

   Although different approaches in qualitative research have their roots in different philosophical assumptions and epistemologies, analytic strategies share many commonalities. These commonalities are also found in thematic analysis which usually includes coding and categorising. (We have explained the analysis specific to each approach in the chapters in Part III.) It must be emphasised, though, that the flexible nature of qualitative research defies prescriptions or 'recipes' for analysis. Analytic processes are flexible and creative as well as iterative. Iteration means that the analysis moves back and forth, with a frequent return to the data. New aspects or elements can be found when revisiting the original data during the analysis process. Occasionally, in the light of further evidence, the data might even be reinterpreted (Holloway, 2008)

The initial steps and practicalities

As stated before, it is essential that students listen to the data closely, read the transcripts several times and gain an overall picture of the meaning of the participants. When doing that, they often feel that they are 'drowning in data'. It is obvious that the data need to be reduced or collapsed as it isn't possible to use everything from the transcript. Researchers reflect on, segment and reduce the data; they need to search for patterns, themes and meaning units which emerge directly from the data. Practical aspects of handling transcripts and images might include underlining, using highlighters or colour pencils to mark certain passages. Text can also be physically cut up and rearranged according to meaning – one of the reasons for having several copies. Alternatively, data can be 'cut up' electronically. There are different ways of analysing the data, and the researcher needs to choose which to adopt, depending on the approach and the analytic stance that is taken.

Coding and categorising

Coding and categorising – indexing the data – are important strategies in QDA for many qualitative approaches when the researcher searches for meaning in the data. Coding only begins after the process of familiarisation has taken place, when the researcher has listened to or watched audio and visual record-ings and read through the transcripts and field-notes several times. Creating analytic codes is essential, as this stops the researcher from getting lost in the data (Mason, 2002). Some researchers start with line-by-line coding, but this can be an arduous process and coding by paragraph is more usual. Others carry out this process more holistically and search for themes or patterns straight away. In any case, when looking at a transcript, listening to a recorded inter-view, or looking at notes from observations, some major concepts and ideas seem to emerge, though they have to be examined more closely. Students need remember that the data are always the initial basis of coding and not to impose their own ideas. Analytic categories need to be grounded in and illustrated by verbatim quotations or extracts from field-notes. These are inserted to demon-strate a point and show evidence from the data. Not only do they illuminate the participants' experience or behaviour, but they also exemplify an argument or illustrate a point which the researcher wishes to make. The quotes help to show how the findings were derived from the data and to build the credibility of the emerging categories or themes. Thus quotes are usually typical for the theme or category. If statements cannot be grounded in the data, it is advisable that the researcher revisits the analytic process.

The code is an identifying name or label given to a data unit or a datum. It is a word used to represent a phenomenon the researcher notices in the text. It must be distinct so that it is obviously different from another code, and there must be a low level of inference; it must be close to concrete description. The coding process often starts with *in vivo* codes, labels that are given to words or concepts that the participants use themselves in the inter-view; for instance, 'supporting the team' or 'it supports my identity' are *in vivo* codes. Gibbs (2007: 47), who gives much practical advice, provides a list of the things that the researcher might want to code. We have shortened and adapted it here:

- Behaviours, acts and activities – how people act, what is going on in the setting from the point of view of the observer or the perception of the participants. *Example*: 'taking control of my weight'.
- Events – what happens in the setting, what do people say about incidents and occurrences? *Example*: 'taking part in the marathon'.
- Meanings – what people say they mean when they speak about conditions, circum-stances and feelings, how people think about the situation. *Example*: 'searching for a running identity'.
- Relationships – how people interact and relate to others. *Example*: 'gaining social support'.
- Conditions and consequences – under which conditions do things happen, what are the consequences of particular types of behaviour. *Example*: 'exercise as relief from stress'.

Developing codes: athletes' experiences of poor coaching

Following transcription of 16 interviews with athletes, Gearity (2011) began the process of analysis. The first stage involved identifying the smallest meaningful units of data, for example 'I never got instruction on how to fix it (hitting)' (p. 7). The second iteration involved clustering similar meaning units into sub-themes. In the case of the code just given, this was placed into the sub-theme of 'not instructing'. The third and final stage involved all sub-themes being compared and clustered to create broad themes, all related to poor coaching. Thus the sub-theme of 'not instructing' was categorised under a larger theme of 'poor teaching by the coach'.

The examples given are merely illustrations. Qualitative researchers do not generally predetermine codes or categories – although some do. (King (2008) discusses this in relation to template analysis.) It can be seen that this differs somewhat depending on whether observations, interviews or images are analysed. For interviews, the researcher analyses transcripts or notes made from the interviews. Observations come in the form of field-notes and images might be explored in detail and themes, patterns or major ideas can emerge from either. Diaries or additional documents such as leaflets, minutes of meetings or newsletters also need close examination.

After all the data have been coded, the process of sorting those codes that are linked will take place: similar codes will be grouped together and a category will emerge. A cluster of similar codes is named a category – a conceptual label for a group of linked codes. As O'Reilly (2005) points out, some codes can overlap different categories. For instance, 'wanting to be a part of the group', 'being with my friends' and 'seeking help from others' might be reduced or collapsed to the category 'building relationships'. Some analysts also call this a theme (or even a construct), especially if they are carrying out thematic analysis. Most students draw diagrams and flowcharts to obtain a good overview of the findings.

Themes of parental experiences in elite youth sport

Harwood et al. (2010) undertook a study of parental experiences in elite youth sport. Data from six focus groups were transcribed and meaningful comments were identified and coded as meaning units. 77 meaning units were found and were organised into 23 themes, clustered around common underlying categories. Four major themes were identified: academy processes and quality of communication, match-related stressors, role conflict between the sport and the family, and school support and education issues. As an example, one parent suggested that 'watching him play, that is stress, I mean it's the most stressful time for me...I wanted him to come off in case he made a mistake. He's a defender as well, and with the youth-team coach coming to watch, I thought, if he touches the ball and makes a mistake, then that's it.' This meaning unit was placed into a sub-theme labelled 'child's level of performance', which subsequently found its way into the major theme of match-related stressors. Other sub-themes in this major theme included anticipating and dealing with reaction to losing and other parents' comments and behaviour (there were eight sub-themes overall).

Searching for themes in the data

The first process of thematic analysis is coding, but researchers sometimes move directly to identifying themes in the data. This is not as detailed a process as coding and categorising and skips the line-by-line coding process. Important issues might be missed, but, on the other hand, this way of analysing is more holistic and looks for core concepts in the data. A theme is a core idea or common thread in the data. These ideas and patterns are not immediately obvious to the researcher but need to be worked out carefully. They tend to be more abstract than codes or categories and can only be established through total immersion in the data. Unfortunately, the use of the term 'theme' varies in research texts, but we attempt here a general understanding of the concept. A major theme is one that occurs frequently in the data. Usually it starts from the ideas of participants, the 'emic' perspective. It is then taken to a broader, more abstract, theoretical level by the researcher – his or her 'etic' view. It does not simply mean 'hearing the voices of the participants' and describing or presenting their view; themes depend on the evaluation and judgement of the researcher. The themes represent an understanding of the phenomenon under investigation. Braun and Clarke (2006: 82) argue that a theme 'captures something important about the data'. Researchers can generate themes by a top-down approach – through reading and reflecting on meaning – or through coding and categorising the data first and then developing themes based on the different categories that have been identified. Either way, these are interpretive processes carried out by the researcher. Themes always need to be supported by evidence from the data. Some textbooks allow students to work from pre-set themes that are determined in advance and find areas and examples to match these. We would not advise this, however, as qualitative research in general is initially inductive and the themes uncovered emerge directly from the data when they have been properly analysed.

Themes and their labels might change in the process of analysis. The final themes show insight into the perspective of the participant and the meaning they and the researcher give to the findings. Themes might be divided into several sub-themes, depending on the length of the research report. To get a clearer view of the findings, researchers often generate a hierarchy of themes, with major or more abstract and theoretical ideas at the top of this. They might also generate typologies (classifications) of people in the setting, for instance runners for pleasure or runners for exercise.

Thematic analysis of exercise addiction and training patterns

Warner and Griffiths (2006) undertook an exploratory qualitative study of exercise addiction, focusing on the positive and negative experiences of exercise. The thematic analysis consisted of transcription, familiarisation through reading the data twice and coding. Once data were coded, the authors identified a number of broad themes. Positive experiences of exercise were: increased health and fitness, stress relief, improved body image, improved self-esteem and social enjoyment. The negative experiences of exercise were grouped into five themes: pain and injury, neglecting other commitments, tiredness, poor performance during exercise and poor body image.

The study by Fraser-Thomas et al. (2008) explored the impact of training patterns and the role of significant others in participation in adolescent swimming. 20 swimmers were interviewed from which a total of 613 codes were identified. These were clustered into five broad themes: training patterns, the influence of coaches, parental influence, peer influence and the influence of siblings.

Computer-aided analysis of qualitative data

Many researchers use computer-aided/assisted qualitative data analysis software (CAQDAS) in the analysis process. Masters or undergraduate students might not use computer-aided analysis unless they are already familiar with it, because it takes time and training to learn the process; their time is limited. However, some PhD candidates undertake computer-aided analysis, in particular when the data set is huge. It can be a valuable tool or a time-consuming hindrance in qualitative research. Indeed there is now a wide range of users (Mangabeira et al., 2004), including some researchers from commercial organisations.

A wide range of sophisticated software packages for computer-aided qualitative research is now available, the best known of which are probably NVivo, Atlas/ti, Nud*ist and HyperRESEARCH. There is also video-analysis software (Koch and Zumbach, 2002/7). Supporters of CAQDAS argue that it helps in the organisation, retrieval and management of data. It is advisable to access an expert or undertake some training to be able to use the package most suited to the particular type of approach to be adopted.

There are a variety of computer analysis processes which are very similar to the strategies that qualitative researchers also use in manual analysis:

- Storing, annotating and tracking texts
- Locating words, phrases and segments of data
- Identifying data units
- Naming and labelling data
- Extracting quotes

The items in this following list were discussed by Tesch (1993) around two decades ago, but it is still useful and valid. Lewins and Silver (2007) argue that the following functions can be carried out, at least partially, by computers:

- Planning and managing the project
- Memoing, including keeping track of ideas as they occur and building on them as work progresses
- Searching for strings, words and phrases
- Coding and recoding into themes and categories
- Storing, retrieving and linking

One of the initial concerns of carrying out computer analysis of qualitative data was mentioned by Seidel (1991), himself a developer of the software package 'ETHNOGRAPH', who believed that computer analysis might distance the researcher from the research, in particular if it was just seen as a mechanical process. He warns researchers of 'analytic madness' in the use of technology. They might collect more data than necessary and make the process overly complex and miss significant ideas in the data. Computers also tempt researchers to count themes or categories rather than look for importance and significance. Fletcher and Arnold (2011), for example, in their study of performance leadership and management in elite sport, despite having 329 pages of transcripts, chose to undertake manual analysis because of the threat that CAQDAS can distance the researcher from the data. We would advise students to be sensitive to the data, not to be rigid and mechanistic and always look for meaning rather than just frequency of themes or categories. In manual analysis, the researcher is closer and more intimately involved with the data. However, computers do help in the management of large amounts of data. Indeed, computers have not only been accepted for simple research tasks, but also in many areas, and for many researchers, they are accepted for qualitative analysis as well, as long as adequate care is taken to immerse oneself and become familiar with the data.

The use of CAQDAS in exploring the use of imagery by athletes in rehabilitation from sport injuries

Driediger et al. (2006) explored the use of imagery by athletes in rehabilitation from sport injuries. Interviews with ten participants with a current injury were undertaken and subsequently transcribed, producing 105 pages of text which

(Continued)

> *(Continued)*
>
> were uploaded to the QSR N4 Programme (the fourth version of NUD*IST). The decision to undertake CAQDAS was based, according to the authors, upon its advantage over manual analysis of allowing the organisation of large amounts of data and the exploration of relationships among coded text.

Interpreting the data

Although data analysis is an important step in research, the act of interpretation of the data cannot be under-estimated. The interpretation of data is a creative enterprise that involves skill and imagination (Geertz, 1973). This perhaps explains one of the common flaws in research reports: findings are often presented well but they are under-interpreted. It is the researchers' job to both *present* and *interpret* their findings. Interpretation of the data starts at the very beginning of the research process. In the early stages of coding and categorising, the researcher makes inferences from the data, as they do during data collection when they reflect on what they observe and hear. One might even suggest that even descriptive phenomenologists, who insist on description above interpretation, cannot help ascribing some significance to their data. Alvesson and Sjőldberg (2009) argue that interpretation relies on the judgement and intuition of the researchers. After all, they were present during the research; they listened to the participants and observed their behaviour; they were aware of the context in which the research took place. They have a privileged position in regard to the data.

The formulation of concepts is important in the interpretation process. Researchers elicit data on the everyday life of participants, which they take to a second level of understanding which is more theoretical and abstract and show the meanings they, as researchers, attribute to the findings. Thus there is an interweaving of the emic and etic views (see Chapters 1 and 13). Denzin (1989) called the understandings of participants first-order constructs, while the researchers' interpretations are second-order constructs. The researchers' interpretations of the analysed data might be revised in the light of the dialogue with the literature, which helps to illuminate and clarify the emergent themes. It must be stressed, however, that the primary data have priority. This is reflected in the reference to the primary data – quotes help to 'clarify the links between data, interpretation and conclusions' (Corden and Sainsbury, 2006: 98). Long rows of quotes or continuous duplication are not needed, however, and frequent, very short quotes might make the study look fragmented (Holloway and Wheeler, 2010). The quotes chosen should show that the data come from a larger number of participants rather than just one or two, unless only one person is interviewed (as is the case occasionally, particularly in phenomenology or narrative research).

Interpreting the data: the personal narrative
of a British Paralympic wheelchair tennis player

Kavanagh (2012) explores the personal narrative of a British Paralympic wheelchair tennis player who experienced a spinal cord injury (SCI) following a motorcycle accident in 2001 that left her paralysed from the waist down. Here is a verbatim excerpt from the findings section of the paper:

Lucy's accident challenged the sense of coherence and predictability of her previous everyday life forcing her to experience and adapt to a world which was unfamiliar, frightening and absent of the natural order which would be part of her normal routine.

When I was in hospital I had 7 weeks on my back and 7 weeks in a brace so you couldn't bend or do anything. You had someone else doing your personal care and washing you, losing all your dignity. It was horrible; I don't think you could do it justice describing it. It was degrading and embarrassing...that was probably one of the hardest things. Life was different...just mundane basic day-to-day stuff, using the bathroom, getting dressed, having a shower. Just things you take for granted.

When working with people following a stroke, Murray and Harrison (2004) reported that the 'loss of me' associated with a life-changing event often meant that people feel distance from the new self, so even their own personhood has an unfamiliarity. In order to move on with her life, Lucy needed to challenge and question the person she had become since the accident and who she would be in the future, thus managing the threads that make up the wider rope of her life path (Ellis-Hill et al., 2008).

As the researcher is the research instrument, interpretation is subjective and depends on the individual, and research students in particular need to be aware that others might have different and alternative interpretations. After all, the qualitative researcher is the research tool, and each individual researcher may think about and develop an understanding of the same findings in a different way. This is effectively demonstrated by Hollway and Jefferson (2000) who end their research report by inviting readers to make their own interpretation of the research findings, indicating that no interpretation takes priority. It is important that the research account is reflexive, that the researcher acknowledges their subjectivity and the influence that they carry on data collection, analysis and interpretation.

Problems with analysis

All researchers occasionally make mistakes in the analysis process. Some problems might emerge when students, in particular, do not know how to start the analysis, hence beginning researchers could start with a limited section of data, for instance just one page or paragraph. It is always important to show the reasons for particular themes or categories and give evidence from the data for them.

'Premature closure' – a term used by Glaser (1978) – occurs when the data are not analysed sufficiently, or when inferences and interpretations are made too quickly or when previous, already existing codes are applied to the data to achieve a quick fix.

Some researchers, in particular novices or students, do not carry out a proper analysis and think that they have analysed the data when they found a few themes and given quotes from participants to show that they have roots in the data. Analysis means that the researcher has examined the data thoroughly and asked questions from and about them.

Summary

- Data analysis depends on the approach adopted and the judgement of the researcher
- QDA is complex and takes time
- Usually, though not always, the data are coded and categorised. Sometimes a more holistic approach of thematic analysis is adopted
- CAQDAS can be a useful tool in data analysis if it is used with care
- The researcher takes the data to the level of interpretation

15

The Quality of Qualitative Inquiry

Most researchers wish to demonstrate validity in their studies. In quantitative research, long-established methods provide guidelines for ensuring quality. The debate in qualitative research is still going on; some writers take a philosophical and theoretical approach (for instance, Seale, 1999; Cho and Trent, 2006), whilst others have developed criteria to judge quality and suggest ways in which validity can be established. There seems to be confusion about terminology, however: while many researchers use the term trustworthiness rather than rigour and validity in qualitative research, following Lincoln and Guba (1985), others feel that validity is a legitimate concept for both quantitative and qualitative research (Maxwell, 2005; Silverman, 2010) and argue for the retention of the term. Some completely reject evaluative criteria (criteriology) as useful for qualitative research (Wolcott, 2009). Indeed, Onwegbuzie and Leech (2007) state that no single idea of validity dominates in qualitative research; researchers do not agree on the concept.

Rigour is one of the terms often used in research to denote validity and reliability. For research to be judged as sound, valid or trustworthy, many researchers believe that it must have rigour. *Rigour* is related to reliability and has its origin in quantitative, natural science research. Of course, it has a different meaning in qualitative inquiry. Gratton and Jones (2010) state that rigour refers to the 'appropriateness of the methodological choice' made by the researcher. Rigour denotes thoroughness, soundness and appropriateness in qualitative research (Golafshani, 2003). However, excessive emphasis on rigour might hinder flexibility or originality in the research, and some qualitative researchers avoid this term.

Validity and reliability

Validity and reliability have been seen as the criteria for quality in quantitative research. In quantitative inquiry, validity is the extent to which a test or an instrument measures what it aims to measure, and that the conclusions are well founded. Reliability is the consistency and repeatability of the measurement. These concepts and definitions as understood by quantitative researchers, however, have no place in qualitative research and many qualitative researchers who use these terms give them alternative meanings.

Validity

In research, validity is the equivalent of the common-sense term of truthfulness and soundness, no matter what type of inquiry researchers adopt. The discussion in qualitative research centres on internal and external validity. In qualitative research *internal validity* is the honesty with which researchers report and present the concerns and thoughts of the participants, and whether the latter find that it describes reality as they see it. Bryman (2008) extends this concept of internal validity by stating that the researcher's empirical observations and their interpretations should match their theoretical ideas. *External validity* exists when the findings and conclusions of the research hold true for other settings and times – that is, if they are generalisable.

Generalisability

Generalisability is not an aim of qualitative studies, and many researchers reject its relevance. As said before, generalisability exists when the findings of research are applicable to other similar settings and populations, i.e. when they can be generalised across a variety of settings. In quantitative research, random sampling ensures that the results of the research are representative of the group under study and through the search for causality and law-like generalities. Generalisabilty is difficult in qualitative inquiry as researchers focus on specific and unique cases and instances, even though they might want to establish patterns and typologies. The concept of generalisability is wholly irrelevant if only a single case or a unique phenomenon is examined.

Many researchers use the term *transferability* in place of generalisability, or 'theory based generalisation', whereby theoretical ideas might be transferred from one context or setting to another.

Objectivity seems to be another criterion used in quantitative research and not in qualitative inquiry. Objectivity means that the research is free of bias and relatively neutral. Qualitative researchers maintain that neutrality and objectivity are not achievable; on the contrary, they acknowledge their subjectivity and examine it for bias or their own assumptions. Carr and Kemmis (1986) call this 'critical subjectivity' (see also reflexivity).

Reliability

The notion of reliability is also widely contested in qualitative research. Reliability refers to the replicability (repeatability) of research. As the researcher is the research tool in qualitative research, the latter is never wholly replicable. Although the study could be repeated, other researchers would rarely find the same results, even under similar circumstances and conditions. Their own location and background influence their data collection and interpretation and they differ in their perception and focus, even when they select the same topic, adopt the same methods and choose a similar sample. Thus a study of a specific group or situation cannot be repeated as each piece of work differs in time and location, though consistency over time might demonstrate a form of reliability.

Alternative criteria for qualitative research

Those who reject conventional ideas about validity and reliability often follow Guba and Lincoln (1989) and their use of different concepts:

Table 15.1   Alternative criteria

Conventional criteria	Alternative criteria
Internal validity	Credibility
External validity	Transferability
Reliability	Dependability
Objectivity	Confirmability

The overall alternative concept used in qualitative research is *trustworthiness*. For the research to have this, it has to be credible, transferable, dependable and confirmable.

Credibility means that the research and its findings are believable, not only by the reader but, in particular, by research participants. The findings of the researcher and the views of participants need to be compatible. Indeed, participants must have confidence in the results of the study and recognise its truth within their own setting and context; the research account should resonate with the participants' own experiences. Dahlberg et al. (2001) specifically claim that the research account should not contain internal contradictions for it to be seen as credible. Credibility can be established through member-checking and a holistic description of the context (see later in this chapter for ways of ensuring trustworthiness).

Transferability is an alternative label for generalisability. Transferability refers to the extent to which findings and conclusions can be transferred to similar settings and situations with similar participants. Hence the context of the research needs detailed description, and the researcher needs to show good judgement on how this context is transferable. The audit trail and 'thick description' are ways of persuading readers that research findings can be transferred to other settings and situations. As Diacin et al. (2003) observe in their study of drug use amongst college athletes, 'the findings from this study are context-bound and not intended to be representative of all inter-collegiate athletes nor generalisable to all inter-collegiate athletics programmes, as context cannot be duplicated. Transferability of findings for making possible connections to other unique inter-collegiate athletics contexts is appropriately left to the reader' (p. 4).

Transferability of findings on the influence of the interpersonal context on sport motivation

Bengoechea and Strean (2007) wanted to gain an understanding of the influence of the interpersonal context on sport motivation. Interviews were undertaken with 12 adolescents. Interviews revealed that interpersonal relationships had five major motivational roles: providers of support, sources of pressure and control, sources of information, socialisation agents and role models. This allowed an explanatory model to be developed to provide a theoretical explanation of the interpersonal motivators. Given the corroboration of the model offered by the literature, it seems likely that the model would be transferable to other contexts. However, the authors themselves warn that the model may not be entirely applicable to adolescent athletes from other backgrounds and this is something that the reader needs to take into account. Like Diacin et al. (2003), the authors suggest that they have provided enough contextual detail that readers should be able to judge for themselves the transferability of the findings.

Dependability is a term similar to reliability and shows that the work can be repeated. However, we have already stated that qualitative research is not replicable, hence dependability means internal consistency over time. This means that the research is consistent or comparable over time, that similar things are treated in a similar way, and that it is similar in quality over time. Dependability is still a contested concept, and overlaps with confirmability.

Confirmability means the extent to which others, readers and peers alike, can confirm the ideas presented in the research. Peer debriefing is a valid way of corroborating and checking confirmability. Readers need an audit trail for confirmation so they can follow researchers to see how they collected and analysed the data and arrived at their findings.

The idea of intersubjectivity has importance for confirmability. Moustakas (1994), for example, states that human beings share the social world and will recognise the essence of the phenomenon under study and confirm the perspectives of the researchers.

Guba and Lincoln (1989) added the concept of *authenticity* a few years after their earlier work (Lincoln and Guba, 1985), a term which has no equivalent in quantitative research. Qualitative research is authentic in the following situations: when its procedures and strategies are appropriate and sound; when a range of alternative explanations have been examined and researchers act ethically; when participants are helped to understand their social reality and through this improve other people's understanding; and when the participants are empowered by the research (this can be followed up in the 1989 text).

How to ensure trustworthiness

Whatever concept is used, most writers believe that qualitative researchers can ensure validity or trustworthiness through particular strategies. These are:

1   Development of an audit trail
2   Member-checks
3   Peer-debriefing (peer review)
4   Triangulation within and between methods
5   Prolonged engagement or immersion in the setting
6   Thick description
7   Searching for alternative explanations or interpretations
8   Reflexivity

The audit trail

The audit or decision trail (a concept developed for qualitative inquiry by Lincoln and Guba, 1985, though Halpern, 1983, initiated the strategy) is the detailed description of the researcher's steps from the beginning to the end of the research process. The term derives from the audit procedure in the financial world in which auditors examine accounts for accuracy. By following this audit trail, readers can judge whether the research has *dependability*. The trail documents the researcher's decision-making and the path they followed throughout the study. It includes descriptions of methods of both data collection and analysis as well as sampling strategies; it even gives specific detail on transcription and coding procedures. The trail also documents memos and field-notes. Although this is difficult to do in short articles, any research project should contain this audit trail.

Ensuring trustworthiness: the Teaching Personal and Social Responsibility Model

Walsh et al. (2010) investigated the extent to which the Teaching Personal and Social Responsibility Model was transferable beyond the scope of a given programme through multiple qualitative methods focusing on the experiences of 13 African-American and Pacific Island students. The authors used several strategies to establish trustworthiness, including member-checking, peer-debriefing, data triangulation and an audit trail. The latter involved a review of all steps taken in the research process, from the initial planning through to the analysis. The materials reviewed within the audit trail included the original research plan, interview protocols, transcriptions, field-notes and various iterations of the coding scheme.

The member-check

One of the ways in which to ensure *credibility* in qualitative research is the member-check (Lincoln and Guba, 1985) which is sometimes called respondent validation, the latter a term taken from quantitative research. Researchers return to participants after interviews and observation to give feedback on the researcher's understanding of their data. Though many books suggest differently, it is not a good idea to go back with interview transcripts and observation field-notes: this is too time-consuming and problematic (Buchbinder, 2011). However, researchers can show their themes or categories as well as their interpretations. They can then ask participants to confirm, challenge or expand on these understandings from inside their own experiences. Cohen and Crabtree (2008), however, suggest that the member-check can be problematic. First, the understandings of the researcher are not just based on the experiences of the participants but are more theoretical and abstract ideas that may be difficult to understand or accept by participants. Second, participants rely on their memories and these may change over time, or they might be influenced by others if they happen to work in the same organisation or are members of the same group.

Member-checking in a study of poor coaching

Gearity (2011) undertook member-checking through sending participants a three-page summary of the findings and encouraging them to modify, dispute or corroborate the conclusions reached. The feedback from participants strongly supported the researcher's own interpretation, therefore the study was considered 'complete'.

Peer-debriefing (peer review)

In the process of peer-debriefing, one or several peers of the researcher review the data and analyse them independent of the researcher (in the first instance). The ideas of the researcher and those of the peers should show some similarity. Of course, the review must be done by individuals who are competent in the analysis of data and knowledgeable about the phenomenon under study; they may be a student's supervisor or an academic or professional colleague. The debriefer will also have access to the categories or themes generated by analysis. Discussion might also take place about the findings and research process and potential biases or prior assumptions of the researcher. Peer-debriefing can take place throughout the whole of the research process and is another means of demonstrating credibility.

Peer-debriefing in studies exploring the relationship between moral reasoning and achievement motivation in rugby, and parental experiences in elite youth sport

Tod and Hodge (2002) explored the relationship between moral reasoning and achievement motivation in rugby. Eight rugby union players were presented with a series of moral dilemmas and were asked for their value reactions. The interviews were repeated a number of times across the season and data were analysed on an ongoing basis. The analysis was presented on a weekly basis to a peer of the researchers to review both the analysis procedures and subsequent interpretations as well as identifying any features from the data that may have been overlooked. This study serves as an effective illustration of how peer-debriefing can be used to help guide the analysis and interpretation rather than it being a procedure used only at the end of the analysis stage.

Harwood et al. (2010) used two methods to enhance trustworthiness in their study of parental experiences in elite youth sport. First, the coding of their focus group data was undertaken by two members of the research team independently from each other. This allowed areas of disagreement to be discussed and the coding to be revised when deemed necessary. The subsequent grouping of codes into themes was openly discussed and challenged at each stage until consensus was reached. The final codes were then reviewed by a third researcher acting as critical friend (Creswell, 1998) who critically probed the key decisions made by the research team. This was supported by a comprehensive member-checking process whereby random participants from each focus group were asked to verify not only their own contributions but also the final thematic analysis and explanatory summary of the key findings.

Triangulation

Triangulation is a way of illuminating a research project from more than one angle – the application of different perspectives to examine a phenomenon.

Its purpose is to establish the *confirmability* of findings. Triangulation can mean that a study combines qualitative and quantitative approaches to investigate a phenomenon or topic. However, triangulation in qualitative research usually takes another path: it is not triangulation *'between methods'* but *'within method'*, meaning that the procedures used might be observation and interviewing, and/or documentary research. Denzin (2009) differentiates between several types, some of which are 'within method' triangulation:

- *Data triangulation,* in which researchers use several data sources and obtain their data from different groups, settings or at different times (multiple sources of data). This is the usual way of triangulating in qualitative research.
- *Investigator triangulation,* when several researchers are involved in the study. This of course rarely happens in student dissertations or theses.
- *Theoretical triangulation,* when more than one theoretical idea is used in the interpretations of the data.
- *Methodological triangulation,* when researchers use two or more methods in one study to answer a similar question (observations, interviews, documents, questionnaires). These are either between-method or within-method triangulation (adapted from Denzin by Holloway and Wheeler 2010).

Methodological triangulation in researching the role of the setting in positive development within elite youth sport from the perspective of coaches

Strachan et al. (2011) examined the role of the setting in positive development within elite youth sport from the perspective of coaches. Data were collected from multiple methods. In-depth semi-structured interviews with five elite youth sport coaches were conducted, which led to the production of 45 pages of single-space transcript. Interviews were complemented by direct observation of coaches on seven opportunities. This produced 30 pages of single-space field-notes. This method allowed the researchers to develop a deeper understanding of the context and provided an opportunity to observe events that participants might have taken for granted or been unwilling to disclose. Interviews were analysed inductively and thematically, and observational data were then analysed deductively using the themes emerging from the interviews, although the authors acknowledged that new and additional themes were generated from the observational stage of the research.

Investigator triangulation when researching the perceived benefits of injury from the perspective of athletes

Wadey et al. (2011) suggest that research into sport injury focuses almost exclusively on the negative impact. Their study examined the perceived benefits of injury from the perspective of athletes. Ten injured athletes were interviewed; each interview lasted between 40 and 60 minutes. Investigator triangulation was used throughout the analysis of the interview data, involving the discussion of coding and categorising until consensus was reached. This was followed by the four authors independently generating causal networks, which were then group discussed to create a single causal network for each participant.

Prolonged engagement

Several decades ago, Lincoln and Guba (1985) and Erlandson et al. (1993) used the terms 'immersion' and 'prolonged engagement' in a setting as a means of reducing reactivity, though of course this can never be wholly eliminated. Learning the routines, rituals and language in the chosen location, the researcher will get to know the participants and become part of the setting. Through prolonged engagement and immersion in a situation, the researcher becomes less visible, does not disturb the setting and can see the situation as it is – or at least as far as this is possible. Participants will still react to the researcher's presence but the impact is lessened.

Prolonged immersion in the setting: the meanings of outdoor physical activity for parentally bereaved young people

Brewer and Sparkes (2011) undertook an ethnographic study to examine the meanings of outdoor physical activity among parentally bereaved young people. Data were generated from a study focusing on the experiences of participants attending the 'Rocky Centre', a childhood bereavement centre. One of the researchers (Brewer) negotiated access as overt participant observer for a two-year period. Access was facilitated by the researcher having attended the centre previously following the death of her father when she was 15. She had also acted as a volunteer at the centre subsequently, during which time good working relationships were established. This allowed open communication during the two years of fieldwork and acceptance from those in the research setting, thus minimising the impact of the presence of the researcher.

Thick description

Thick description is a concept developed by Geertz (1973), initially rooted in the ideas of the philosopher Ryle. It is the description and interpretation of behaviour in context (see Chapter 1). The context in particular needs detailed portrayal and, as Denzin (2001) claims, thick description is not about fact and appearance but about emotions, meanings and intentions of individuals in a specific environment. Thick description is analytical and theoretical and explores the interpretations of experience and the meanings and motives of the participants involved in a study.

Thick description: the experiences of lesbian college coaches

Krane and Barber (2005) studied the experiences of lesbian college coaches with particular reference to the tensions between what they believed was best for the well-being of their athletes and what was best for the coaches' professional well-being. The authors noted that the lesbian sporting environment has been described as 'silent'; thus they stressed the importance of thick description in their study. First, they presented as much of the data as possible through direct quotes to allow the voices of participants to be heard, providing a rich source of information separate from the researchers' interpretations. However, second, noting that such voices needed to be situated within a larger perspective to enhance their meaningfulness, the experiences of the coaches were framed within a social identity perspective. Third, within the findings section of the paper, the coaches clearly articulated the social norms of the environment as well as portraying the cultures of womens' athletics and their own specific athletic departments.

Searching for alternative interpretations

Alternative explanations are interpretations that differ from the initial and main explanations which seemed to be appropriate in the research. Competing explanations or interpretations will then be developed and reviewed to find the one that is most likely to describe or explain the phenomenon. It means that researchers challenge their own initial assumptions and become aware of alternatives.

Seeking alternative explanations: the goals of recreational exercisers, and racial identity development in a bi-racial athlete

Rogers et al. (2008) explored the goals of recreational exercisers through interviewing 11 participants. Although the study focused on achievement goals, the authors clearly identified a rival explanation of the data. This put emphasis on motivations to participate rather than predetermined targets of achievement goals.

Stanley and Robbins (2011) explored racial identity development in a bi-racial athlete and used the Stage-Model Variant Approach as a guiding theoretical framework. Although the study focused on one framework, the authors adopted a rival explanations method whereby alternate theories were also considered as the best fit to the data. Thus social identity theory was adopted as an alternative means of interpretation. The data generated demonstrated a closer fit to the Stage-Model Variant Approach, thus this was the explanatory model that was adopted by the authors.

Reflexivity

Reflexivity refers to a researcher's awareness of themselves and of their relationship with the research and its processes. Qualitative researchers see this concept as significant. Reflexivity is not only used throughout the research but also becomes a means by which to expose and critically reflect on the researchers' own assumptions and show where they are located in culture, time and space, as well as in the research itself. Reflexivity relates to the audit trail in that researchers show how they acquire knowledge and why they interpret it in the way they do. It involves a measure of self-criticism. Reflexivity helps researchers to recognise their own biases in data collection, analysis and writing that might skew the inquiry. It thus enhances trustworthiness.

Reflexivity when doing research in a sports club in rural Canada

Fortune and Mair (2011) discuss the issues emerging from their critical reflection on field research in a sports club in rural Canada. Noting the importanceof locating themselves in the research process, they identified a number ofchallenges:

1 *Role relationships*, specifically with regard to their status as young women, with one of the researchers being a student and the other being a research professor. The relationship between the two researchers and with the participants was reflected on.
2 *Participation*, specifically their decisions on how much or how little to participate in the setting and when to remain in the role of observer.
3 *Performances*: the extent to which the researchers found themselves 'performing' to get closer to participants, to establish trust and generate understanding, and to develop a sense of street credibility.
4 *Personal issues, backgrounds and experiences*, specifically how their past experiences and identities shaped their relationships with participants.
5 *Balance and distance*, in particular the balance between complete distance from participants and going native.

The authors state that their analysis demonstrates how their key findings were partly shaped by their emotional connections to particular people in the sports club and the extent to which their individual selves influenced their data collection and analysis. They were also able to reflect on how their decisions were shaped by each other. As such 'examining our own actions and beliefs through the eyes of another researcher provided us both with an opportunity to reflect critically on research decisions that may otherwise get taken for granted' (p. 480).

The debate between traditionalists and modernists over validity has not been completed. Problems also exist between specific approaches in qualitative research which occasionally differ in the way in which they manage validity or deny its importance. Truth itself is a problematic and not a unitary concept. Whatever criteria qualitative researchers use, or even if they are sceptical of criteriology and feel that validity and reliability are obsolete concepts, they still have to demonstrate that their research is trustworthy and credible.

Summary

- Researchers do not agree on the concepts of validity and reliability
- Some writers suggest that such conventional concepts have no place in qualitative research
- Certain strategies ensure the quality and truth value of the research: member-check, peer-debriefing, triangulation, search for alternative cases and explanations, the audit trail, thick description and reflexivity
- Whatever concepts researchers use or whatever beliefs they adhere to, they should make sure that the research is relevant, believable and truthful

16

Writing Up Qualitative Research

Writing up research findings is an important task for researchers, not only because they want do justice to their work but also because the final report will be in the public domain, to be reviewed by others. There are different outlets for the dissemination of data; each has different styles and conventions. Researchers generally submit their findings to external examiners, to supervisors, to commissioning or funding agencies, to an academic journal for peer review or to a trade (or professional) magazine or newspaper. As Gratton and Jones (2010) point out, writers must take into account the potential readership; there is a clear difference between reports that are written for practitioners, for funding bodies, or for the academic audience.

Practitioners and funders tend to be interested in the results and implications of the research for practice, and less concerned with methodological, philosophical and theoretical issues, while academics see the latter as important and place a high value on detailed accounts of how the data were collected and analysed; they are also keen to witness the researcher's grasp of the relevant literature in the field. For this reason, it is not uncommon that a researcher writes up two reports, one for 'industry' and one for academia.

In all these reports, anonymity and confidentiality are normally essential.

For a PhD thesis or a Masters dissertation, the candidate will have guidelines for presentation, and these should be followed. Although conventions for writing up exist, these guidelines may vary from one institution to another, even within one country. Wolcott (2009) advises researchers to create a style sheet similar to that offered by academic journals to prospective writers, so that consistency in spelling, referencing, headings and other aspects is achieved. Our experience shows that many students lack consistency in style and spelling, and this can negatively impact on the overall impression.

This chapter presents a typical layout for a qualitative research report; however, we advise researchers to check that this conforms to their institution's own conventions. In general, the format of the report *should* match the research design. In a qualitative thesis, the first two chapters, the introduction, which contains the research rationale, the initial literature review and the methodology, set the frame for the research. Readers, reviewers and examiners must be introduced to the research context, to the location of the research in the literature and to the procedures and processes of the study. The bulk of the literature is tied to the emergent themes and is therefore located in the findings chapters, where a dialogue takes place between the researcher's own findings and the literature. This location of the literature marks the qualitative thesis out from the quantitative; the latter is preceded by a lengthy literature review. The structure of the qualitative study thus reflects the inductive reasoning associated with qualitative research.

Writing in the first person

When writing up their dissertation, especially the introduction and methodology chapters, it is better that qualitative researchers write in the first person. As Bateman (2009) comments, routine suppression of the first person prevents authors from taking overt responsibility for their work. By writing in the first person, the author conveys the sense that they are actively involved in the research process, that it has not been conducted in an objective, distanced way, with no personal bias. Researchers should use the first person to describe what they themselves chose to do. For instance, they would not say, when speaking about their own actions, 'the author chose a sample' or 'the researcher used the interview method'. They might write, 'I chose a purposive sample' or 'I collected the data through ...' Geertz (1988) warned over two decades ago against the 'author evacuated text', whilst Charmaz and Mitchell (1996) speak of the 'myth of silent authorship' and encourage the inclusion and presence of the writer in the text. A text without of authorial presence undermines the acknowledgement of the influence of the researcher on the research process by qualitative researchers. Writing in the first person is also more engaging; it carries more immediacy and resonance for the reader. It sounds pompous and dull when writers state 'the researcher has found ... the author does ... the writer considers ...' (Holloway and Wheeler, 2010). It is important, however, that the first person is not overused, and that the dissertation doesn't descend into anecdotal or unsubstantiated musings.

However, this is not a universally accepted view, and students and researchers should check policy with their departments and publishers. As Wolcott observes:

> Because the researcher's role is ordinarily an integral part of reporting qualitative work, I write my descriptive accounts in the first person. I urge that others do (or in some cases, be allowed to do) the same. I recognise that there are still a few

academics and academic editors on the loose who insist that scholarly work be reported in the third person. I think the practice reflects a belief that impersonal language intensifies an author's stronghold on objective truth.

Those who do not wish to use the first person might choose the passive form; for instance, 'a purposive sample was chosen'. However, this distances the researcher from the project, and conveys an abstention from authority. (2009: 17)

Using the first person: learning the social norms of playing with injury

Malcom's (2006) investigation of the process by which novice athletes learned the social norms of ignoring injuries and playing through pain demonstrates the use of the first person in the methods and discussion sections of the article. For example, when discussing the strategy of downplaying injuries, she reported her own experiences, noting that 'I was acting as first base coach during one game in 1996 and Trisha hit a single. As she stood on first base, Trisha complained to me that her finger hurt and I did not respond to her. Instead I consciously and deliberately ignored her complaint. In my mind, Trisha was not acting appropriately' (p. 505). A further example explored the reactions to injury: 'often, their words were harsh and their body language indicated a heightened state of irritation and frustration. In one example, Becca was complaining that her hands hurt. I realised that Becca's pain was caused by the fact that she kept hitting the ball off the end of the bat' (p. 506).

The format of the report

The structure of a qualitative report is often organised in the following sequence, though there may, as indicated previously, be departmental and institutional differences in advice given to students, which should be considered:

- Title page
- Abstract
- Table of contents
- List of tables and figures (if appropriate)
- Acknowledgement and dedication
- Introduction

  o Background and rationale (justification) for the study, including its aim
  o Initial literature review (or overview of the literature)

- Methodology and research design

  o Description and justification of methods
  o The sample and the setting

- ○ Specific techniques and procedures (such as interviewing or observation)
- ○ Data analysis
- ○ Trustworthiness (or validity)
- ○ Entry issues and ethical considerations
- ○ Limitations

- Findings/results and discussion

  - ○ This takes the form of several chapters where the primary research findings are linked with the literature, and where theoretical implications are drawn

- Conclusion and implications
- Reflections on the research
- References
- Appendices

Qualitative writing may differ substantially from a quantitative report, although commonalities exist. The main distinction lies in the length of the literature review (see Chapter 4) and of the findings chapters. The findings and discussion are the most important elements of the final write-up. The individual elements of the report are now considered below.

Title page

The title page in a dissertation or thesis contains the title, the name of the researcher, the year and the name of the educational institution at which the student was enrolled. There is generally a pro forma for the title page at most universities.

The title of the dissertation is important as it acts as the main signpost for the reader on what to expect and as the main guide in terms of information collection as well as the presentation and content of the dissertation. The title needs to be specific and indicate the core of the research; a vague title does not stimulate the interest of the reader. It should reflect the aim of the research, though students should not repeat the aim word for word in the title.

Examples of titles

Real cyclists don't race: informal affiliations of the weekend warrior (O'Connor and Brown, 2007)

'If you let me play': Young girls' insider-other narratives of sport (Cooky and McDonald, 2005)

Seeing is believing: telling the 'inside story' of a beginning Masters athlete through film (Kluge et al., 2010)

The title (and abstract) of a study is the first and most immediate contact the reader has with the research, and its impact on judging and receiving the work is high. We argue for a concise but informative title which sounds interesting and engaging. The title is initially a working title; it may change as the research develops, in order to encompass emergent ideas. Thus the final submission may well have a different title, although the general focus of the dissertation should remain the same. It is important then that the title is reviewed at the end of writing to make sure that it captures the essence of the study (though universities have rules about the last date of final title submission).

As the above examples indicate, writers often use explanatory subtitles. Silverman (2005), for instance, prefers two-part titles. Punch (2006) meanwhile advises that the title should not be long but contain all essential information. Novice researchers sometimes include unnecessary redundancies in the title such as 'A study of ...' and 'Aspects of ...' or 'Inquiry', 'Analysis' and 'Investigation'. These clutter up the title.

Abstract

This is a brief summary of about 250–300 words (a maximum of one side of A4), which provides the reader with a quick overview of the research question and aim, the methods adopted and the main findings of the study. It might include the implications of the study in one or two succinct sentences. The abstract will normally be written last, but it appears at the beginning of the dissertation (on the page after the title and before the table of contents) to enable a potential reader to make a decision as to whether the content is likely to be of interest. Writers should keep to the word limit specified and be selective about the content.

There follow two examples of an abstract, one for a journal article and one for a thesis. The abstract for a thesis or dissertation is generally a little longer than that for an article.

Example of an abstract for an article (Russell, 2004)

On versus off the pitch: the transiency of body satisfaction among female rugby players, cricketers and netballers

In this study, I investigated the development of body satisfaction among women rugby players, cricketers and netballers. I also sought to assess the impact of sport participation on both athletic and 'feminine' identity.

(Continued)

(Continued)

Semi-structured interviews were conducted with ten rugby players, ten cricketers and ten netballers. The interviews focused on the experience of playing sport and the impact sport had made on respondents' perceptions. Using Interpretative Phenomenological Analysis to explore the interview data, it was found that, although sport participation did lead to positive perceptions of their bodies, this effect was transient. Once placed in a social environment, body satisfaction decreased and women's perceptions of their bodies changed because of a perceived demand to conform to socially accepted and expected norms of (heterosexual) physical attractiveness. Fear of being perceived as lesbian and the perceived naturalness of body concern were also identified.

Example of an abstract for a PhD thesis (Gellweiler, 2011)

The staging of many sport events, ranging from small to mega-events, increasingly rely on the availability of a workforce of unpaid helpers. Whilst much research has been carried out in the past regarding the reason why people decide to volunteer at sport events, little is known about how this type of volunteering is experienced by the individual. Adopting an experiential focus, this study contributes to the existing body of knowledge and enhances the understanding of this particular form of volunteering by exploring the question – *What is it like to be a sport event volunteer?*

Using different strands of the concept and theory of role to serve as parameters for this study, the lived experiences of volunteers who assisted at the World Firefighters Games 2008 are analysed and discussed. The research approach that was adopted for this study draws from the work of Hans-Georg Gadamer in the form of hermeneutic phenomenology which is an interpretative approach towards collecting and analysing data about a specific phenomenon. Incorporating the hermeneutic circle that advocates the idea that understanding of a phenomenon is co-created by both the researcher and the research participants, hermeneutic phenomenology is concerned with exploring rather than merely describing contextual aspects and structures of lived experiences.

A total of 18 semi-structured interviews involving volunteers who helped with the World Firefighters Games 2008 in Liverpool were conducted. The interviews were audio-recorded and transcribed verbatim. Using the approach of van Manen towards analysing the collected data, a number of themes and sub-themes emerged which are presented in the thesis in a manner that reflects the nature of the hermeneutic circle.

Besides providing a working definition of the term – *sport event volunteering* – the findings of the study critically evaluate the meaning that the volunteers attach to the role and how they make sense of their role as helpers involved in staging large sporting events. The interpretation of the collected data suggests that the enactment of the volunteer role is informed

by individuals' expectations and needs, e.g. with regards to role alloca-
tion, trust, recognition and reciprocity, and the experience of anti-climax
and loss after their volunteer engagement has come to an end. Furthermore, the critical synthesis of how the individual manages his/her volunteer
role suggests that sport event volunteers can be understood as *bricoleurs*
who craft rather than merely take and perform this particular role.

Beside contributing to existing research on sport-event volunteering with these findings and by identifying further research avenues
relating to sport event volunteering that can be explored in future, the
findings of these studies might inform the work of practitioners in the
respective research fields.

The abstract is the 'public face' of the research as it appears on databases,
websites and in abstract books, so it is of major importance in the research.
Thus care should be taken with writing style and content.

Acknowledgement and dedication

Acknowledgement of others' help is important. Traditionally all researchers
use this section to give credit to those who supported, advised or supervised the research, and they also acknowledge the input of participants.
Often the writing is dedicated to particular individuals such as parents or
spouses. It is a personal decision as to whether or not to dedicate the dissertation in this way.

Table of contents

Academic research reports have a table of contents before its main chapters
begin. It cannot be finished before the whole project is finalised and written.
This gives the reader the first view of how the dissertation is structured. It
should list sequentially the chapters and the major sub-divisions of chapters,
each identified by a heading and located by a page number. The precise
structure will need to be tailored to the particular dissertation. Care must be
taken to make sure that the numbers in this section and in the text correlate,
as students often make mistakes in this area.

A list of tables and a list of figures may follow this section of the dissertation,
if required, though not many of these will be used by the qualitative researcher.
A list of abbreviations or acronyms, or a glossary of terms employed and written in alphabetical order, is also useful. In the text itself, terms should be
written in full the first time they are mentioned, with the abbreviations in
brackets. Subsequently, abbreviations can be used.

Introduction

Background and rationale

In the introduction the writer sets the scene for the study and informs the audience about the research topic. The introduction places the research in context and details the aim of the research – the overall purpose of the project. Some institutions will ask students to choose an aim *and* several objectives, though this is felt to be rather prescriptive for qualitative research. In case students are asked to provide objectives, a short definition is offered below. The research aim is a general statement of what is to be achieved overall – an aspiration of the study – whereas the objectives identify the key tasks that need to be undertaken (Gratton and Jones, 2010), i.e. the steps that lead to the aim. Each objective can stand alone as a completely researchable unit, though the combined results of each objective should present the solution to the aim. If objectives are felt to be necessary, it is usually advised that between four and six are provided.

Aim and objectives: the lived experiences of sport event volunteers

'Looking through the kaleidoscope: perspectives on the lived experiences of sport event volunteering' (Gellweiler, 2011)

Aim

To explore the lived experience of sport-event volunteering from a role perspective in order to contribute to a better understanding of this form of volunteering.

Objectives

1 To develop a working definition of sport-event volunteering;
2 To discover and critically evaluate what meanings sport-event volunteers attach to and how they make sense of their role as helpers involved in staging large sporting events; and
3 To critically synthesise how this role is managed by the individual volunteer.

The second part of the introduction concerns the rationale for the research. Researchers need to justify the chosen topic, and to state its relevance. It is useful for the researcher to ask the 'So what?' question, as this will be covered in the viva. Writers explain why they have become interested in the question, how their project relates to the general topic area and what gap in knowledge might be filled by the new research. Implications for practice and policy will also be drawn out.

Justifying the study: the behaviour and perceptions of mixed-martial arts spectators

MacIntosh and Crow (2011) justified their research into the behaviour and perceptions of mixed-martial arts spectators at a live event by suggesting that understanding the sport spectator is key to successfully positioning the (MMA) brand within a given sponsorship context. In light of the rise of and interest in MMA, exploring sport spectator perceptions, opinions and behaviour is important for informing marketing practices.

Initial literature review

This section can stand on its own as a separate chapter, or it can become an integral part of the introduction. Though the literature in qualitative studies has a different place from that in quantitative research (see Chapter 4), the researcher must nevertheless show early on what relevant research in the *general* area of the study has been conducted. This helps the reader to appreciate how the research fills a gap in knowledge, and serves to underscore the academic relevance of the research. The initial review of the key literature should identify how current research fits in with the existing state of knowledge or understanding of the topic. Reference to the methods used in previous research must also be made. By the end of the introductory section, the reader should be in no doubt that qualitative research, in the form suggested by the researcher, was most appropriate to meet the research aim.

However, it is neither necessary in qualitative reports to explore every piece of known research in the field at the start of the study, nor to give a critical review of *all* the literature but just that of the main foundational studies, those which are specifically relevant, and up-to-date recent research (see Chapter 4).

Methodology and research design

The methodology chapter includes many sections, such as research design and methodology, the methods, including data collection, sampling, detailed interviewing or observation procedures as well as a description of the data analysis. In qualitative research, the methodology is of particular interest because the researcher is the main research tool and has to make explicit the path of the research, so that the reader is able to follow his/her decision trail. Hence the methodology section is often longer than the equivalent in a quantitative study.

Description and justification of methodological approach

The research design includes the methodology adopted and the reasons and justification for it. Researchers should also explain the fit between the research question and the methodology.

The sample and setting

The sample is described in detail. The writer provides a profile of participants: who they were, how many were chosen and the reasons for the choice. Researchers tell the reader how they obtained their sample and portray the setting in which the study took place. If there is theoretical sampling, this must also be explained.

Writing about the sample: physical activity in African-American women

In their study on physical activity in African-American women, Harley et al. (2009) included the following information on sampling in their methods section:

1 *Sampling method*: criterion sampling (African-American women between 25 and 45 with a commitment to physical activity).
2 *Recruitment of participants*: the sample was recruited through gate-keepers to African-American sorority alumni associations, who provided a list of potential participants.
3 *Screening*: participants were screened using the criteria outlined above.
4 *Justification of sample size* of 15 interviewees: the data were considered to lead to theoretical saturation.
5 *Characteristics of participants*: age, body mass index, levels of physical activity and commitment to physical activity.

Specific techniques and procedures

In this section, researchers describe the procedures they used, such as interviewing, observation or focus groups. The outline should not be a general essay on procedures but a step-by-step description of the work in hand so that the reader can follow it closely. Enough detail must be given so that a reader might draw inspiration from the study. Lack of instruction and advice given to the reader as to how the subject was approached generally and analysed specifically leads to a weak dissertation, and to an average or below average mark. It is also expected that reference to relevant research texts is made.

Data analysis

The data analysis needs to be explained and should include the ways in which data were coded and categorised and how theoretical constructs were generated from the data, how thematic analysis was carried out, or how the more holistic analysis in phenomenology proceeded. It is useful, and essential in dissertations or theses, to give examples from the study. A detailed account of the chosen type of analysis is required. If computer analysis was used, this should be stated and justified.

Trustworthiness

This section will demonstrate how the researcher ensured the validity (trustworthiness) of the research (see Chapter 15).

Entry issues and ethical considerations

It must be stated how the participants were approached, for instance whether researchers advertised on a notice board or approached the potential participants personally. How did researchers gain permission from gatekeepers (those in the position of power to grant access to the setting)?

Importantly, researchers should make explicit how the ethical principles were followed in the study, and how the participants' rights were protected. To have permission from ethics committees might be essential, but this does not necessarily ensure that the researcher behaves ethically. The integrity of any research depends not only on its rigour but also on its ethical adequacy. Ethical issues are many and varied but any research requires a consideration of such issues in order to ensure the protection of the participants, especially if the research involves sensitive or vulnerable groups, such as children, or involves experimental research designs.

Findings and discussion

Researchers can choose to separate their findings and discussion, but this is not very readable or engaging; therefore the findings and discussion are often integrated. Some writers start their findings section or chapter with a diagrammatic portrayal of major research themes, followed by a brief discussion of each theme. Findings are then often presented under thematic headings and discussed in the light of related literature. However, postgraduate students should never forget that they have the freedom and flexibility to change the structure as long as it has inner logic.

Showing themes: an ethnography of long-distance runners

The following figure is a diagrammatic portrait of one of the main themes to emerge from Shipway's (2010) ethnographic study of long-distance runners: *A Desire for a Healthy Lifestyle.*

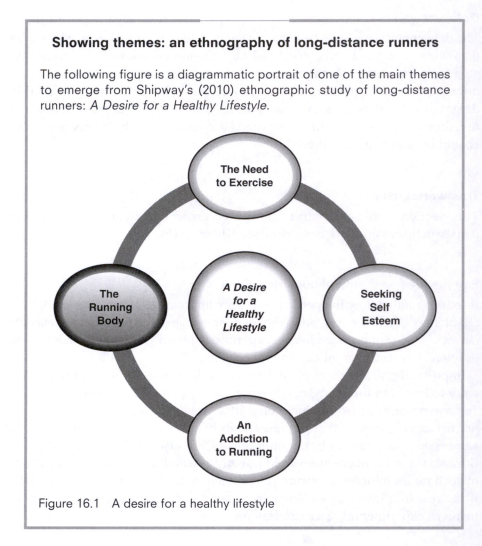

Figure 16.1   A desire for a healthy lifestyle

In each chapter or section, the collected data are discussed first: the researcher's own data have primacy. The relevant literature is integrated into the discussion where it fits best and serves as additional evidence for the particular category or as a challenge to the findings of the researcher. A dialogue with the literature needs to be ongoing. Researchers should ask themselves the following questions when writing up the findings: Do their findings confirm or contradict the literature? Does their research make an original contribution to the literature?

The use of quotes from participants

Direct, verbatim quotes from interviews or excerpts from the field-notes are inserted in the findings section or chapter at an appropriate place to show some (not all) of the data from which the results emerged. Quotes help the reader to judge how the themes were derived from the data and help to establish credibility. Researchers must ensure that the quotes are directly connected with the themes they seek to illustrate. Quotes show that the ideas discussed are based in the data. Quotes are selected from the mass of data collected as faithful and effective indicators of the theme being presented. When deciding which quotes to use to illustrate a point, the researcher must ensure that there is a match between the data and the analytic point they are making. As Corden and Sainsbury (2006: 98) point out, quotes help to 'clarify the links between data, interpretation and conclusions'. They also note that participants value the inclusion of their own words as they feel their voices have been heard and represented. Researchers must think carefully about ethical issues when using quotes such as, for instance, protecting the identity of participants in a study with an easily identifiable population.

There are two common flaws in presenting qualitative findings. First, there is a tendency to simply summarise what participants have said without illustrating with quotations. This makes the research account less engaging to read, as quotations bring the account to life. On the other hand, a common flaw is linked to a lack of analysis. Students often give a collection of lengthy quotes without synthesis or interpretation. This is not analysis. Researchers have to develop their theoretical ideas and interpretations, which they illustrate with relevant quotes from the participants. Researchers need to substantiate and give evidence for all firm claims that they make but they also interpret and make meaning from the stories of their participants.

Conclusion and implications

Researchers should not under-estimate the importance of well-crafted arguments; students in particular often pay inadequate attention to the conclusion (Gratton and Jones, 2010). The conclusion should include at least three sections. First, it should offer a summary of the main themes, and the primary research findings should be set in the context of the latest literature, but not in great detail as this has been covered in the discussion section. The original research aim should be revisited at this stage so that the success of the research in achieving its goal can be judged. Some researchers tend to start new arguments, but nothing new can be developed in the conclusion.

Second, researchers can make implications and recommendations for practice but should not list them. Recommendations are based *directly* on the findings of the study which has just been completed; all too often they are not linked sufficiently to the findings, or they are based on the work of other researchers. It might be useful to consider the following questions when writing this section: which sector or sectors can learn from your findings? What changes can be made as a result of your findings? What new practices can be introduced because of what you have discovered? Or what aspects of good practice should the sector continue with? Often, though not always, the research was conducted in the first place in order to benefit industry or society in some way.

Making recommendations for practice: performance leadership and management in elite sport

Fletcher and Arnold (2011) investigated performance leadership and management in elite sport. They interviewed 13 national performance directors of Olympic sports to explore best practice for preparing Olympic teams. They were able to conclude their paper by identifying specific recommendations to be made. These were the need for leaders and managers to identify and disseminate their vision; to optimise their resources and processes; to challenge and support their people; and to transform individuals' attitudes and group cohesion. To achieve the above, they concluded that national performance directors would need to develop their knowledge and competencies across all these domains of practice.

Third, it is conventional to include a measure of reflection and self-criticism in this chapter or section, where researchers take a critical stance to their study. They demonstrate how the research could be improved, extended or illuminated from another angle. At this stage they might point to its limitations and their own biases, which they might not have made explicit in the main body of the study, and describe some of the problems they encountered. Finally, suggestions for further research on the topic are made. The question researchers ask is: Where do we go from here?

Identifying further research: the constraints to downhill skiing among Chinese-Canadians and Anglo-Canadians

Hudson et al. (2010) explored the constraints to downhill skiing among Chinese-Canadians and Anglo-Canadians using interviews and focus groups. They concluded that there was a strong influence of culture as a constraining influence and they identified a number of additional barriers not present in the literature. The authors argued in their conclusion that this allowed a greater understanding of the development of a person's preference for participation in such activities. They recommended the need for further analysis of the role of both culture and ethnicity in the understanding of constraints. Finally they outlined the limitations to their study, notably the difficulty in collecting and analysing data across different cultures and their study's focus on winter sports only.

Referencing

The terms 'references' and 'bibliography' are often used interchangeably, and there is often confusion over which heading writers should use. Strictly speaking, a reference list includes all works cited in the text, whereas a bibliography refers to wider reading undertaken but not cited (Gratton and Jones, 2010). Writers can create two sections, or Wolcott (2009) advises that a heading 'references and select bibliography' be used for both categories. Many researchers just have a list of references.

It is critical that researchers reference any work that they cite accurately, giving a detailed description of the source from which they obtained their information. From the very early stages, researchers will need to be organised and keep an *accurate* record. The following simple rules should be adhered to:

- always keep a record of what you have read;
- always keep a full bibliographical reference, in the correct form, of everything that you read, including the page numbers;
- if you copy a quotation into your notes, do so fully and without abbreviations. *Check it thoroughly* and remember to include the page number in your notes and give it when you quote directly from a book or article; and
- compare the references in the text with the selected bibliography and make sure that every reference is included.

For academic studies the Harvard system of referencing is generally used, but the author must always check the guidelines beforehand to save time later on in the process. Sloppy references are often the cause of criticism: we sometimes find that student referencing is incomplete or insufficient, and this has a negative impact on examiners, readers or on the assessment of the study.

Appendices

The appendices (plural of appendix) are placed at the very end of the study after the references in the order in which they appear in the chronology of the study. The attention of the reader should be drawn to the content of the appendices at the relevant parts of the dissertation. The appendices are not a dumping ground, however, for material which researchers couldn't find a place for in the main body. They may contain background information or data that might be important for further reference but is not directly related to the main thrust of the argument. Information of *direct* relevance to the written text must be included in the main body of the study.

Examples of appendices include: an interview guide, an interview transcript, extracts from field-notes, a formal letter to participants requesting their help and a letter of approval from the ethics committee.

Checklist before submission

Before submission, the following checklist, modified from that produced by Gratton and Jones (2010), can be used to identify omissions and areas for improvement.

About your dissertation

- Does the title clearly indicate the nature of the study?
- Does your abstract give the reader a clear idea of what is in the document? Have you ensured that it gives precise, but short, details about the findings?
- Is your table of contents well structured and does it give a picture of what's included?

Focus and justification

- Have you introduced your dissertation adequately – to set the scene?
- Do you have you a clear focus?
- Have you got a clearly constructed and suitable aim?
- What is the rationale behind your dissertation? Why is it important that the research has been undertaken? Who are the potential readers?
- Why should the reader read your piece of work? Is it saying something worthwhile?

Literature

- Have you managed to identify and access the work of key writers in your particular area?
- How up-to-date are your references?
- Is there an initial overview that demonstrates the gap in knowledge?
- Have you used a variety of sources or are you over reliant upon a certain author(s)?
- Do you adopt a critical approach to the literature?
- Have you identified how your dissertation relates to what has been done before?

Methodology

- Have you explained the rationale behind your chosen approach?
- Are your research methods the most appropriate given your aim?
- Does the researcher state how he or she gained access to the participants?
- Were the rights of participants safeguarded (including their right to withdraw from the study)?
- Are issues of anonymity and confidentiality discussed in relation to the study?
- Are issues of power taken into account?
- If vulnerable clients are included in the sample, is this inclusion justified?
- Are major ethical issues discussed?
- Has the study been approved by ethics committees and review boards?

- Does the researcher explain the trustworthiness (validity) of the study?
- How are the data collected, transcribed and stored?
- Is the data analysis systematic and detailed? Any limitations? Anything you might have done differently?

Findings and discussion

- Are your findings clearly presented?
- Do you interpret your data or merely describe? Are you critical?
- In the discussion, do you tie your emergent findings to the literature?
- Are your arguments coherent, logical and sound?
- Is the presentation of the findings appropriate for a qualitative approach?

Conclusions and recommendations

- Do you return to your research aim?
- Do the conclusions come directly from the data?
- Are implications for practice drawn out? Do they emerge directly from the findings of the study?
- In evaluating your own progress and dissertation outcomes, what limitations would you identify?
- Do you make recommendations for future research?

General presentation

- Is your content logically structured?
- Is the work well presented?
- Have you stayed within the word limit?
- Have you made appropriate use of supportive materials to enhance presentation, i.e. graphs, tables, illustrations?
- Have you conducted a thorough read through, to eliminate careless spelling and typos, poor grammar and poor sentence construction?
- Are you writing in the most appropriate tense?
- Is your writing too informal?
- Do you link your various chapters and make use of signposting to help the reader?
- Do you set out your intentions clearly in your introduction?
- Have you set out your references with the required detail and in the recommended format?
- Have you acknowledged all sources used? Have you made appropriate use of appendices? Are there any unnecessary appendices?

Telling the tale: creativity and originality

In a qualitative report, writers tell a story which should be vivid and interesting as well as credible to the reader. This sometimes means writing and rewriting drafts until a storyline can be discerned clearly. The communicative element is of special importance in the presentation of qualitative research so it can make an impact on its readers and remind them that the participants are 'real' people. Holloway (2005: 282) reminds researchers that scientific writing need not be incomprehensible but should capture the audience's attention, have immediacy and present a good story. The research account needs to be evocative, to resonate; therefore it is important to pay attention to writing style, to hone creative skills

To achieve resonance, researchers need to cultivate their creative writing skills. Caulley (2008) argues, however, that many qualitative research accounts are boring to read, and advocates the use by qualitative researchers of creative non-fiction techniques to make their reports 'vivid and vital' (p. 424). The first paragraph is crucial in attracting and maintaining the reader's interest, as is the title, which should stimulate curiosity if it is well crafted. The use of the first person is also recommended, as it carries the immediacy of an eye-witness account. Every paragraph of the report should be scrutinised for fluency of argument and style, in the same painstaking way that a novelist would approach their writing. Finally, 'closings are just as important as openings' (p. 447); a common flaw of the conclusion of research reports is that they are rushed, as though the researcher ran out of time and energy. Therefore time must be left to craft a well-written and engaging conclusion.

Throughout the write-up it is important to consider the style of communication. The qualitative account should not just be a conventional write-up but also a good story with elements of tension and persuasion. This is what makes it distinct from other types of research.

The research reports we have discussed in this chapter follow fairly conventional lines, albeit with some flexibility. Some qualitative studies, however, include elements of performance art, films or poetry. Lately students, in particular, aim for presenting more innovative forms of presenting their research; for instance we have seen films or videos based on some of the writing and which integrate scholarly and creative work. Indeed this could be very useful in the sports and exercise arena, as pointed out by Douglas and Carless (2008) who describe how performance has the potential to affect an audience emotionally, how it provides fresh appreciation of a study: 'we had seen our academic work connecting with others, taking on something, a life of its own perhaps, in a way that neither of us had thought possible' (online). Sparkes and Douglas (2007) add that the responses of students who have used the technique of poetic representation have been positive particularly in allowing them to think about and understand topics differently.

Sparkes and Douglas (2007) suggest that 'as part of the emergence of new writing practices in the social sciences, qualitative researchers have begun to harness the potential of poetic representations as a means of analysing social worlds and communicating their findings to others' (p. 170). In their study of the motivations of elite female golfers, Sparkes and Douglas offer a useful guide to students as to how to produce a poetic representation of data. They include a section of a transcript in the paper and show how a poem was created by drawing directly from the data. An excerpt from the poem is presented below:

My Dad

Dad was a keen golfer

Seemed the natural thing to do

My Dad was out playing golf

And that's what I wanted to do

I got a little club cut down.

I would have been bout four

I remembered being chuffed to bits

Playing 3 holes 6 then 9

I disliked hitting bad shots

Expected all to be good

I had a wicked temper,

So my Dad – he sent me home.

Source: Sparkes and Douglas (2007: 178)

Sparkes and Douglas reflect that producing effective poetic representations is not an easy task. Additionally, not all data sets lend themselves to the creation of poetic forms.

Publishing and presenting the research

If the findings are significant, the researcher has the responsibility to disseminate them to a wider group. Burnard (2004) notes that the research project is not properly finished until the findings have been published and Evans (2008: 1) even adds that 'research that is not written up is wasted'. The most traditional way of disseminating findings is through books and journal articles. Keen and Todres (2007) describe some of the more non-traditional forms of dissemination, which might include theatrical performances, using art and photographs, dance and poetry.

> ### Performing research: the nature of sport fandom
>
> Parry and Eastwood (2010) explored the nature of contemporary sport fandom through an interactive performance at a conference. Parry's presentation involved audience participation and the use of props such as flags, hats and scarves. These were distributed to those delegates who attended Parry's presentation. Delegates were encouraged to act out and experience the world of the sports fan. This mode of dissemination was considered to be more instructive than a traditional oral presentation.

Books

Sometimes researchers produce a book based on their thesis or a chapter in an edited book. Most publishers have guidelines for writing book proposals that the researcher can use. The proposal goes to an editorial board which decides whether the book is worth publishing, in their view, and commercially viable. Commercial considerations are the main concern of publishers, and these depend on the general appeal of the piece of research. Editors are, of course, also concerned about the quality of the content and the ability of the researcher to write clearly and in an accessible style.

Articles

More often, students who have carried out research publish an article in a professional or academic journal, often with their supervisor. The length and style of the article will depend on the type of journal. Articles have higher standing in research circles than chapters in books because they are refereed by experts in the field. For articles that focus on methodological issues, the two journals *Qualitative Research* and *Qualitative Inquiry* are useful. *Qualitative Research* is published in Britain while *Qualitative Inquiry* is published in the USA. There are a number of sports journals which accept qualitative research articles such as *Qualitative Research in Sport, Exercise and Health*, *Sociology of Sport Journal*, *International Review of Sport Sociology* and many more.

Journals that are intended to assist practitioners advocate language that is more accessible for professionals. In these journals one can find articles which describe findings and address the implications of these findings for practice. Some articles are meant for lay readers. Although most researchers do not write for this readership, whilst occasionally an article in a specialist magazine could actually help members of a group or the general population.

All students carrying out PhD or MPhil and even MA/MSc research should attempt writing articles; some universities encourage this during the process of the research, whilst others suggest writing after completion of the research degree. There is an academic tradition that candidates publish with their supervisors who, of course, have had an input in the research and will help in refining the article, critiquing it and possibly writing sections for it. Nevertheless, the student's name should be first on the list of authors.

Summary

The main points to remember when writing up research are listed below:

- Qualitative research provides flexibility for writing research accounts
- The structure of a qualitative report might be different from that of a quantitative study
- Ethical issues and access must be addressed
- The findings and discussion are the major part of the study in which the literature is integrated
- Reports in qualitative health research need a strong conclusion with implications for the profession and/or clinical practice directly based on the findings
- The research should be presented in an interesting way which communicates with the reader
- To be of use in practical terms, the research needs to be disseminated

Glossary

Abstract: A short summary of the research including research topic, methods, aim, procedures such as sampling, data sources, data collection and analysis, and findings and implications.

Aide mémoire (or aide memoir): Words or phrases to remind researchers of the focus or the agenda of the research during in-depth interviewing.

Assumption: A belief, conjecture or preconception of the researcher based on a hunch or experience which has not been verified by evidence.

Audit trail: A detailed description of all the steps taken by the researcher in the research.

Authenticity: A term used to show that the findings of a research project are authentic and represent the participants' perspectives.

Autoethnography: An ethnographic approach where writers or researchers explore their own experiences which then become the focus of the research.

Bias: A predisposition, inclination or even distortion in the processing of research (a problematic concept rooted in quantitative research).

Bracketing (in phenomenology)*:* A process by which researchers set aside their assumptions about the phenomenon under study so that they can understand the phenomenon from the inside.

CAQDAS: Computer aided/assisted qualitative data analysis software.

Case study: Research on a unit of study (an individual, a group, an event) with clear boundaries.

Category: A group of concepts – a unit of analysis – which shares traits and is given a label by the researcher.

Causality: A link between cause and effect – where the cause generates the effect.

Coding (in qualitative analysis): Examining and breaking down the data into pieces of text and naming them.

Concept: An abstract idea produced by specific instances.

Confidentiality: A principle in ethics where the communication between researcher and participants is kept private and not disclosed under the name of the participant (but see confidentiality in research).

Constant comparison (in grounded theory): A technique in data collection and analysis where incoming data are compared with those previously collected.

Construct: A construct is built on concepts or categories and has a high level of abstraction and theory.

Constructionism (social constructionism): A belief or supposition that human beings create their own social reality, and that the social world cannot exist independently of human beings.

Contextualisation: Researchers locate people, data and processes in their specific social context.

Context sensitivity: An awareness of context

Core category (in grounded theory): A central phenomenon which links or integrates all other categories in the research.

Criterion (pl. criteria): A standard by which something is judged.

Critical theory: The view that people can critically evaluate social phenomena and change society in order to become emancipated. It has its origin in Marxism.

Data (plural but often used as singular): The information collected by researchers which they analyse to draw their findings and conclusions.

Data analysis: Organisation, reduction and transformation of the gathered data.

Deductive reasoning: Reasoning that proceeds from general principles to explain specific cases.

Delimitations: The boundaries of the research showing what is included or excluded.

Description: A detailed account of the features of a phenomenon, setting or situation.

Design (research design): The plan of the research, including strategies and procedures for sampling, data collection and analysis.

Deviant case: An occurrence or instance that is contrary to what has been found in the rest of the data; an example where some elements of the data do not fit into the working propositions or initial explanations of the researcher.

Emic perspective: The 'insider's' point of view which is culture-bound (see also *etic perspective*), a term used specifically in anthropology.

Epistemology: The theory of knowledge, an area of philosophy concerned with the nature of human knowledge.

Ethnography: Anthropological (or sociological) research concerned with a description of a culture or group and its members' experiences and interpretations. An ethnography is the completed product of ethnographic research.

Etic perspective: The outsider's point of view, the perspective of the observer or researcher (see also *emic perspective*).

Exclusion criteria (singular: criterion): Conditions/factors/people that are excluded on the selection of sample.

Exhaustive description (in phenomenology): Writing that is comprehensive and captures the participants' experience in depth and exhaustively.

External validity: See *generalisability*.

Field: The general area and/or the setting of the research.

Field-notes: Notes and records made by the researcher from observations in the field.

Fieldwork (initially a term from anthropology): The collection of data 'in the field' by observation, interviewing, etc., outside the laboratory or library.

Focus group: A group of individuals with experience of a particular phenomenon who provide information about it.

Gatekeepers: People who have the power to allow or restrict access to an organisation, a setting, or participants for research.

Generalisability: The extent to which the findings of a qualitative study can be generalised, that is, applied to other settings or situations.

Grounded theory: A research approach which generates theory from the data through constant comparison, initially developed by Strauss and Glaser.

Hermeneutics: A phenomenological research approach which focuses on the interpretation and meaning of text rather than the description of a phenomenon.

Hypothesis: An assumption, theory or tentative statement based on limited evidence of a relationship between variables which can be tested, verified or falsified.

Idiographic methods: An approach to knowledge where methods focus on the unique rather than the general. These differ from *nomothetic methods* that seek law-like generalities subsuming individual cases.

Immersion: The process whereby researchers are engaged and involved in the field.

Inclusion criteria (singular: criterion): Factors or conditions that are taken into account or will be met in the choice of sample (see also *exclusion criteria*).

Induction: A reasoning process in which researchers move from specific instances to the general.

Informant: An individual who, as a member of the group under study, participates in the research and helps the researcher to interpret the culture of the group (see also *key informant*).

Informed consent: A voluntary agreement of participants to take part in a study after they have been informed of and understand its nature and aim.

Interviewer effect (also observer effect): The effect of the researcher's (interviewer's or observer's) presence on the research.

Interview guide: An array of questions which might be used flexibly in in-depth interviews. (Not 'interview schedule' as in quantitative research.)

In vivo code: A verbatim term from participants (see *grounded theory*).

Iteration: Repetitive movement between parts of the research text and the whole, between raw data and analysed data.

Key informant: (in ethnography): A member of a culture or group who is an expert on its customs and rules.

Limitations: Restrictions in the scope of the research.

Member-check: Feedback from participants and verification of their perspectives.

Memoing: Records and notes from the field of varying degrees of abstraction.

Method: Strategy for collecting, analysing and interpreting data.

Methodology: The framework of theories and principles on which methods and research strategies are based.

Narrative: The account of experiences and related events.

Nomothetic: Having law-like generalities, tendency to generalise (see also *idiographic methods*).

Objectivity: A neutral and unbiased stance, not distorted by feelings or personal assumptions, and free from individual perceptions.

Ontology: A branch of philosophy concerning the nature of being, related to assumptions about reality and existence.

Paradigm: A theoretical framework (pattern, model) to reality recognised by a community of scholars. A position that provides the researcher with a set of principles to guide the research.

Participant: A person who takes part in qualitative research.

Participant observation: Observation in which researchers/observers participate in the setting they study.

Phenomenon: The central occurrence, event or experience to be researched (see *phenomenology*).

Phenomenology: A philosophical approach which explores the study of consciousness. In research it explores the meaning of individuals' lived experience through their own description.

Pilot study: A small-scale trial run or feasibility study of research (not usual in qualitative research).

Positivism: A philosophical approach to scientific methods which aims to find general laws and regularities (oriented towards cause and effect) based on the methods of the natural sciences.

Premature closure: Arriving too early at an explanation before the research is fully analysed.

Progressive focusing: Starting with broad questions which become gradually more specific in the research.

Pseudonym: Fictitious name given to participants to keep their anonymity.

Purposive (or purposeful) sampling: A sample chosen by certain criteria relevant to the research question.

CAQDAS: Computer assisted qualitative data analysis.

Raw data: Unanalysed data.

Reflexivity: Reflecting on and critically examining one's own position and influence in the research.

Research account: A written record or report of a research study.

Reliability: Consistency of a research tool.

Research aim: The statement by researchers of what they want to achieve, related to the research question.

Research question: A statement which identifies the problem or question that guides a study.

Rigour: Accuracy and truthfulness.

Saturation: A state where no new data of importance to the specific study and developing theory emerge.

Serendipity: An unexpected discovery and a pleasant surprise.

Storyline: The plot of a story.

Subjectivity: A personal and individual perspective influenced by one's own background and assumptions based on experience.

Symbolic interactionism: An interpretive approach in sociology that focuses on meaning in interaction, particularly language and signals.

Tacit knowledge: Informal or implicit knowledge often unrecognised and not articulated.

Theoretical sampling: A sampling technique which proceeds on the basis of emerging concepts and is guided by developing theory (see *grounded theory*).

Theoretical sensitivity: Sensitivity and awareness of meaning in the data.

Theory: A set of concepts, principles and propositions that explains phenomena.

Thick description: Dense detailed and conceptual description which depicts events and actions within a social context.

Triangulation: A way of validating the research by using different methods (the most common way), data-collection approaches, investigators or theoretical perspectives in the study of one phenomenon (e.g. qualitative and quantitative methods, interviews and observation).

Validity: The extent to which the research does what it intends to do – the extent to which the researcher's findings are accurate, reflect the purpose of the study and represent reality (validity in qualitative research differs from that in quantitative research).

(This glossary has been developed from a variety of sources but mainly from Holloway and Wheeler, 2010: 337–42.)

References

Abrams, W.L. (2000) *The Observational Handbook: Understanding how Consumers Live with Your Product*. Chicago: NTC Business Books.

Adams, A., Anderson, E. & McCormack, M. (2010) Establishing and challenging masculinity: the influence of gendered discourses in organized sport. *Journal of Language and Social Psychology*, 29(3): 278–300.

Alexander, N. (2009) Brand authentication: creating and maintaining brand auras. *European Journal of Marketing*, 43(3/4): 551–62.

Allen-Collinson, J. (2009) Sporting embodiment: sports studies and the (continuing) promise of phenomenology. *Qualitative Research in Sport and Exercise*, 1(3): 279–296.

Allen-Collinson, J. & Hockey, J. (2007) Grasping the phenomenology of sporting bodies. *International Review of the Sociology of Sport*, 42(2): 115–31.

Allport, G. (1943) *The Use of Personal Documents in Psychological Society*. New York: Social Science Research Council.

Alvesson, M. & Sjőldberg, K. (2009) *Reflexive Methodology: New Vistas for Qualitative Research*. Los Angeles: Sage.

Andrews, G., Sudwell, M. & Sparkes, A. (2005) Towards a geography of fitness: an ethnographic case study of the gym in British bodybuilding culture. *Social Science and Medicine*, 60(4): 877–91.

Angrosino, M. (2007) *Doing Ethnographic and Observational Research*. London: Sage.

Aspers, P. (2004) *Empirical Phenomenology: An Approach for Qualitative Research*. Papers in Social Research Methods, Qualitative Series 9. London: LSE.

Atkinson M. (2008) Triathlon, suffering and exciting significance. *Leisure Studies*, 27(2): 165–180.

Atkinson, P. (1997) Narrative turn or blind alley? *Qualitative Health Research*, 7(3): 325–344.

Atkinson, P. & Delamont, S. (2006) Rescuing narrative from qualitative research. *Narrative Inquiry*, 16(1): 164–172.

Atkinson, P., Coffey, A., Delamont, S., Lofland, J. & Lofland, L. (eds) (2007) Introduction to Part One. In *Handbook of Ethnography*, London: Sage (paperback edition), pp. 9–10.

Atkinson P. & Silverman D. (1997) Kundera's immortality: the interview society and the invention of the self. *Qualitative Inquiry*. 3(3): 304–325.

Barker C. (2011) *Cultural Studies: Theory and Practice*. London: Sage.

Bateman, R. (2009), Pursuit of knowledge is being hamstrung by heavy-handed editing, *THE*, 16–22 July, p. 25.

Bavinton, N. (2007) From obstacle to opportunity: parkour, leisure, and the reinterpretation of constraints. *Annals of Leisure Research*, 10(3-4): 391–412.

Bazeley, P. (2004) Issues in mixing qualitative and quantitative approaches to research. In Buber, R., Gadner, J. & Richards, L. (eds) *Applying Qualitative Methods to Marketing Management Research*. Basingstoke: Palgrave Macmillan pp. 141–156

Bell, J. & Hardy, J. (2009) Effects of attentional focus on skilled performance in golf. *Journal of Applied Sport Psychology*, 21(2): 163–77.

Bengoechea, E. & Strean, W. (2007) On the interpersonal context of adolescent sport motivation. *The Psychology of Sport and Exercise,* 8(2): 195–217.

Bergman, M. (2011) The good, the bad and the ugly in mixed methods research and design. *Journal of Mixed Methods,* 5(4): 271–75.

Berry, K., Kowalski, K.C., Ferguson, L.J. & McHugh, T. F. (2010) An empirical phenomenology of adult women exercisers' body self-compassion. *Qualitative Research in Sport and Exercise,* 2(3): 293–392.

Bishop, D., Karageorghis, C. & Loizou, G. (2007) A grounded theory of young tennis players' use of music to manipulate emotional state. *Journal of Sport and Exercise Psychology,* 29(5): 584–607.

Bloodworth, A. & McNamee, M. (2010) Clean Olympians? Doping and anti-doping: the views of talented young British athletes, *International Journal of Drug Policy,* 21(4): 276–82.

Bloor, M., Frankland J.,Thomas, M. & Stewart, K. (2001) *Focus Groups in Social Research.* London: Sage.

Blumer, H. (1969) *Symbolic Interactionism: Perspective and Method.* Englewood Cliffs, NJ: Prentice- Hall.

Bott, E. (2010) Favourites and others: reflexivity and the shaping of subjectivities and data in qualitative research. *Qualitative Research,* 10(2): 150–73.

Bowen, G. (2008) Naturalistic inquiry and the saturation concept. *Qualitative Research,* 8 (1): 137–152.

Brannen, J. (2005) mixed methods research: a discussion paper. Southampton: ESRC National Centre for Research Methods.

Braun, V. & Clarke, V. (2006) Using thematic analysis in psychology. *Qualitative Research in Psychology,* 3(2): 77–101.

Brewer, J.D. (2000) *Ethnography.* Buckingham: Open University Press.

Brewer, J. & Sparkes, A. (2011) Meanings of outdoor physical activity for parentally bereaved young people in the United Kingdom: insights from an ethnographic study. *Journal of Adventure Education and Outdoor Learning,* 11(2): 127–43.

Bringer, J.D., Brackenridge, C.H. & Johnstone, L.H. (2002) Defining appropriateness in coach athlete sexual relationships. *Journal of Sexual Aggression,* 8(2): 83–98.

Bringer, J.D., Brackenridge, C.H. & Johnstone, L.H. (2006) Swimming coaches' perceptions of sexual exploitation in sport: a preliminary model of role conflict and role ambiguity. *The Sports Psychologist,* 20(4): 465–79.

Bruner J. (2000 *Making Stories: Law, Literature, Life.* New York: Farrar, Straus & Giroux.

Bruner, M., Munroe-Chandler, K. & Spink, K. (2008) Entry into elite sport: a preliminary investigation into the transition experiences of rookie athletes. *Journal of Applied Sport Psychology,* 20(2): 236–52.

Brustad, R. (2008). Qualitative research approaches. In Horn, T. (ed) *Advances in Sport Psychology* (3rd edn). Champaign, IL: Human Kinetics, pp. 31–43.

Brustad, R. (2009) Validity in context – qualitative research issues in sport and exercise studies: a response to John Smith. *Qualitative Research in Sport and Exercise,*1(2): 112–115.

Bryman, A. (2007) Barriers to integrating qualitative and quantitative research. *Journal of Mixed Methods,* 1(1): 8–22.

Bryman, A. (2008) *Social Research Methods* (3rd edn). Oxford: Oxford University Press.

Buchbinder, E. (2011) Experiences of the validation interview. *Qualitative Social Work,* 10(1): 106–22.

Burke, H., Jenkins, L. & Higham, V. (2010) Transcribing your own qualitative data. *Realities Toolkit #08.* Manchester: ESRC National Centre for Research Methods.

Burnard, P. (2004) Writing a qualitative report. *Nurse Education Today,* 24(3): 174–79.

Byrne, B. (2004) Qualitative interviewing. In Seale, C. (edn.) *Researching Society and Culture* (2nd edn). Oxford: Alden Press, pp. 179–192.

Caelli, K. (2001) Engaging with phenomenology: is it more of a challenge than it needs to be? *Qualitative Health Research*, 11(2): 273–81.

Caelli, K., Ray, L. & Mill, J. (2003) 'Clear as mud': toward a greater clarity in generic qualitative research. *International Journal of Qualitative Methods,* 2(2): Article 1. www.ualberta.ca/~iiqm/backissues/pdf/caellietal.pdf. (accessed 5/1/11).

Carless, D. & Douglas, K. (2008) Narrative, identity and mental health: how men with serious mental illness re-story their lives through sport and exercise. *Psychology of Sport and Exercise,* 9(5): 576–94.

Carless, D. & Douglas K. (2009) We haven't got a seat on the bus for you' or 'all the seats are mine': narratives and career transition in professional golf. *Qualitative Research in Sport and Exercise,* 1(1): 51–66.

Carr, W. & Kemmis, S. (1986) *Becoming Critical: Education, Knowledge and Action Research.* Lewes: Falmer.

Carspecken, P.F. (2009) A very short, fairly interesting and reasonably cheap book about qualitative research. [Book review online.] *International Journal of Multiple Research Approaches,* 3(1): 108–12. http://search.informit.com.au/documentSummary ,dn = 083364895023207;res = IELHSS.

Caulley, D. (2008) Making qualitative research reports less boring: the techniques of writing creative nonfiction. *Qualitative Inquiry,* 14(3): 424–49.

Charmaz, K. (2006) *Constructing Grounded Theory: A Practical Guide through Qualitative Analysis.* London: Sage.

Charmaz, K. & Mitchell, R.G. (1996) The myth of silent authorship: self, substance and style in ethnographic writing. *Symbolic Interaction,* 19(4): 285–302.

Chenail , R.J., Cooper, R. & Desir, C. (2010) Strategically reviewing the research literature in qualitative research. *Journal of Ethnographic and Qualitative Research,* 4(2): 88–94.

Cho, J. & Trent, A. (2006) Validity in qualitative research revisited. *Qualitative Research,* 6(3): 319–40.

Clark, T. (2010) On 'being researched': why do people engage with qualitative research. *Qualitative Research,* 10(4): 399–419.

Cohen, D. & Crabtree, B. (2008) Evaluative criteria for qualitative research in health care: controversies and recommendations. *Annals of Family Medicine,* 6(4): 331–119.

Colaizzi, P. (1978) Psychological research as a phenomenologist views it. In Vallé, R. & King, M. (eds) *Existential Phenomenological Alternatives for Psychology.* New York: Oxford University Press, pp. 48–71.

Cooky, C. & McDonald, M. (2005) 'If you let me play': young girls' insider-other narratives of sport. *Sociology of Sport Journal,* 22(2): 158–77.

Cooley, C.H. (1922) *Human Nature and the Social Order.* New York: Scribner's

Cope, C.J., Eys, M.A., Schinke, R.J. & Bosselut, G. (2010) Coaches' perspectives of a negative informal role: the 'cancer' within sport teams. *Journal of Applied Sport Psychology,* 22(4): 420–36.

Corbin, J. & Morse, J.M. (2003) The unstructured interactive interview: issues of reciprocity and risks when dealing with sensitive topics. *Qualitative Inquiry,* 9(3): 335–54.

Corbin, J. & Strauss, A. (2008) *Basics of Qualitative Research: Techniques and Procedures for Developing Grounded Theory* (3rd edn). Los Angeles: Sage.

Corden, A. & Sainsbury, R. (2006) Using verbatim quotations in reporting qualitative social research: researchers' views. University of York: ESRC.

Cortazzi, M. (1993) *Narrative Analysis.* Abingdon: Routledge.

Creswell, J. (1994) *Research Design: Qualitative and Quantitative Approaches.* Thousand Oaks, CA: Sage.

Creswell, J. (1998). *Qualitative Inquiry and Research Design.* London: Sage.

Creswell, J. (2007) *Qualitative Inquiry and Research Design* (2nd edn). Thousand Oaks, CA: Sage.

Creswell, J.W. & Plano Clark, V.L. (2011) *Designing and Conducting Mixed Methods Research.* Thousand Oaks, CA: Sage.

Crossley, N. (2008) (Net)Working out: social capital in a private health club. *British Journal of Sociology*, 59(3): 475–500.

Crust, L., Keegan, R., Piggott, D. & Swann, C. (2011) Walking the walk: a phenomenological study of long-distance walking. *Journal of Applied Sport Psychology*, 23(3): 243–62.

Czarniawska, B. (2004) *Narratives in Social Science Research*. London: Sage.

Czech, D. & Bullet, E. (2007) An exploratory description of Christian athletes' perceptions of prayer in sport: a mixed methodological pilot study. *International Journal of Sports Science & Coaching*, 2(1): 49–56.

Dahlberg, K., Drew, N. & Nyström, M. (2001) *Reflective Lifeworld Research*. Lund: Studentlitteratur.

Darker, C., Larkin, M. & French, D. (2007) An exploration of walking behaviour – an interpretative phenomenological approach. *Social Science and Medicine*, 65(10): 2172–83.

Darko, N. (2011) 'Get up, and shut up, you play like Tarzan and Moan like Jane': Rugby Union men and their suppression of body anxiety. *International Journal of Sport and Society*, 2(2): 49–65.

Daymon, C. & Holloway, I. (2011) *Qualitative Research Methods in Public Relations and Marketing Communications*. London: Routledge.

De Bosscher, V, Shibli, S. van Bottenburg, M., De Knop, P. & Truyens, J. (2010) Developing a method for comparing the elite sport systems and policies of nations: a mixed research methods approach. *Journal of Sport Management*, 24(5): 567–600.

Denzin, N.K. (1989) *The Research Act: A Theoretical Introduction to Sociological Methods* (3rd edn). Englewood Cliffs, NJ: Prentice Hall.

Denzin, N. (1997) *Interpretive Ethnography: Ethnographic Practices for the 21st Century*. London: Sage.

Denzin N.K. (2001) *Interpretive Interactionism*. (2nd ed). Thousand Oaks: Sage.

Denzin, N.K. (2009) *The Research Act: Theoretical Introduction to Sociological Methods*. (4th edn). New Brunswick, NJ: Aldine Transaction.

Denzin, N. & Lincoln, Y. (1998) *Collecting and Interpreting Qualitative Materials*. London: Sage.

Deutscher, I. (1966) Words and deeds: social science and social policy. *Social Problems*, 13(3): 235–54.

Deutscher, I. (1970) Words and deeds: social science and social policy. In Filstead, W.J. (ed.) *Qualitative Methodology: Firsthand Involvement with the Social World*. Chicago: Markham Publishing, pp. 27–51.

DeWalt, K. & DeWalt, B. (2010) *Participant Observation: A Guide for Fieldworkers* (2nd edn). Walnut Creek, CA: Altamira Press.

Diacin, M., Parks, J. & Allison, P. (2003) Voices of male athletes on drug use, drug testing, and the existing order in intercollegiate athletics. *Journal of Sport Behavior*, 26(1): 1–16.

Dickinson, J. & Robbins, D. (2009) 'Other people, other times and special places': a social representations perspective of cycling in a tourism destination. *Tourism and Hospitality Planning & Development*, 6(1): 69–85.

Dorgo, S. (2009) Unfolding the practical knowledge of an expert strength and conditioning coach. *International Journal of Sports Science & Coaching*, 4(1): 17–30.

Douglas, K. & Carless, D. (2008) *Nurturing a Performative Self*. Forum Qualitative Sozialforschung/Forum: *Qualitative Social Research*, 9(2), Art. 23, http://nbn-resolving.de/urn:nbn:de:0114-fqs0802238

Driediger, M., Hall, C. & Callow, N. (2006) Imagery use by injured athletes: a qualitative analysis. *Journal of Sports Sciences*, 24(3): 261–72.

Eatough, V. & Smith, J. (2006) I was like a wild wild person: understanding feelings of anger using interpretative phenomenological analysis. *British Journal of Psychology*, 97(4): 483–498.

Elliot, J. (2005) *Using Narrative in Social Research: Qualitative and Quantitative Approaches.* London: Sage.

Ellis-Hill, C., Payne, S. & Ward, C. (2008) Using stroke to explore the Life Thread Model: an alternative approach to understanding rehabilitation following an acquired disability. *Disability and Rehabilitation,* 30(2): 150–159.

Emden, C. (1998) Conducting narrative analysis. *Collegian,* 5(3): 34–9.

Erlandson, D.A., Skipper, B.L., Allen, S.D. & Harris, E.L. (1993) *Doing Naturalistic Inquiry.* Newbury Park, CA: Sage.

Evans, R. (2008) Getting the message across. *Qualitative Researcher,* 8: 1.

Ferrand, C., Tetard, S. & Fontaine, P. (2006) Self-handicapping in rock climbing: a qualitative approach. *Journal of Applied Sport Psychology,* 18(3): 271–80.

Fetterman D.F. (2010) *Ethnography: Step by Step* (3rd edn). Thousand Oaks: Sage.

Filo, K., Funk, D. & O'Brien, D. (2008) It's really not about the bike: exploring attraction and attachment to the events of the Lance Armstrong Foundation. *Journal of Sport Management,* 22(5): 501–25.

Finlay, L. (2008) *Introducing phenomenological research.* Available from: www.lindafinlay.co.uk.

Fletcher, D. & Arnold, R. (2011) A qualitative study of performance leadership and management in elite sport. *Journal of Applied Sport Psychology,* 23(2): 223–42.

Fortune, D. & Mair, H. (2011) Notes from the sports club: confessional tales of two researchers. *Journal of Contemporary Ethnography,* 40(4): 457–84.

Frank, A.W. (1995) *The Wounded Storyteller: Body, Illness, and Ethics.* Chicago: University of Chicago Press.

Fraser-Thomas, J., Cote, J. & Deakin, J. (2008) Understanding drop-out and prolonged engagement in adolescent competitive sport. *Psychology of Sport and Exercise,* 9(5): 645–62.

Friman, M., Nyberg, C. & Norlander, T. (2004) Threats and aggression directed at soccer referees: an empirical phenomenological psychological study. *The Qualitative Report,* 9(4): 652–72.

Gadamer, H. (1975) *Truth and Method.* (Originally published in 1960. Translated by G. Barden & J. Cumming; 2nd edn 1989.) New York: Seabury Press.

Gearity, B. (2011) Poor teaching by the coach: a phenomenological description from athletes' experience of poor coaching. *Physical Education and Sport Pedagogy,* 17(1): 79–96.

Geertz, C. (1973) *The Interpretation of Cultures.* New York: Basic Books.

Geertz, C. (1988) *Works and Lives: The Anthropologist as Author.* Stanford, CA: Stanford University Press.

Gellweilier, S. (2011) *Through the Kaleidoscope: The Lived Experiences of Sport Event Volunteers.* Unpublished PhD thesis, School of Tourism, Bournemouth University.

Gibbs, G.R. (2007) *Analyzing Qualitative Data.* Los Angeles: Sage.

Gillon, R. (2003) Ethics needs principles – four can encompass the rest – and respect for autonomy should be 'the first among equals'. *Journal of Medical Ethics,* 29(5): 307–12.

Giorgi, A. (ed.) (1985) *Phenomenology and Psychological Research.* Pittsburgh, PA: Duquesne University Press.

Giorgi, A. (1997) The theory, practice and evaluation of the phenomenological method as a qualitative procedure. *Journal of Phenomenological Psychology,* 28(2): 235–60.

Giorgi, A. & Giorgi, B. (2008) Phenomenology. In Smith, J. (ed.) *Qualitative Psychology: A Practical Guide to Research Methods.* London: Sage, pp. 25–50.

Giulianotti, R. (1995) Participant observation and research into football hooliganism: reflections on the problems of entree and everyday risks. *Sociology of Sport Journal,* 12(1): 1–20.

Glaser, B.G. (1978) *Theoretical Sensitivity.* Mill Valley, CA: Sociology Press.

Glaser, B.G. (1992) *Basics of Grounded Theory Analysis.* Mill Valley, CA: Sociology Press.

Glaser, B. G. (with the assistance of Judith Holton) (2004). Remodeling Grounded Theory [80 paragraphs]. *Forum Qualitative Sozialforschung/Forum: Qualitative Social Research*, 5(2): Art. 4. Available at http://nbn-resolving.de/urn:nbn:de:0114–fqs040245. Revised: 4/2011 (accessed 20/8/12).

Glaser, B.G. & Strauss, A.L. (1967) *The Discovery of Grounded Theory*. Chicago: Aldine.

Gobo, G. (2008) *Doing Ethnography.* London: Sage.

Goffman, E. (1969) *The Presentation of Self in Everyday Life*. London: Penguin Books. (First published by Anchor Books in 1959.)

Golafshani, N. (2003) Understanding reliability and validity in qualitative research. *The Qualitative Report,* 8(4): 597–607.

Gold, R. (1958) Roles in sociological field observation. *Social Forces*, 36(3): 217–23.

Granskog, J. (2003). Just "Tri" and "Du" it: the variable impact of female involvement in the triathlon/duathlon sport culture. In Bolin, A. & Granskog, J. (eds), *Athletic Intruders Ethnographic Research on Women, Culture, and Exercise.* New York: State University of New York Press, pp. 27–52.

Gratton, C. & Jones, I. (2010) *Research Methods for Sport Studies.* London: Routledge.

Greene, S. & Hogan, D. (2005) *Researching Children's Experiences: Approaches and Methods.* London: Sage.

Greenbaum, T. (1998) *The Handbook for Focus Group Research* (2nd edn). Lexington, KY: Lexington Books/DC Heath and Co.

Grogan, S., & Richards, H. (2002). Body image: focus groups with boys and men. *Men and Masculinities, 4* (3): 219–233.

Groom, R., Cushion, C. & Nelson, D. (2011) The delivery of video-based performance analysis by England youth soccer coaches: towards a grounded theory. *Journal of Applied Sport Psychology,* 23(1): 16–32.

Groves, S., & Laws, C. (2003): The use of narrative in accessing children's experiences of physical education. *European Journal of Physical Education*, 8(2): 160–174.

Guba, E. & Lincoln, Y. (1989) *Fourth Generation Evaluation.* Newbury Park: Sage.

Gucciardi, D., Gordon, S. & Dimmock, J. (2008) Towards an understanding of mental toughness in Australian football. *Journal of Applied Sport Psychology*, 2(3): 261–81.

Guillemin, M. & Gillam, L. (2004) Ethics, reflexivity and ethically important moments in research. *Qualitative Inquiry*, 10(2): 261–80.

Hadjistavropoulos, T. & Smythe, W. (2001) Elements of risk in qualitative research. *Ethics and Behavior,* 11(2): 163–74.

Halai, A. (2006) Ethics in qualitative research: issues and challenges, *Multi-disciplinary qualitative research in developing countries.* Aka Khan University, Karachi, 26 November.

Halpern, E. (1983) Auditing naturalistic inquiries: the development and application of a model. Unpublished doctoral dissertation, Indiana University.

Hamm-Kerwin, S., Misener, K. & Doherty, A. (2009) Getting in the game: an investigation of volunteering in sport among older adults. *Leisure\Loisir,* 33(2): 659–85.

Hammersley, M. (1992) *What's Wrong with Ethnography?* Abingdon: Routledge

Hammersley. M. (2010) Reproducing or constructing? Some questions about transcription in social research. *Qualitative Research,* 10(5): 551–61.

Hammersley, M. & Atkinson, P. (2007) *Ethnography: Principles in Practice* (3rd rev. edn). Andover: Routledge.

Hanton, S., Cropley, B., Neil, R., Mellalieu, S. & Miles, A. (2008): Experience in sport and its relationship with competitive anxiety. *International Journal of Sport and Exercise Psychology,* 5(1): 28–53.

Harley, A., Buckworth, J., Katz, M., Willis, S., Odoms-Young, A. & Heaney, C. (2009) Developing long-term physical activity participation: a grounded theory study with African-American women. *Health Education & Behavior,* 36(1): 97–112.

Harris, M. (1976) History and significance of the emic/etic distinction. *Annual Review of Anthropology*, 5(1): 329–50.

Harris, M. (1979) *Cultural Materialism: The Struggle for a Science of Culture*. New York: Vintage.

Harwood, C., Drew, A. & Knight, C. (2010) Parental stressors in professional youth football academies: a qualitative investigation of specialising stage parents. *Qualitative Research in Sport and Exercise*, 2(1): 39–55.

Heidegger, M. (2010[1927]) *Being and Time* (translated by Joan Stambaugh, revised by Dennis J. Schmidt). Albany, NY: State University of New York Press.

Hofstede, G. (2001) *Culture's Consequences: Comparing Values, Behaviors Institutions and Organizations across Nations* (2nd edn). Thousand Oaks, CA: Sage

Holloway, I. (2005) Qualitative writing. In Holloway, I. (ed.) *Qualitative Research in Health Care*. Maidenhead: Open University Press, pp. 270–86.

Holloway, I. (2008) *A–Z of Qualitative Research in Healthcare*. Oxford: Blackwell.

Holloway, I. & Todres, L. (2003) The status of method: flexibility, consistency and coherence. *Qualitative Research*, 3(3): 345–7.

Holloway, I. & Wheeler, S. (2010) *Qualitative Research for Nursing and Healthcare*. Oxford: Wiley-Blackwell.

Hollway, W. & Jefferson, T. (2000) *Doing Qualitative Research Differently: Free Association, Narrative and the Interview Method*. London: Sage.

Holt, N. (2003) Coping in professional sport: a case study of an experienced cricket player. *Athletic Insight*, 5(1). Available from http://www.athleticinsight.com/Vol5Iss1/CricketPlayerCoping.htm (accessed 17 February 2012).

Holt, N.L. & Dunn, J.G.H. (2004) Toward a grounded theory of the psychosocial competencies and environmental conditions associated with soccer success. *Journal of Applied Sport Psychology*, 16(3): 199–219.

Holt, N. & Sparkes, A. (2001) An ethnographic study of cohesiveness in a college soccer team over a season. *The Sport Psychologist*, 15(3): 237–59.

Holt, N. & Tamminem, K. (2010) Improving grounded theory research in sport and exercise psychology: further reflections as a response to Mike Weed. *Psychology of Sport and Exercise*, 11(6): 405–13.

Holt, N.L., Tamminen, K.A., Black, D.E. et al. (2008) Parental involvement in competitive sport settings. *Psychology of Sport and Exercise*, 9(5): 663–685.

Hudson, S., Hinch, T., Walker, G. & Simpson, B. (2010) Constraints to sport tourism: a cross-cultural analysis. *Journal of Sport and Tourism*, 15(1): 71–88.

Hunger, I., Sparkes, A. & Stelter, R. (2003) Qualitative methods in sport sciences: a special FQS issue. *Forum Qualitative Sozialforschung*, 4(1): Art. 2. http://nbn-resolving.de/urn:nbn:de0114–fqs030124 (accessed 20/8/12).

Husserl, E. (2012) *Ideas Pertaining to a Pure Phenomenology and to a Phenomenological Philosophy*. (First book in his collected works, first published in 1913 and translated by F. Kersten) Cluwer: Academic Publishers.

Hydén, L.C. & Bülow, P.H. (2003) Who's talking: drawing conclusions from focus groups – some methodological considerations. *International Journal of Social Research Methodology* 6(4): 305–21.

Jennings, G. (2010) *Tourism Research* (2nd edn). Milton: Wiley.

Johnson, R.B. & Onwuegbuzie, A.J. (2004) Mixed method research: a paradigm whose time has come. *Educational Researcher*, 33(7): 14–26.

Johnston, M. & Paulsen, N. (2011) The influence of club and sponsor images and club-sponsor congruence in the Australian Football League. *International Journal of Sport Management and Marketing*, 9(1/2): 29–53.

Jones, A. (2010) Phenomenological examination of depression in female collegiate athletes. Master's thesis. Paper 3813. Available at http://scholarworks.sjsu.edu/etd_theses/3813 (accessed 21/8/12).

Jones, D., Richeson, N., Croteau, K. & Farmer B. (2009) Focus groups to explore the perceptions of older adults on pedometer-based intervention research. *Research Quarterly for Exercise and Sport*, 80(4): 710–17.

Jones, I. (1997) Mixing qualitative and quantitative methods in sports fan research. *The Qualitative Report*, 3(4), December. Available at www.nova.edu/ssss/QR/QR3-4/jones.html (accessed 14 January 2012).

Jones, I. (1998) Football fandom: football fan identity and identification at Luton Town Football Club. Unpublished PhD thesis: University of Luton.

Jones, R.K. (2000) The unsolicited diary as a qualitative research tool for advanced capacity in the field of health and illness. *Qualitative Health Research*, 10(4): 555–67.

Jovchelovitch, S. & Bauer, M. (2000) Narrative interviewing. In Bauer, Martin W. & Gaskell, G. (eds) *Qualitative Researching with Text, Image and Sound: A Practical Handbook*. London: Sage, pp. 57–74.

Jowett, S. & Timson-Katchis, M. (2005) Social networks in sport: parental influence on the coach-athlete relationship. *The Sport Psychologist*, 19(3): 267–87.

Kavanagh, E. (2012) Affirmation through disability: one athlete's personal journey to the London Paralympic Games. *Perspectives in Public Health*, 132(2): 68–75.

Kawulich, B.B. (2005). Participant observation as a data collection method [81 paragraphs]. *Forum Qualitative Sozialforschung/Forum: Qualitative Social Research*, 6(2): Art. 43. Available at http://nbnresolving.de/urn:nbn:de:0114–fqs0502430 (accessed 19/8/12).

Keegan, R., Harwood, C., Spray, C. & Lavallee, D. (2009) A qualitative investigation exploring the motivational climate in early career sports participants: coach, parent and peer influences on sport motivation. *Psychology of Sport and Exercise*, 10(3): 361–72.

Keen, S. & Todres, L. (2007) Communicating qualitative research findings: an annotated bibliographic review of non-traditional dissemination strategies. Occasional Paper, Bournemouth University.

Keller, C., Fleury, J., Perez, A., Ainsworth, B. & Vaughan, L. (2008) Using visual methods to uncover context. *Qualitative Health Research*, 18(3): 428–36.

Kerr, A. & Emery, P. (2011) The allure of an 'overseas sweetheart': a Liverpool FC brand community. *International Journal of Sport Management and Marketing*, 9(3–4): 201–19.

Kerry, D. & Armour, K. (2000) Sport sciences and the promise of phenomenology: philosophy, method, and insight. *Quest*, 52(1): 1–17.

Kidd, P. S. & Parshall, M.B. (2000) Getting the focus and the group: enhancing analytical rigor in focus group research. *Qualitative Health Research* 10(3): 293–308.

Kilbourn, B. (2006) The qualitative doctoral dissertation proposal. *Teachers College Record*, 108(4): 529–76.

Kimball, A. & Freysinger, V. (2003) Leisure, stress, and coping: the sport participation of collegiate student-athletes. *Leisure Sciences*, 25(2–3): 115–41.

King, N. (2008) *Template Analysis*. Available at www2.hud.ac.uk/hhs/research/template_analysis/index.htm (accessed 14/3/12).

Kitzinger, J. & Barbour, R. (1999) Introduction: the challenge and promise of focus groups. In Barbour, R. & Kitzinger, J. (eds) *Developing Focus Groups Research: Politics, Theory and Practice*. London: Sage, pp. 1–20.

Kluge, M., Grant, B., Friend, L. & Glick, L. (2010) Seeing is believing: telling the 'inside story' of a beginning Masters athletes through film. *Qualitative Research in Sport and Exercise*, 2(2): 282–92.

Koch. S. & Zumbach. J. (2002/7) The use of video analysis software in behavior observation research: interaction patterns in task-oriented small groups. *Qualitative Sozialforschung/ Forum: Qualitative Social Research*, 3(2): Art. 18. Available at http://nbnresolving.de/urn:nbn:de:0114–fqs0202187.Revised 2/2007 (accessed 17/5/12).

Kozinets, R. (1998) *Netnography: Doing Ethnographic Research Online*. London: Sage.

Krane V. and Baird S.M. (2005) Using research methods in applied sport psychology. *Journal of Applied Sport Psychology,* 17 (2): 87–107.

Krane, V. & Barber, H. (2005) Identity tensions in lesbian intercollegiate coaches. *Research Quarterly for Exercise and Sport,* 76(1): 67–81.

Kristiansen, E., Roberts, G.C. & Sisjord, M.K. (2012) Coping with negative media content: the experience of professional football goalkeepers. *International Journal of Sport and Exercise Psychology,* 9(4): 295–307.

Krueger, R. & Casey, M. (2009) *Focus Groups: A Practical Guide for Applied Research.* Thousand Oaks, CA: Sage.

Kvale, S. (1996) *Interviews: An Introduction to Qualitative Research Interviewing.* Thousand Oaks, CA: Sage.

Kvale, S. & Brinkman S.: *Interviews: Learning the Craft of Qualitative Research Interviewing.* (2nd edn). Thousand Oaks, CA: Sage.

Labov, W. & Waletzky, J. (1967) Oral versions of personal experience. In Helm, J. (ed.) *Essays on Verbal and Visual Arts.* Seattle, WA: University of Washington Press, pp. 12–14.

Lake, R. (2011) 'They treat me like I'm scum': social exclusion and established-outsider relations in a British tennis club. *International Review for the Sociology of Sport.* published first online http://irs.sagepub.com/content/early/2011/09/24/10126902114 24523 (accessed 13/3/12)

Langdridge, D. (2007) *Phenomenological Psychology.* Edinburgh: Pearson Education.

Langseth, T. (2011) Liquid ice surfers – the construction of surfer identities in Norway. *Journal of Adventure Education & Outdoor Learning,* 12(1): 1–21.

Lavallee, D. & Robinson, H. (2007) In pursuit of an identity: a qualitative exploration of retirement from women's artistic gymnastics. *Psychology of Sport and Exercise,* 8(1): 119–41.

Lehoux, P., Poland, B. & Daudelin, G. (2006) Focus group research and the patient's view. *Social Science and Medicine,* 63(8): 2091–104.

Leidl, D. (2009) Motivation in sport: bridging historical and contemporary theory through a qualitative approach. *International Journal of Sports Science & Coaching,* 4(2): 115–75.

Lewins, A. & Silver, C. (2007) *Using Software in Qualitative Research: A Step-by-Step Guide.* London: Sage.

Li, M., Pitts, B. & Quaterman, J. (2008) *Research Methods in Sport Management* Morgantown, West Virginia: Fitness Information Technology.

Lieblich, A., Tuval-Mashiach, R. & Zilver, T. (1998) *Narrative Research: Reading, Analysis and Interpretation.* Thousand Oaks, CA: Sage.

Lincoln Y. & and Guba, E. (1985) *Naturalistic Inquiry.* Beverly Hills, CA: Sage.

Lindeman, E.C. (1924) *Social Discovery: An Introduction to the Study of Functional Groups.* New York: Republic.

Loizos, P. (2000) Video, film and photographs as research documents. In Bauer, M. & Gaskell, G. (eds) *Qualitative Researching with Text, Image and Sound.* London: Sage, pp. 93–107.

Lugosi, P. (2006) Between overt and covert research. *Qualitative Inquiry,* 12(3): 541–61.

Lyons, K. & Dionigi, R. (2007) Transcending emotional community: a qualitative examination of older adults and masters' sports participation, *Leisure Sciences,* 29(4): 375–89.

MacIntosh, E. & Crow, B. (2011) Positioning a brand within the controversial sport of mixed martial arts. *Journal of Sponsorship,* 4(2): 163–77.

Malcom, N. (2006) 'Shaking it off' and 'toughing it out': socialisation to pain and injury in girls' softball. *Journal of Contemporary Ethnography,* 35(5): 495–525.

Mangabeira W., Lee, R. & Fielding N. (2004) Computers and qualitative research. *Social Science Computer Review,* 22(2): 167–76.

Mann, C. & Stewart, F. (2000) *Internet Communication and Qualitative Research: A Handbook for Researching Online.* London: Sage.

Markula, P. (2006) Body-movement-change: dance as performative qualitative research. *Journal of Sport and Social Issues*, 30(4): 353–63.

Marshall, C. & Rossman, G. (2006) *Designing Qualitative Research* (4th edn). Thousand Oaks, CA: Sage.

Martens, R (1987). Science, knowledge, and sport psychology. *The Sport Psychologist*, 1(1): 29–55.

Mason, J. (2002) *Qualitative Researching* (2nd edn). London: Sage.

Mason, J. (2006) Mixing methods in a qualitatively driven way. *Qualitative Research*, 4(1): 9–25.

Mason, J. (2011) Knowing the in/tangible. Working paper #17: University of Manchester.

Maxwell, J. (2005) *Qualitative Research Design: An Interactive Approach* (2nd edn). Thousand Oaks, CA: Sage.

Mayoh, J., Bond, C. & Todres, L. (2011) An innovative mixed methods approach to studying the online health information seeking experiences of adults with chronic health conditions. *Journal of Mixed Methods Research*, 20(10): 1–13.

McCabe, J. & Palmer, C. (2007) An application of ethnographic method in an investigation into girls' attitudes towards trampolining in Physical Education. *Journal of Qualitative Research in Sports Studies*, 1(1): 77–88.

McCormack. M. & Anderson, A. (2010) The re-production of homosexually-themed discourse in educationally-based organised sport. *Culture, Health & Sexuality*, 12(8): 913–27.

McDonald, I. (2007) Body practice, performance art, competitive sport: a critique of Kalarippayattu, the martial art of Kerala. *Contributions to Indian Sociology*, 41(2): 143–68.

McDonough, M., Sabiston, C. & Crocker, P. (2008) An interpretative phenomenological examination of psychosocial changes among breast cancer survivors in their first season of dragon boating. *Journal of Applied Sport Psychology*, 20(4): 425–40.

McGarry J. (2009) Defining roles, relationships, boundaries and participation between elderly people and nurses within the home: an ethnographic study. *Health and Social Care in the Community*, 17(1): 83–91.

McKenna, J., Delaney, H. & Phillips, S. (2002) Physiotherapists' lived experience of rehabilitating elite athletes. *Physical Therapy in Sport*, 3(2): 66–78.

McMahon, J. & Penney, D. (2011) Empowering swimmers and their bodies in and through research. *Qualitative Research in Sport, Exercise and Health*, 3(2): 130–151.

Mead, M. (1934) *Mind, Self and Society*. Chicago: University of Chicago Press.

Melendez, M. (2008) Black football players on a predominantly white college campus: psychosocial and emotional realities of the black college athlete experience. *Journal of Black Psychology*, 34(4): 423–51.

Mellick, M. & Fleming, S. (2010) Personal narrative and the ethics of disclosure: a case study from elite sport. *Qualitative Research*, 10(3): 299–314.

Merton, R.K. & Kendall, P.L. (1946) The focused interview. *American Journal of Sociology*, 51: 541–57.

Moran, D. (2000) *Introduction to Phenomenology*. London: Routledge.

Morgan, D. (1998) *Focus Groups as Qualitative Research*. Thousand Oaks, CA: Sage.

Morse, J. (1991) Approaches to qualitative-quantitative methodological triangulation. *Nursing Research*. 40(2): 140–3.

Morse, J. (2003a) A review committee's guide for evaluating qualitative proposals. *Qualitative Health Research*, 13(6): 833–51.

Morse, J. (2003b) Principles of mixed-method and multi-method research design. In Tashakkori, A. & Teddlie, C. (eds.) *Handbook of Mixed Methods in Social and Behavioral Research*. London: Sage, pp. 189–208.

Morse, J. M. (2003) Principles of mixed-method and multi-method research design. In Tashakkori, A. & Teddlie, C. (eds) *Handbook of Mixed Methods in Social and Behavioral research*. London: Sage, pp. 189–208.

Moustakas, C. (1994). *Phenomenological Research Methods*. Thousand Oaks, CA: Sage.

Mulhall, A. (2003) In the field: notes on observation in qualitative research. *Journal of Advanced Nursing*, 41 (3): 306–313.

Munroe-Chandler, K., Hall, C., Fishburne, G. J. & Hall, N. (2007) The content of imagery use in youth sport. *International Journal of Sport and Exercise Psychology*, 5(2): 158–74.

Murray, C. & Harrison, B. (2004) The meaning and experience of being a stroke survivor: an interpretative phenomenological analysis. *Disability Rehabilitation*, 26(13): 808–816.

O'Connor, J. & Brown, T. (2007) Real cyclists don't race: informal affiliations of the weekend warrior. *International Review for the Sociology of Sport*, 42(1): 83–97.

Oliver, E., Hardy, J. & Markland, D. (2010) Identifying important practice behaviours for the development of high level youth athletes; exploring the perspectives of elite coaches, *Psychology of Sport and Exercise*, 11(6): 433–43.

Ollis, S., Macpherson, A. & Collins, D. (2006) Expertise and talent development in rugby refereeing: an ethnographic enquiry. *Journal of Sports Sciences*, 24(3): 309–22.

Olofsson, L., Fjellman-Wiqlund, A. & Soderman, K. (2010) From loss towards restoration: experiences from anterior cruciate ligament injury. *Advances in Physiotherapy*, 12(1): 50–7.

Onwuegbuzie, A. & Leech, N. (2007) Validity and qualitative research: an oxymoron? *Quality and Quantity*, 41(2): 233–45.

Opdenakker, R. (2006) Advantages and disadvantages of four interview techniques in qualitative research [44 paragraphs]. *Forum Qualitative Sozialforschung/Forum: Qualitative Social Research*, 7(4): Art. 11. Available at http://nbn-resolving.de/urn:nbn:de:0114fqs0604118 (accessed 21 April 2011).

O'Reilly, K. (2005) *Ethnographic Methods*. London: Sage.

Ortiz, S. (2004) The ethnographic process of gender management: doing the 'right' masculinity with wives of professional athletes. *Qualitative Inquiry*, 11(2): 265–90.

Paley, J. & Eva, G. (2005) Narrative vigilance: the analysis of stories in health care. *Nursing Philosophy*, 6(2): 83–97.

Palmer, C. (1996) A life of its own: the social construction of the Tour de France, Unpublished PhD thesis. Department of Anthropology: University of Adelaide.

Parker, A. & Tritter, J. (2006) Focus group method and methodology: current practice and recent debate. *International Journal of Research & Method in Education*, 29(1): 23–37.

Parkington, S., Parkington, E. & Olivier, S. (2009) The dark side of surfing: a study of dependence in big wave surfing. *The Sport Psychologist*, 23(2): 170–185.

Parry, K. & Eastwood, A. (2010) You'll never walk alone. Paper presented at the 8th International Qualitative Research Conference, 6–8 September, Bournemouth University, England.

Patton, M. (2002) *Qualitative Research and Evaluation Methods* (3rd edn). Thousand Oaks, CA: Sage.

Pearson, G. (2009) The researcher as hooligan: where participant observation means breaking the law. *International Journal of Social Research Methodology* 12(3): 243–255.

Perlman, D. & Karp, G. (2010) A self-determined perspective of the Sport Education Model. *Physical Education & Sport Pedagogy*, 15(4): 401–18.

Perrin-Wallqvist, R. & Carlsson, E. (2011) Self-image and physical education – a phenomenological study. *The Qualitative Report*, 16(4): 933–48.

Perry, C. & Hoffman. B. (2010) Assessing tribal youth physical activity and programming using a community-based participatory research approach. *Public Health Nursing*, 27(2): 104–14.

Phoenix, C., Smith, B. & Sparkes, A. (2007) Experiences and expectations of biographical time among young athletes: a life course perspective. *Time and Society*, 16(2/3): 247–68.

Pitney, W. (2002) The professional socialization of certified athletic trainers in high school settings: a grounded theory investigation. *Journal of Athletic Training,* 37(3): 286–92.

Pitts, M. & Miller-Day, M. (2007) Upward turning points and positive rapport-development across time in the researcher – participant relationship. *Qualitative Research,* 7(2): 177–201.

Polkinghorne, D. (1988) *Narrative Knowing and the Human Sciences.* Albany NY: State University of New York Press.

Pope, C. & Mays, N. (2006) Observational methods. In Pope, C. & Mays, N. (eds) *Qualitative Research in Health Care.* Oxford: Blackwell, Chapter 6.

Punch, K. (2006) *Developing Effective Research Proposals* (2nd edn). London: Sage.

Richardson, L. (1990) Narrative and sociology. *Journal of Contemporary Ethnography,* 19(1): 116–35.

Ricoeur, P. (1984) *Time and Narrative.* Vols 1–3. Chicago: University of Chicago Press.

Riessman, C. (1993) *Narrative Analysis.* Newbury Park, CA: Sage.

Riessman, C. (2008) *Narrative Methods for the Human Sciences.* Los Angeles: Sage.

Roberts, J., Jones, R., Harwood, C., Mitchell, S. & Rothberg, S. (2001) Human perceptions of sports equipment under playing conditions. *Journal of Sports Sciences,* 19(7): 485–97.

Rogers, H., Morris, T. & Moore, M. (2008) A qualitative study of the achievement goals of recreational exercise participants. *The Qualitative Report,* 13(4): 706–34.

Rose, E. & Parfitt, G. (2007) A quantitative analysis and qualitative explanation of the individual differences in affective responses to prescribed and self-selected exercise intensities. *Journal of Sport & Exercise Psychology,* 29(3): 281–309.

Roy, A. (2001) Beyond disability and ethnicity challenges: narrative of a Paralympian. *International Journal of Sociology and Anthropology,* 3(11): 430–435.

Rubin, H. & Rubin, I. (2005) *Qualitative Interviewing: The Art of Hearing Data* (2nd edn). Thousand Oaks, CA: Sage.

Russell, K. (2004) On versus off the pitch: the transiency of body satisfaction among female rugby players, cricketers, and netballers. *Sex Roles,* 51(9–10): 561–74.

Sandelowski, M. (2000) Combining qualitative and quantitative sampling, data collection and analysis techniques in mixed methods studies. *Research in Nursing and Health.* 23(3): 246–255

Sands, R. (2002). *Sport Ethnography.* Champaign, IL: Human Kinetics.

Schensul, S., Schensul, J. & LeCompte, M. (1999) *Essentials of Ethnographic Methods: Observations, Interviews and Questionnaires.* Walnut Creek, CA: Altamira Press.

Schulenkorf, N. & Edwards, D (2010) The role of sport events in peace tourism. In Moufakkir, O. & Kelly, I. (eds) *Tourism, Progress and Peace.* Wallingford: CABI, pp. 99–117.

Scott, J. (1990) *A Matter of Record: Documentary Sources in Social Research.* Cambridge: Polity Press.

Seale, C. (1999) *The Quality of Qualitative Research.* London: Sage.

Seale, C. (2004) *Researching Society and Culture.* London: Sage.

Seidel, J. (1991) Method and madness in the application of computer technology to qualitative data analysis. In Fielding, N.G. & Lee, R.M. (eds) *Using Computers in Qualitative Research.* London: Sage, pp. 107–18.

Seidman, I. (2006) *Interviewing as Qualitative Research: A Guide for Researchers in Education and the Social Science.* (3rd edn). New York: Teachers College Press.

Seldén, L. (2005) On grounded theory – with some malice. *Journal of Documentation,* 61(1): 114–29.

Seymour, W. (2001) In the flesh or online? Exploring qualitative research methodologies. *Qualitative Research,* 1(2): 147–68.

Shaw, M. (2010) Perceptions of exercise among school-aged children with asthma. PhD dissertation, University of Arizona.

Shipway, R. (2010) on the run: an ethnography of long distance running. Unpublished PhD thesis, Bournemouth University.

Silk, M., Slack, T. & Amis, J. (2000) Bread, butter and gravy: an institutional approach to televised sport production. *Culture, Sport, Society*, 3(1): 1–21.

Silverman, D. (2005) *Doing Qualitative Research: A Practical Handbook* (2nd edn). London: Sage.

Silverman, D. (2007) *A Very Short, Fairly Interesting and Reasonably Cheap Book about Qualitative Research*. Los Angeles: Sage.

Silverman D. (2010) *Doing Qualitative Research: A Practical Handbook* (3rd edn). London: Sage.

Smith, B. & Gilbourne, D. (2009) Editorial. *Qualitative Research in Sport and Exercise*, 1(1): 1–2.

Smith, B. & Sparkes, A. (2002) Men, sport, spinal cord injury and the construction of coherence: narrative practice in action. *Qualitative Research*, 2(2): 143–71.

Smith, B. & Sparkes A. (2005) Men, sport, spinal cord injury, and narratives of hope. *Social Science and Medicine*, 61(5): 1095–1105.

Smith, B. & Sparkes, A. (2008) Changing bodies, changing narratives and the consequences of tellability: a case study of becoming disabled through sport. *Sociology of Health & Illness*, 30(2): 217–36.

Smith, B. & Sparkes, A. (2009a) Narrative inquiry in sport and exercise psychology: what can it mean and why might we do it? *Psychology of Sport and Exercise*, 10(1): 1–11.

Smith, B. & Sparkes, A. (2009b) Narrative analysis and sport and exercise psychology: understanding lives in diverse ways. *Psychology of Sport and Exercise*, 10(2): 279–88.

Smith, B. & Sparkes, A. (2011) Exploring multiple responses to a chaos narrative. *Health*, 15(1), 38–53.

Smith, J., Flowers, P. & Larkin, M. (2009) *Interpretative Phenomenological Analysis: Theory, Method, Research*. London: Sage.

Smith, J. & Osborn, M. (2008) Interpretative phenomenological analysis. In Smith, J. (ed.) *Qualitative Psychology: A Practical Guide to Methods*, London: Sage (2nd edn). pp. 53–80.

Smithson, J. (2000) Using and analysing focus groups: limitations and possibilities. *International Journal of Social Research Methodology*, 3(2): 103–19.

Soundy, A., Faulkner, G. & Tailor, A. (2007) Exploring variability and perceptions of lifestyle physical activity among individuals with severe and enduring mental health problems: a qualitative study. *Journal of Mental Health*, 16(4): 493–503.

Spaaij, R. (2008) Men like us, boys like them: violence, masculinity, and collective identity in football hooliganism. *Journal of Sport & Social Issues*, 32(4): 369–92.

Sparkes, A. (2002) *Telling Tales in Sport and Physical Activity: A Qualitative Journey*. Champaign, IL: Human Kinetics.

Sparkes, A. & Douglas, K. (2007) Making the case for poetic representations: an example in action. *The Sport Psychologist*, 21(2): 170–90.

Sparkes, A., Partington, E. & Brown., D. (2007) Bodies as bearers of value: the transmission of jock culture via the 'Twelve Commandments'. *Sport, Education and Society*, 12(3): 295–316.

Spindler, G. & Spindler, L. (1982). Roger Harker and Schonhausen: from the familiar to the strange and back again. In: Spindler, G. (ed.), *Doing the Ethnography of Schooling*. New York: CBS College Publishing, pp. 20–47.

Spowart, L., Burrows, L. & Shaw, S. (2010) I just eat sleep and dream of surfing: when surfing meets motherhood. *Sport and Society*, 13(7/8): 1186–203.

Spradley, J. (1979) *The Ethnographic Interview*. Fort Worth, TX: Harcourt Brace Johanovich College Publishers.

Spradley, J. (1980) *Participant Observation*. Fort Worth, TX: Harcourt Brace Johanovich College Publishers.

Stake, R.E. (2010) *Qualitative Research: Studying How Things Work*. New York: The Guilford Press.

Stanley, C. & Robbins, J. (2011) Racial identity and sport: the case of a bi-racial athlete. *International Journal of Sport and Exercise Psychology,* 9(1): 64–77.

Stegelin, A. (2003) The development and maintenance of collective efficacy with a women's community college baseball team. Unpublished MSc degree, University of Florida.

Stewart, A (2008) From the boxer's point of view: a study of cultural production and athletic development among amateur and professional boxers in England. Unpublished doctoral dissertation, University of Luton.

Stewart, C., Smith, B. & Sparkes, A. (2011). Sporting autobiographies of illness and the role of metaphor. *Sport in Society*, 14(5): 577–93.

Stewart, D., Shamdasani, P. & Rook, D. (2007) *Focus Groups: Theory and Practice*. Thousand Oaks, CA: Sage.

Strachan, L., Côtè, J. & Deakin, J. (2011) A new view: exploring positive youth development in elite sport contexts. *Qualitative Research in Sport, Exercise and Health*, 3(1): 9–32.

Strauss, A. (1987) *Qualitative Analysis for Social Scientists*. New York: Cambridge University Press.

Strauss, A. & Corbin, J. (1990) *Basics of Qualitative Research: Grounded Theory Procedures and Techniques*. Newbury Park, CA: Sage.

Strauss, A. & Corbin, J. (1998) *Basics of Qualitative Research: Techniques Procedures for Developing Grounded Theory*, (2nd edn). Thousand Oaks, CA: Sage.

Taylor, C. & Gibbs, G.R. (2010) Preparing data. Online QDA Web Site. Available at onlineqda.hud.ac.uk/Intro_QDA/preparing _data.php (accessed 14/8/11).

Teddlie, C. & Tashakkori, A. (2009) *Foundations of Mixed Methods Research: Integrating Quantitative and Qualitative Approaches in the Social and Behavioural Sciences*. Thousand Oaks, CA: Sage.

Terrell, S. (2011). Mixed-methods research methodologies. *The Qualitative Report*, 17(1): 254–80. Retrieved from www.nova.edu/ssss/QR/QR17-1/terrell.pdf (accessed 16/9/11).

Tesch, R. (1993) Personal computers in qualitative research. In LeCompte, M.D. & Preissle, J. with Tesch, R. (eds) *Ethnography and Qualitative Design in Educational Research* (2nd edn). Chicago: Academic Press, pp. 279–314.

Thomas, M., Bloor, M., Frankland, J. (2007) The process of sample recruitment: an ethno-statistical perspective. *Qualitative Research*, 7(4): 429–446.

Thomas, O., Lane, A. & Kingston, K. (2011) Defining and contextualizing robust sport-confidence. *Journal of Applied Sport Psychology*, 23(2): 189–208.

Thomsen, S., Bower, D. & Barnes, M. (2004) Photographic images in women's health, fitness and sports magazines and the physical self-concept of a group of adolescent female volleyball players. *Journal of Sport & Social Issues*, 28(3): 266–83.

Tod, D. & Hodge, K. (2002) Moral reasoning and achievement motivation in sport: a qualitative inquiry. *Journal of Sport Behavior,* 24(3): 307–27.

Todres, L. (2002) Humanising forces: phenomenology in science; psychotherapy in technological culture. *Indo-Pacific Journal of Phenomenology*, 2(1): 1–11.

Todres, L. and Holloway, I., (2006). Phenomenological research. In: Gerrish, K. and Lacey, A. (eds) *The Research Process in Nursing* (2nd edn) Oxford: Blackwell Science, pp. 224–238.

Todres, L. & Wheeler, S. (2001) The complementarity of phenomenology, hermeneutics and existentialism for nursing research. *International Journal of Nursing Studies*, 38(1): 1–8

van Maanen, J. (2011) *Tales of the Field: On Writing Ethnography*. Chicago: University of Chicago Press.

van Manen, M. (1998) *Researching Lived Experience* (2nd edn). New York: State University of New York Press.

Vergeer, I. & Lyle, J. (2007) Mixing methods in assessing coaches' decision-making. *Research Quarterly for Exercise and* Sport, 78(3): 225–35.

Vicsek, L. (2007) A scheme for analysing focus groups. *Qualitative Sozialforschung/ Qualitative Social Research*, 6(4): 20–34.

Waddel-Smith, A. (2010) A qualitative analysis of motivation of elite female triathletes. Masters thesis, San Jose University. Available at http://scholarworks.sjsu.edu/etd_theses/3830 (accessed 1/3/11).

Wadey, R., Evans, L., Evans, K. & Mitchell, I. (2011) Perceived benefits following sport injury: a qualitative examination of their antecedents and underlying mechanisms. *Journal of Applied Sport* Psychology, 23(2): 142–58.

Walsh, D., Ozaeta, J. & Wright, P. (2010) Transference of responsibility model goals to the school environment: exploring the impact of a coaching club program. *Physical Education and Sport Pedagogy*, 15(1): 15–28.

Warner, R. & Griffiths, M. (2006) A qualitative thematic analysis of exercise addiction: an exploratory study. *International Journal of Mental Health Addiction*, 4: 13–26.

Warr, D. (2005) It was fun… but we usually don't talk about these things': analyzing sociable interaction in focus groups. *Qualitative Inquiry.* 11(2): 200–225.

Warren, C. & Hackney, J. (2000) *Gender Issues in Ethnography* (2nd edn). London: Sage.

Weed, M. (2006) The story of an ethnography: the experience of watching the 2002 World Cup in the pub. *Soccer & Society.* 7(1): 76–95.

Weed M. (2009) Research quality considerations for grounded theory research in sport and exercise psychology. *Psychology of Sport and Exercise,* 10(5): 502–10.

Weeden C. (2005) A qualitative approach to the ethical consumer: the use of focus groups for cognitive consumer research in tourism. In Richie, B.W., Burns, P. & Palmer, C. (eds) *Tourism Research Methods: Integrating Theory With Practice*. Wallingford: CABI, pp. 179–90.

Wertz, F., Charmaz, K., McMullen, L., Josselson, R., Anderson, R. & McSpadden, E. (2011) *Five Ways of Doing Qualitative Analysis*. New York: The Guilford Press.

Weinberg, R. & McDermott, M. (2002) A comparative analysis of sport and business organisations: factors perceived critical for organisational success. *Journal of Applied Sport Psychology,* 14(4): 282–98.

Weissensteiner, J., Abernethy, B. & Farrow, D. (2009) Towards the development of a conceptual model of expertise in cricket batting: a grounded theory approach. *Journal of Applied Sport Psychology,* 21(3): 276–92.

Wengraf, T. (2001) *Qualitative Research Interviewing: Biographic Narrative and Semi-Structured Methods*. Thousand Oaks, CA: Sage.

Wheeler, S. (2012) The significance of family culture for sports participation. *International Review for the Sociology of Sport*, 46(2): 235–252.

Whitehead, T. (2006) *Workbook for Descriptive Observations of Social Settings, Acts, Activities and Events*. Workbooks: University of Maryland.

Whitehead, S. & Biddle, S. (2008) Adolescent girls' perceptions of physical activity: a focus group study. *European Physical Education Review* 14(2): 243–62.

Whitson, D. (1976). Method in sport sociology: the potential of a phenomenological contribution. *International Review of Sport Sociology*, 11(4): 53–68.

Whyte, W. (1943) *Street Corner Society: the Social Structure of an Italian Slum*. Chicago, University of Chicago Press.

Wibek, V., Abrandt, M. & Gren, D. (2007) Learning in focus groups: an analytical dimension for enhancing focus group research. *Qualitative Research*, 7(2): 249–67.

Wilkins, K. & Woodgate, R. (2008) Designing a mixed methods study in paediatric oncology research. *Journal of Pediatric Oncology Nursing*, 25(1): 24–33.

Williams, M. (2003) *Making Sense of Social Research*. London: Sage.

Willig, C. (2008) A phenomenological investigation of the experience of taking part in 'extreme sports'. *Journal of Health Psychology*, 13(5): 690–702.

Wolcott, H. (1994) *Transforming Qualitative Data: Description, Analysis, and Interpretation*. Thousand Oaks, CA: Sage.

Wolcott, H. (2009) *Writing Up Qualitative Research* (3rd edn). Thousand Oaks, CA: Sage.

Wright, R. (2007) Planning for the great unknown: the challenge of promoting spectator-driven sports event tourism. *International Journal of Tourism Research*, 9(5): 345–59.

Young, D., Gittelsohn, J., Charleston, J., Felix-Aaron, K. & Appel, L. (2001) Motivations for exercise and weight loss among African-American women: focus group results and their contribution towards program development. *Ethnicity & Health*, 6(3–4): 227–45.

Index